THE
SEARCH
FOR
JUSTICE

THE

SEARCH

FOR

JUSTICE

A Defense Attorney's Brief
on the O.J. Simpson Case

Robert L. Shapiro

WITH LARKIN WARREN

WARNER BOOKS

A Time Warner Company

Warner Books, Inc., 1271 Avenue of the Americas, New York, NY 10020

 A Time Warner Company

Printed in the United States of America
First Printing: April 1996
10   9   8   7   6   5   4   3   2   1

ISBN: 0-446-52081-0
LC: 96-60025

For Linell, Brent, and Grant

The Timeline

1994

June 12. Nicole Brown Simpson and Ronald Lyle Goldman are stabbed to death, their bodies found in the front courtyard of the former's Brentwood condominium on Bundy Drive.

June 13. In Chicago, O.J. Simpson is notified of his former wife's death. He returns to Los Angeles from a Hertz business trip, is temporarily handcuffed, and taken downtown by police for questioning. That evening, Robert Shapiro is contacted on Simpson's behalf and asked to become defense counsel.

June 16. The funerals of the victims are held.

June 17. As he's about to be arrested for murder, O.J. slips out of Robert Kardashian's home and goes on Bronco ride with friend A.C. Cowlings. When he returns to his home on Rockingham, Simpson is taken into custody.

June 24. Grand jury recused.

July 8. Six-day preliminary hearing results: Judge Kathleen Kennedy-Powell rules there is ample evidence for O.J. Simpson to stand trial on two counts of first-degree murder.

July 22. O.J. pleads "absolutely 100 percent not guilty" to the charges. Judge Lance A. Ito assigned to hear case.

Aug. 18. Defense counsel files motion to obtain personnel records of Detective Mark Fuhrman.

Sept. 2. District attorney files motion to sequester jury.

Sept. 9. District attorney announces that the People will not seek the death penalty.

Sept. 19. Although Judge Ito finds that detectives acted with a "reckless disregard for the truth," he upholds the legality of the search of Simpson's home.

Sept. 26. First day of jury selection. Process will ultimately take five weeks.

Nov. 3. Jury panel selected: eight black, one white, one Hispanic, two mixed race; eight women, four men.

Dec. 8. Alternate jury selected.

1995

Jan. 4. Defense waives Kelly-Frye hearing, which would have challenged prosecution's DNA evidence.

Jan. 11. The jury is sequestered. Hearing held re defense arguments against admissibility of domestic-abuse evidence.

Jan. 13. Prosecutor Christopher Darden and defense attorney Johnnie Cochran have heated exchange over racist language, specifically the *n* word, regarding the upcoming testimony of Mark Fuhrman.

Jan. 24. First day of trial. Prosecutors Marcia Clark and Christopher Darden deliver opening arguments.

Jan. 25. Johnnie Cochran makes opening statement for the defense.

Jan. 27. O.J. Simpson's book, *I Want to Tell You*, is published.

Feb. 3. Nicole Brown's sister Denise testifies to O.J.'s mistreatment of her sister.

Feb. 12. Jurors, judge, and attorneys for both prosecution and defense take field trip to O.J.'s home and Bundy Drive crime scene.

March 15. Detective Mark Fuhrman, cross-examined by defense attorney F. Lee Bailey, adamantly denies using the word "nigger" at any time in previous ten years.

April 11. L.A.P.D. criminalist Dennis Fung testifies. Under cross-examination by defense attorney Barry Scheck, he concedes litany of procedural errors.

April 21. After three sheriff's deputies are reassigned, jurors protest, at first refusing to come to court, later showing up dressed in black.

May 4. Wrongful death suit filed on behalf of Frederick Goldman and Kim Goldman, Ron Goldman's father and sister.

May 10. DNA testimony begins with testimony of Dr. Robin Cotton.

May 15. O.J. tries on the bloody gloves in front of the jury. They don't fit.

July 6. The prosecution rests its case against O.J. Simpson.

July 10. Arnelle Simpson, O.J.'s daughter, is first witness called in defense case.

Aug. 15. Controversy over possible conflict of interest re Judge Ito, his wife, L.A.P.D. captain Margaret York, and Mark Fuhrman tapes. Marcia Clark asks Ito to recuse himself from Simpson trial.

Aug. 16. Clark changes her mind on Ito recusal. In turn, Ito will ask a second judge to rule on relevancy of Captain York's testimony.

Aug. 18. Superior court judge John Reid rules that Captain York is not relevant to Simpson trial and need not testify.

Aug. 29. Portions of Fuhrman tapes are played in court, with jury absent.

Aug. 31. Judge Ito rules that jury will hear only two excerpts of controversial tapes. Attorney Robert Tourtelot, who represented Fuhrman in potential lawsuit against Shapiro, resigns as Fuhrman's lawyer.

Sept. 5. The jury hears excerpts from Fuhrman tapes.

Sept. 6. With jury absent, Mark Fuhrman appears on stand, invoking his Fifth Amendment privilege against self-incrimination.

Sept. 7. The defense announces that O.J. Simpson won't testify on his own behalf and requests that the judge instruct jury as to reason for Fuhrman's further nonappearance. Judge agrees, but prosecution objects. The question goes to appeals court.

Sept. 8. Appeals court rejects Ito's jury instruction.

Sept. 11. Defense refuses to rest their case due to the unresolved question of judge's instruction to jury re Fuhrman. In an unprecedented move, Ito orders prosecution to begin its rebuttal.

Sept. 18. Prosecution conditionally rests its case.

Sept. 19. Detective Vannatter is cross-examined by Shapiro on statements he made to mob informants, the Fiato brothers, about why police went to O.J.'s residence.

Sept. 21. Ito gives jury the option of finding O.J. guilty of second-degree murder.

Sept. 22. Both defense and prosecution rest their cases. In a statement to judge waiving his right to testify, O.J. says, "I did not, could not, and would not have committed this crime." Judge Ito gives jury instructions.

Sept. 26 and 27. Clark and Darden deliver prosecution's closing arguments.

Sept. 27 and 28. Cochran and Scheck deliver defense's closing arguments. Cochran makes controversial statements to the jury comparing Fuhrman to Hitler, which creates furor both inside the courtroom and out.

Sept. 29. The case goes to the jury.

Oct. 2. After less than four hours, jury announces that it has reached a verdict.

Oct. 3. Jury finds O.J. Simpson not guilty of two counts of murder.

Ethics code 7–19. *An adversary presentation counters the natural human tendency to judge too swiftly in terms of the familiar that which is not yet fully known; the advocate [for the defense], by his zealous preparation and presentation of facts and law, enables the tribunal to come to the hearing with an open and neutral mind and to render impartial judgments. The duty of a lawyer to his client and his duty to the legal system are the same: to represent his client zealously within the bounds of the law.*

American Bar Association Code of Professional Responsibility

Prologue

The most frequent question a defense attorney is asked (and this goes double for one involved in high-profile criminal cases) is "How do you sleep at night?" I heard it myself almost daily during the O.J. Simpson trial, especially when the prosecution was presenting its case and the evidence against my client was mounting. The second thing I heard, especially from people who know me well and feel comfortable leaning on me just a little harder, was "In your heart, don't you know he did it?"

My answer to the second question is simple: "I wasn't there, you weren't there. Ultimately, it is a matter to be decided by the court."

My answer to the first question—How do I sleep at night?—is a little longer.

We live in a nation founded on the principles of freedom and liberty. We fought dearly for those principles, and we pay a continuing price. The Constitution—and, in particular, the ten amendments that make up the Bill of Rights—is where that price is clearly set out, in plain and simple English. Of those first ten amendments, five are specific as to the rights of citizens who find themselves in an adversarial relationship with the judicial process: the Fourth Amendment protects the people against unreasonable search and seizure; the Fifth sets out the protections of due process, including self-incrimination; the Sixth ensures a public trial and the assistance of counsel; the Seventh guarantees the right of trial by jury; and the Eighth prohibits cruel and unusual punishment. It is the provisions in this document and nothing else—not good intentions, not patriotism, not capitalism, not orthodoxy—that stand like a sentry between us and our becoming a police state.

The Bill of Rights and an attorney's rules of professional conduct require (they do not *suggest*) that anyone accused of a crime is entitled to a lawyer, as well as a trial. A defense attorney's job is not to "get someone off" but rather to represent someone's interests when the formidable resources of the state are arrayed against that person. And we aren't allowed to adjust our efforts to fit the circumstances, no matter the crime, no matter how morally questionable the person accused of it may appear to be, no matter our public or private assumptions of that person's guilt or innocence. A surgeon doesn't do less than his best when he's confronted with a person he detests on the operating table; neither does a lawyer. They *cannot:* Their respective professional codes of ethics forbid it. In my home state of California, the Business and Professions Code Section 6068(h) expressly forbids an attorney "ever to reject, for any consideration personal to himself, the cause of the defenseless or the oppressed."

Prosecution attorneys and defense attorneys are officers of the court, both bound by the same rules of evidence and the same rules of professional conduct. However, our advocacy roles are different. The prosecutor's responsibility, according to the American Bar Association's Code of Professional Conduct, is "to seek justice, not merely to convict." The defense attorney's responsibility is "to represent his client zealously within the bounds of the law." The resulting adversarial presentation "counters the natural human tendency to judge too swiftly in terms of the familiar that which is not yet fully known."

In *Berger v. United States* (1935), the Supreme Court stated that the prosecutor "is the representative not of an ordinary

party to a controversy, but of a sovereignty . . . whose interest
. . . in a criminal prosecution is not that it shall win a case, but
that justice shall be done." Justice means different things to
different people. There is legal justice and moral justice. When
most people talk about justice, they're talking about moral justice. Did someone commit a crime or not? If so, that person
should be tried, convicted, and punished. If not, he or she
should be acquitted. As a defense attorney, however, I must
view justice as our (that is, our country's) system of legal justice, which is based not on the assumption of guilt but on the
presumption of innocence. Guilt must be *proven* by the prosecution. And it must be proven beyond a reasonable doubt and to
a near certainty within the rules of constitutional law.

Reasonable doubt is a standard of common sense that is at
the heart of our system of justice. Neither the prosecution nor
the defense instructs the jury on that standard; the judge must
do it. And judges have been wrestling with the intricacies and
complexities of jury instruction, in both the state and federal
courts, in nearly every single trial since the beginning of our
criminal justice system. Ultimately, the questions before a jury
are, Have they proved this case to your satisfaction? Are you
sure? If someone near and dear to you—yourself, your rela-
tives, your children—were on trial, and this type of evidence
was presented against that person, would you be confident that
you had made the right decision? Or would you be uneasy?
Would you think, Did I do the right thing? Could I be wrong?
If you're 90 percent certain, that still leaves 10 percent doubt.
And if you have doubts—rational doubts, based not on speculation but on *fact*—then you have no right to convict. Judge
William Blackstone anticipated society's struggle with this
when he said, more than two hundred years ago, "It is better
that ten guilty persons escape than one innocent suffer."

Society has become so afraid of crime that Americans seem
increasingly willing to forego the Bill of Rights, convinced that
it protects the sinners rather than the sinned-against. "Well, the
Founding Fathers couldn't have foreseen gang wars," goes the

rationale. Or crack, or insider trading, or contraband automatic weapons, or drugs, or sexual abuse, or pornography, or serial killers. To that, I would counter that neither could the Founders have envisioned the possibility that guilt or innocence might rest on a small laboratory slide containing an even smaller amount of deoxyribonucleic acid—DNA. Reasonable doubt takes on a new meaning in a case informed by science and determined by fallible human beings who interpret, manipulate, and define this data.

It's convenient, when confronted with the virulence of modern crime, to forget history, both ancient and recent, which is full of object lessons illustrating what happens when the rules that govern a people's conscience are, for whatever "expedient" reason, set aside. As the country's perception of crime goes up—and its intellectual understanding of the justice system correspondingly goes down—everybody decides that the solution to "the problem" is tougher sentencing, more jails, and bigger prisons. The results of that decision are questionable. Nationally, one-third of male African American adults ages eighteen to twenty-five are either in jail, on probation, or on parole. In California, the legitimate desire for safe streets has led to the "three-strikes-and-you're-out" law. However, most prosecutors and many judges have begun to feel that the system has been slowed down because of this law, as real menaces to society are put in a holding pattern awaiting trial while the court wrestles with the problem of the man with two prior convictions who's arrested for stealing a slice of pizza and now faces life imprisonment.

In the face of society's anger, it's almost inevitable that defense attorneys, rather than criminals, begin to carry the onus of crime. No longer seen as protectors of anyone's rights, or of constitutional rights, lawyers are hired guns, paid to "get the guy off," and the public doesn't care for us very much. That is, until that moment in many people's lives when they or someone near and dear to them is arrested for something as simple as drunk driving or as complicated as insider trading. And then the first question asked is "Where are my rights?"

Until and unless that moment happens, crime isn't committed by "us"; therefore, those accused of crimes aren't "us," and "they" are not entitled to the same constitutional protections that "we" are entitled to. Or, as one defense attorney once put it, "Everybody in town hates my guts—until two o'clock in the morning, when their kid gets arrested."

To be sure, defense attorneys have brought some of the criticism upon themselves, by their courtship of and relationship with the press. There's a natural symbiosis between big trials and the media, with both caught up in the playing-field drama of game plans, strategy, key players, winning and losing. The tremendous egos that motivate us to win in the courtroom are not immune to the adulation that comes outside as attorneys spin their successes, in the process becoming everything from talk-show staples to Sunday-morning-TV pundits. Little wonder that in this environment the "celebrity attorney" becomes a pop-culture icon. It's one thing to garner respect, congratulations, and praise from one's peers and friends; it's another thing entirely to glance up during a Lakers game and see one's face juxtaposed with Jack Nicholson's on the massive video screen in the Great Western Forum.

The "Dream Team" glitz shouldn't blind society to the fact that defense attorneys, in addition to zealously representing clients, also offer an ongoing and vital civics lesson in the rights of individuals. We cannot ignore the role of popular culture in shaping—or misshaping—public perceptions and expectations. Cop shows, both fictional and nonfictional, routinely portray illegal search and seizure, the physical abuse of suspects, and manipulation of evidence, all in the interests of "getting the bad guy" by the end of the hour, minus, of course, the time expended for commercials. But trials, and the people in them, are all too real. These days, anybody can accuse anybody of anything; indeed, in civil suits, anybody can *sue* for anything. What if a neighbor doesn't like you, or a business competitor wants to weaken you, and so files a false report of wrongdoing? What if your ex-wife calls the IRS and tells them you're cheating on your income taxes? Or your ex-husband calls the vice squad and tells them you're running a prostitution ring? Do you want the police coming into your home or office, going through your records, going through your closets, without a warrant? What happens if your spouse is killed and you have no immediate alibi? Suspicion always focuses on the surviving spouse, yet most of us could never account for all of our minute-to-minute whereabouts on any given day or date, especially during the times that we are alone. These days, an accusation is enough to destroy a life; an indictment and trial holds that life up to the examination and judgment of a society. A defense attorney's job is to see to it that the man or woman who stands under that scrutiny doesn't stand alone.

The terms "Dream Team" and "Trial of the Century" didn't come from me, and I was never comfortable with either of them. My primary focus from the beginning of the Simpson case was to vigorously defend my client and to assemble a team of experts to strengthen that defense. Within a day or two it was clear that this would become a highly visible case, although I couldn't know at that point the degree to which the public would continue to demand information and coverage. I believed that the visibility would be good for two things: first, for lawyers (especially criminal lawyers, who have historically always been demeaned) to demonstrate how professional they can be, so that the public would come to understand what the real role of a criminal lawyer is; and second, to serve as some kind of positive symbol at a time when race relations were seriously frayed, especially in my own city. We had been through the Rodney King and Reginald Denny trials, and the riots and the soul-weariness that came with them. We had been through, in my lifetime, the promise of the civil rights movement, which now seems to have come undone. Perhaps, I thought, my being a white Jewish lawyer defending a black man accused of killing two white people, one of whom was Jewish, would strengthen what had become weakened. Perhaps a vigorous defense team that included a respected African-American attorney, and an equally vigorous prosecution team led by a Jewish woman and another black man, could somehow convey the message that the American system of justice is ultimately more important than any racial or religious element within it. Unfortunately, I was wrong on all counts. I was clearly, clearly wrong. Was I naive? Perhaps. But even now I would argue that optimism and idealism—which keep me in this business—are difficult to sustain without sustaining some naiveté as well.

I am not omniscient, and I have no better way of judging guilt or innocence than anyone else. However, I do know one thing for certain: Legally, the result of the trial is correct. This was a solid case of reasonable doubt, and I knew that before the trial itself ever began. Based on the evidence presented to this jury, "not guilty" was the only verdict that could have been returned.

That doesn't mean a significant number of Americans aren't sitting out there this minute thinking, "O.J. probably did it." But under our system, "probably did it" is not sufficient to convict someone. You cannot ask the question on one side of the coin—How does the defense attorney sleep, knowing that sometimes the guilty go free?—without confronting the question on the flip side: How could any of us sleep if innocent people were put away? Or executed?

I take pride in what I do. I am a professional, I have a constitutionally mandated job, and I work hard at it. Therefore, I'm able to function as a lawyer and survive as a human being. And so I sleep very well.

Chapter One

On Monday, June 13, I was heading back to my Century City office after spending the morning in the Los Angeles Municipal Court. Two different clients, two different preliminary hearings. One was a minor theft case, and I had filed a motion for continuance so we could get additional discovery. The second was more complicated: a white-collar case where a client had allegedly taken money for discounted airline tickets. Just as I pulled into the building's parking garage, the car phone rang. It was Dale Gribow, an old friend and Loyola Law School classmate.

"Bob, have you heard the news about O.J. Simpson?" he asked.

"No," I answered, mildly curious. "What about him?" Although we weren't close friends, O.J. and I knew each other in passing, and with many mutual friends in Los Angeles, we had often run into each other over the years at various charity events and parties, including one Fourth of July party at his house in Laguna with my wife, Linell, and my two sons, Brent and Grant.

"It's incredible," Dale said. "Nicole's been murdered, and O.J.'s been taken down to the Parker Center by the police for questioning."

"I can't believe it!" I said. "Dale, what else do you know about this?"

He didn't have many details; the news reports were still pretty sketchy. All he knew so far was that there had been a stabbing, there was supposedly a second victim, although he didn't know who it was, and Simpson had reportedly made some kind of statement to the police.

"Actually, one of the reasons I called was to see if you were representing him," Dale said.

This wasn't an out-of-the-blue question: Dale knew I had represented many high-profile clients in the past, and there had been some athletes and celebrities on that list. Not this time.

"No," I said. "This is the first I've heard about this. And nobody's contacted me."

For the rest of the afternoon, local TV anchors repeated the same information I'd heard from Dale. Howard Weitzman, a Los Angeles attorney, had reportedly been retained by Simpson. Weitzman, an excellent lawyer and a friend of mine, had represented John DeLorean in the famous narcotics case where DeLorean was accused of offering to sell large amounts of cocaine to federal agents, a charge that he was subsequently acquitted of, and Weitzman was currently representing pop singer Michael Jackson. As the news reports accelerated throughout the day and mild gossip and speculation began to buzz throughout the office, all I could think of was that someone I knew had been murdered just ten minutes away from where I was sitting. In fact, I could look out my office window and see Brentwood in the distance.

That night, Linell and I went to a private party at the House of Blues. A great blues singer was behind the microphone, Cher would be entertaining later, and the champagne was flowing. At about nine o'clock, a security guard came up to me and said, "You have an emergency phone call, Mr. Shapiro," telling me I was welcome to take the call in the club's private office. My heart started to pound—all I could think was that something had happened to one of our boys. Murmuring a quick excuse to

Linell, I followed the guard into the office, where I picked up the phone to hear a totally unfamiliar voice on the other end of the line.

"You don't know me, Mr. Shapiro," the man said. "My name is Roger King. I'm the chairman of Kingworld, and a dear friend of O.J. Simpson's. He needs a good lawyer right now, and I think you're the man to represent him. I'd like to engage you on his behalf."

King, whose company owns and syndicates such television programs as *Wheel of Fortune, Jeopardy,* and *Oprah,* had a reputation as a respected and powerful businessman. And he was clearly someone who could cut to the chase when the situation required it.

"Mr. King, I can appreciate what you're asking me," I said, "and I take it as a compliment. But I understand he already has a lawyer. Besides, it's pretty late in the evening, and at any rate, I couldn't consider going forward without talking to O.J. himself. We would need to meet personally."

"I'm going to get O.J. on the line right now," King insisted, "so you can talk to him about this tonight."

King then tried to reach O.J. at his home, but whoever answered there said O.J. couldn't be disturbed right now for a phone call; he was understandably occupied with other things. King and I continued talking about the situation for about half an hour, during which he kept repeating his intention to retain me immediately.

"You're obviously a loyal friend," I said, "and this is a generous thing that you want to do for O.J. But let's wait until I talk to him before we go any further."

When I returned to the table, Linell had grown concerned. She was relieved to hear that the call wasn't about the boys, and when I told her about my conversation with King, she asked, "What are you going to do?"

"I don't know yet," I said. "It has to wait until tomorrow." Wanting to enjoy the rest of the evening, I didn't tell anyone else at the table about the phone call.

Later that night, I heard from Roger King again as he put me in touch with the head of legal affairs for a motion picture company that had released some of O.J.'s films. I reiterated that no matter how urgent the matter seemed to everyone, we had to put it to rest until I could actually meet with O.J. Finally, I called Alan Schwartz, one of O.J.'s longtime friends, in New York. Schwartz, the founder of ABS (a national women's apparel manufacturer and retailer), had also been a friend of mine for some time. A hardworking, hands-on man who is at his factory every day at six-thirty in the morning, his opinion of this case and my participation in it would prove to be a big part of my decision. Alan assured me that he had in fact spoken both to O.J. and Skip Taft, O.J.'s personal attorney, and that they would call me in the morning.

I arrived at my office early the next day. I had watched the morning TV news programs and wanted an opportunity to read as much of the newspaper coverage as I could before talking to Simpson himself.

I had learned that Nicole had been killed, along with a second person, a young man whose name was Ronald Goldman. The deaths were the result of multiple stabbings, and the crime scene was out in front of the Bundy Drive condominium that Nicole had purchased shortly after she and O.J. had been divorced in 1993. The two young children of O.J. and Nicole, Sydney and Justin, were unharmed—they had evidently been asleep in their rooms when the murders took place—and were now with Nicole's parents, Louis and Juditha Brown, down in Orange County.

After being notified of Nicole's death, O.J., who had been in Chicago on business, had returned to Los Angeles early Monday morning. He was met at the airport by his longtime assistant, Cathy Randa, and Skip Taft. Minutes after they pulled into the driveway at his home on Rockingham, he was in handcuffs, in full view of his companions and the press already assembled in the street in front of his house.

Simpson had reportedly given the police a statement, but his attorney, Howard Weitzman, had not been present for it. My inner alarm went off when I heard this. It was clear from the TV and news reports (not to mention the initial handcuff incident at his house) that the police considered the man a suspect. What on earth was he doing talking to them, or anyone else for that matter, without legal counsel present?

By the time O.J.'s call came, I had learned as much as I could. I had never talked to him on the phone before. In spite of an obvious tension, his voice was measured, much as it had been whenever we had met. Despite my awareness of the tragedy, I realized that this was an important moment. This was one of the greatest football players in history, a man who was still a major sports figure even though he hadn't been on the gridiron for the last fifteen years. He was calling to seek my advice, my counsel, and he wanted it immediately.

"What are you doing right now?" I asked.

"I'm just sitting here with Skip Taft and my friend Bob Kardashian. We would like to meet with you."

"O.J., stay where you are, I'm coming right over," I said. "Don't go anyplace, and don't talk to anybody else."

As I drove, I wondered about the meeting ahead. For one thing, O.J. was represented by my friend Howard Weitzman, which created a somewhat awkward situation. In addition, the first meeting with a potential client is always an anxious situation, especially when the focus of suspicion is already on him. I hadn't agreed to anything yet, and I didn't have much information. Even without the specifics, I knew that if I was going to take this case, I needed to start thinking like a prosecutor. Since I had actually been one early in my career (and in the Los Angeles D.A.'s office, too), it wasn't so hard to do. What, I wondered, did they have? Was it possible that O.J. could have killed Nicole?

Some defense attorneys say that they never ask clients whether or not they committed the crime, because they don't want the burden of knowing. I disagree. I want to know, I have to know, it's in my client's best interests that I do know. I'm never afraid to ask the question right at the beginning, and I keep asking it throughout a case. I want a client's confidence, and I want him to have mine, so that we can operate as a single entity. No surprises, no plot twists. I want the truth, no matter what it is, and I want the inconsistencies up front.

When a client says "I'm guilty," what he means is "I'm responsible"—for setting in motion certain events that culminated in a crime or act of violence. To the public, a defendant is either guilty or not guilty. But a criminal attorney recognizes that the law is not black and white—everything is shades of gray. In a death case, is it murder? Is it manslaughter? Or is it justifiable homicide? In a burglary, is it first-degree or second-degree? What is the difference between assault with a deadly weapon and assault with intent to commit murder? All have the same basic elements, but each has tremendously different legal consequences. It is up to the courts to ascertain the level of responsibility and the penalty, if any, to be paid for it.

For example, the first time I talked with Marlon Brando's son Christian, who had been charged with first-degree murder for shooting his sister's boyfriend, Dag Drollet, he told me, "I killed him."

"Killing him doesn't mean you murdered him," I said, explaining that there were extenuating circumstances, and thus different degrees of responsibility, that we hadn't yet explored. And indeed, as I began to learn the details of the case, I concluded that Christian wasn't guilty of murder. At best it was manslaughter, and possibly accidental death as the result of negligence.

I hired expert investigators (including two who would later work with me on the Simpson case) to do a complete reconstruction of the shooting, which indicated that the victim was in an upright position at the time he was shot. This, we argued, was evidence of a struggle between two men, not, as the police had concluded, the premeditated murder of a sleeping man by someone standing over him. And later, in fact, when Marlon was walking barefoot in the room, he stepped on the spent bullet-shell casing; the detectives had missed it in a two-day search. It was imbedded in the floor, beneath the carpet, at a location and angle that proved the theory of our reconstruction; the shot was fired while Drollet was upright. Thus, the level of Christian's responsibility was quite different than the police had originally believed, allowing him to plead guilty to voluntary manslaughter, which carries a sentence of three to sixteen years. First-degree murder would have been twenty-five years to life.

On another occasion, a man walked into my office after shooting his wife and dumping her body on the freeway.

"You should surrender yourself immediately," I told him.

It turned out that he had a significant defense. He had been living in a destructive marriage with a woman who insisted on having sex with a mutual friend of theirs and required her husband to watch. Slowly but surely he was pushed beyond his capacity to think or act in a rational way. Guilty, yes, but of what? Murder? First degree? Second? None of the above. He was found guilty of manslaughter and sentenced to five years.

What if he had told me he didn't do it and I had built a defense on that? And then found out about the bad marriage and sex angle later—from the prosecution, as they cross-examined my witness? I don't want any surprises; I want everything up front from day one. I remembered the strategy one veteran lawyer told me that he always used on his clients at their first meeting: "You tell me what happened, and then *I'll* tell *you* what happened." What, I wondered as I drove, was I about to hear from O.J. Simpson?

∞

Skip Taft has a small law firm, and adjacent to his suite of offices is a room that resembles someone's personal study or den, with star-studded pictures on the wall, a large television, a couch, a sound system, and a lot of sports memorabilia. Decorated with classic American pieces and a large wooden partner's desk, this is O.J.'s office, which for years has served as the center of his business and professional activities and his sports corporation,

Orenthal Productions. When I arrived, O.J. was waiting anxiously with his two friends.

Leroy "Skip" Taft, a tall, lanky man in his late fifties who had been a star basketball player at USC, and O.J.'s personal attorney and business manager for many years, was clearly stressed out. Bob Kardashian, who was only slightly less agitated than Taft, is, after Allen "A.C." Cowlings, probably O.J.'s oldest friend. They met on a tennis court twenty-five years ago. O.J. was an usher at Kardashian's wedding; Kardashian was with O.J. when he first met Nicole and had stayed friends with both of them throughout their separation and divorce. A business and entertainment entrepreneur who received a law degree in 1969, Kardashian was and has remained O.J.'s closest advisor.

No one can deny the charisma and kinetic energy that O.J. Simpson projects, and I saw from the minute I walked into the room that his frustration, added to the grief and stress of the previous days, was barely contained within the four walls. Clean-shaven, wearing a T-shirt and a pair of slacks, he was in control, but it was clear that he wanted to get his innocence across quickly and without any equivocation whatsoever. Essentially, everything I'd heard and read in the newspapers so far accurately depicted the previous thirty-six hours.

After attending his daughter Sydney's dance recital, O.J. had flown to Chicago on the Sunday night red-eye to play in a Monday morning golf tournament sponsored by Hertz, the auto-rental company for which he had been a longtime spokesman. At 6:05 L.A. time on Monday morning, he received a phone call at his hotel room from L.A.P.D. Detective Ron Phillips informing him that Nicole Brown Simpson, his former wife, had been murdered.

After making a number of phone calls to family members, O.J. got on a plane back to Los Angeles, landing before noon. Skip Taft and Cathy Randa met him and drove him back to Brentwood. Immediately upon entering the grounds of his home on Rockingham Drive, he was handcuffed on orders by L.A.P.D. Detective Philip Vannatter.

Skip Taft had called O.J.'s attorney, Howard Weitzman, who had represented Simpson in 1989 when he pleaded no contest to charges of spousal abuse. Weitzman prevailed upon Vannatter to take the cuffs off, and at noon O.J. was then taken downtown by the detectives, with Taft and Weitzman following in their car.

In the police car on the way down to the station, O.J. told the police that when he'd gotten the call in his hotel room about Nicole's death, he was completely distraught. "I just kind of went bonkers for a little bit," he told them.

There's been much speculation about why O.J. gave his statement without a lawyer being present. It was clear to me from our first meeting that he was a very strong-willed person, used to making his own decisions, running his own show, and his position was that he was completely innocent, and so he had no reason to hide behind lawyers. In fact, he talked quite freely to the police in the car on the way to the police station—they even took notes during the ride, about where he was in Chicago and what he was doing there. At that point in time he was under great emotional and physical stress. The mother of his children had been murdered; and he'd made the Chicago round-trip in less than twelve hours, with little more than an hour's sleep. Not only was he suffering from shock and grief but sleep deprivation as well. Even before he'd gone to Chicago, he'd been up the previous morning at five to play his routine Saturday golf game. The man was in no condition to answer questions or reconstruct his previous twenty-four hours to police or anybody else. And yet, he had insisted he was capable of doing it.

Once they got to the station, Detective Vannatter told Weitzman, "We want to talk to O.J., but we'd really like to talk to him alone. If he wants a lawyer present, we won't talk to him right now."

Weitzman and Taft both insisted that they be present for O.J.'s statement. But the police held to their position: If there were lawyers, there would be no interview. And O.J. wanted to talk to them. So Weitzman reluctantly said, "Well, my client is more than willing to cooperate. However, I must ask that you tape-record the conversation." This the police agreed to do.

Although Weitzman was widely criticized for allowing the interview to happen—and I was among those being critical—I soon understood that in order to prevent O.J. from doing or saying something he'd set his mind on, he almost had to be physically tackled. As a boxer—middleweight class, albeit an amateur—I would have tried.

"Gentlemen," I would've said to the police, "my client is exhausted and grieving. He's been up all night; today he has to prepare to bury the mother of his children. He's more than willing to cooperate, but right now, under doctor's orders, he's going to bed." And that, for at least a couple of days, would have been that.

O.J.'s statement to the police about his whereabouts the previous twenty-four hours was exculpatory—that is, he accounted for his whereabouts—and after they taped it, they told him he was allowed to go back home.

After I went over all of this with Taft and Kardashian, I said I wished to talk with Simpson alone. When they left the room, I explained the attorney-client privilege of confidentiality to O.J. "I'm not here to judge you," I said. "You can tell Taft one thing, Kardashian another, but if you want my help, what you need to tell me is the truth." I stopped a moment, preparing to ask the question that would decide where we went from here. "O.J., did you do this?"

Although his face was haggard, his eyes were steady when he looked directly at me and responded in a strong voice. "I did not do this," he said firmly. "Nicole and I were together for a long time, Bob. We had our problems, sure, but we shared two beautiful children together, and she was a great mother." He paused, and then said, "Besides, I have such a good life. Four great kids. Fame, fortune, and wonderful friends. How could anyone think I would destroy all of it? I wouldn't. I couldn't do this. I didn't do this." It struck me then that this man had, until this week, led a charmed life, repeatedly overcoming obstacles that would have daunted others—and he was completely able, he believed, to overcome this one as well.

It was time to get down to serious business. Once suspicion is focused on someone, a client must prepare for the prosecution to come at him with everything they've got. And the hardest thing to come to grips with is that once the system locks in, a client's innocence will have nothing to do with the outcome of a case.

Even as we spoke, the district attorney's office was gearing for battle as if it were mounting a military invasion, complete with heavy artillery. I knew that they would have the best lawyers, the best investigators. Indeed, what we later learned was that it was the largest effort ever expended by a prosecuting agency. There's been a lot of talk about the "Dream Team"— how many lawyers there were on it, how much it cost. Given what was coming at O.J. from the prosecution, we might've been forgiven for believing that we were outgunned. There are eight to nine thousand members of the Los Angeles Police Department and nine hundred deputy district attorneys. It is the largest prosecutorial agency in the world. In an ordinary murder case, two deputy district attorneys would've been assigned; in this case, there would be forty-five working full-time, not to mention the rest of the L.A.P.D. resources, as well as the assistance of the Chicago police department, the FBI, and Interpol.

Reaching for a sports analogy, I thought about my own experience and training as an amateur boxer. Boxing and trial law have a great deal in common. The contest is not about mass or weight; it's about speed, agility, quick thought, and footwork. You have to think on your feet, and can never show any fear, no matter how badly you've been slowed or hurt by the opposition. Not only must you know what the other side is thinking, you must think it before them, and think quicker. There is an axiom in boxing: A good big man will beat a good small man. We had to be better than good. In short, we had to start thinking like the prosecution—how they were building their case and how we were to counter it. It was ironic to discover later that while we began to think like the prosecution, the district attorney's office hadn't yet started thinking strategically at all, and the police, in their rush to judgment, their "sure thing," were running around making mistakes.

To find out exactly what the police knew and what evidence, or lack of it, they had would require getting expert witnesses of our own, putting together a parallel investigation of our own, and moving quickly to get our own people in the field before any more time passed. There was no time to lose. Time was of the essence and we were already two days behind.

There was no way to know for certain if O.J. was the primary suspect, the only suspect, or if in fact he would be charged at all. At this point, it appeared to me that he believed the whole matter would be dealt with and cleared up simply and quickly. I didn't want to dampen his natural optimism; I knew he would need to draw on it as events unfolded. However, as his advocate, it was my job to be pragmatic and prepare for the worst. First, there was the matter of Taft and Kardashian and their roles.

Taft, as O.J.'s business attorney, was certainly covered by the attorney-client privilege and had separated himself because of his professional representation. However, Kardashian's status, because he knew all the important players intimately, was crucial to us. Kardashian's ex-wife, Kris, now married to former Olympian Bruce Jenner, had been Nicole's close friend; they shared the same circle of girlfriends and their children played together. Kardashian, as a lawyer O.J. had been relying upon for advice, had and would continue to have access to information that would be difficult for me to get; conversely, this information would be invaluable to the prosecution. Although he hadn't practiced law in years, his knowledge of the case and people involved were essential. I wanted his help.

It was then decided that Howard Weitzman, whose firm specialized in civil cases and who had been primarily doing civil litigation, would be asked to step aside. Skip immediately met with Weitzman to tell him that I'd been retained by O.J. I then talked to Weitzman, who was extraordinarily gracious. We discussed the transition, and he subsequently issued a public statement that in the interests of his client, given both their close personal relationship and his own professional commitments, he thought it was best to withdraw. There were rumors at the time that the reason Weitzman left the case was that O.J. had made a confession to him. That is categorically not true.

There were also rumors (which continue to this day) that at one point we were prepared to enter a plea bargain. This, too, is categorically untrue. Since my client steadfastly maintained his innocence from the beginning and never once wavered, there was never a plea bargain considered, by anyone.

The words "plea bargain" are right up there with "legal loophole" and "technicalities" in their negative connotation; they make it sound like the courts are helping criminals get away with something. Prosecutors, on the other hand, refer to the process as "case resolution" or "case disposition." These terms more correctly reflect the role of lawyers, which is to resolve a case to everyone's satisfaction. Nobody holds it against either party when a settlement is negotiated in a civil case, but when you try negotiation in a criminal case, the media takes it to the street. However, plea bargaining is *not* detrimental to the justice system; in fact, the system would completely founder without it. Ninety percent of cases are resolved by pleas. Imagine if they all went instead to trial. The court system would bog down almost instantly, and cases would be systematically dismissed, one after the other.

That said, it doesn't mean that prosecutors give away cases. Each case has a certain value in terms of what can be proven, what the real offense is, and what the fair sentence should be based on the individual, the individual's record, and the likelihood of recurrence. When a case comes up, judges, defense, and prosecuting lawyers ask what the logical end result of the case will be—and if we can get there without a trial. First of all, is the defendant willing to plead guilty and admit responsibility to something? And if so, to what? These are the questions we faced on Christian Brando's case, for instance, and I had dealt with them as well on behalf of other clients. But in this case, suffice it to say that O.J. Simpson wouldn't have considered pleading guilty to any charge, let alone first-degree murder. And the district attorney wouldn't have offered anything less.

∞

Speed is essential in criminal cases. Memories fade, evidence dissipates. Since we had few facts to go on, the people who had seen or been with O.J. throughout the day of the crime were clearly going to be key witnesses, and there were two in particular who were key to establishing his innocence. Brian "Kato" Kaelin had spent much of the evening of the murder with O.J., and Allan Park was the limo driver who had picked him up and taken him to the airport. I wanted to talk to both of them immediately.

I wished to talk to them both that very night, before their stories eroded from repetition, before anyone had a chance to interrogate them at length with techniques that might favor a particular point of view. And I wanted to tape-record the interviews so that no one could dispute later what questions were asked and answered, or suggest that the questions were improper, or that undue pressure was put on either man.

From Skip Taft's office I called Allan Park, and with Skip present and his secretary coming in and out, we talked over the speaker phone. Park was a conscientious young man who had just begun working part-time for Town and Country Limousine, the company that O.J. used regularly. The company's owner, Dale St. John, happened to live across the street from Park, and was O.J.'s normal driver, but on this night he was unavailable and had sent Park in his place.

Park told us that he had arrived at O.J.'s about 10:25 P.M.

(twenty minutes early, he said), parked outside the gate, got out of the car and had a cigarette, and then had gone up to the gate at 10:40 and rung the buzzer. When no one replied after several attempts, Park got back into the car and called his boss, who told him that O.J. always ran late and that he should wait until at least 11:15. As they were talking, Park saw Kato Kaelin coming around the side of the house with a flashlight. Almost simultaneously (at around 10:57, he estimated), he also saw someone go into the house. When Park saw the lights go on in the house, he then buzzed the intercom again. O.J. answered it and, according to Park, told him he'd overslept and been in the shower and that he would be down in just a few minutes.

It was Kaelin who opened the gate so that Park could drive the limo up to the front door. He'd felt or heard thumping sounds near the back of the house, Kaelin told him, and that's why he had the flashlight. He wondered if perhaps it had been an earthquake, or perhaps a prowler.

O.J. showed up about five minutes later, in a hurry because he knew it would be a race to the airport. As he would later tell the police, "I was doing my little crazy what I do. . . . Anybody who has ever picked me up says that O.J.'s a whirlwind, he's running, he's grabbing things, and that's what I was doing."

After his luggage was loaded into the limo, O.J. went into the kitchen to get a better flashlight in order to check the grounds with Kato. When he looked at the kitchen clock, he knew he didn't have enough time, and he headed back to the limo. At 11:15, he and Park took off for the airport.

After ending my discussion with Park, I then interviewed Kato Kaelin at Skip Taft's office. Kaelin, at first glance, looks like the kind of person you'd never want to be your witness; you'd much rather have him appear for the other side. But his shaggy surfer-dude hair, fragmented grammar, and off-handed manner are deceptive. In fact, although the police had already interviewed him once, when they were first at Rockingham the morning of the murders, their interview wasn't particularly thorough or focused. I wondered if they had been somewhat misled by his style.

As Kato and I talked, I discovered he was a college graduate who'd played college football. A divorced single father with a ten-year-old daughter—which accounted for his great empathy with Justin and Sydney Simpson—Kaelin had much more intelligence than he was ever given credit for. Although he was very nervous in trying to recollect exactly what had taken place—because he didn't want to make any mistakes—he had a good memory and he understood the facts. He was especially torn because of his intense love and loyalty for Nicole. He didn't want to take any sides, he simply wanted to be as straightforward as possible; and in doing so, he gave me reason to believe that O.J. was not involved in these deaths in any way.

An aspiring actor, Kato had met Nicole in Aspen about two years earlier, after she and O.J. had been divorced. Although they were never romantically involved, they became close friends. She and the children lived in a house on Gretna Green, and Kaelin had boarded for a while in the guesthouse there, paying five hundred dollars a month for rent.

When Nicole purchased the condominium on Bundy, Kaelin agreed that perhaps it was no longer appropriate for him to be living under the same roof with her and the children, so while maintaining his close friendship with her, he temporarily moved to the guesthouse on O.J.'s Rockingham estate.

He told us that after O.J. returned from his daughter Sydney's dance recital early Sunday evening (Nicole and her family had gone on to dinner at Mezzaluna restaurant), he and O.J. went out and picked up burgers and fries at McDonald's, then returned to the house at around 9:45. O.J., who had been on the go since 5:00 A.M., still hadn't packed for his red-eye trip to Chicago that night and went right into the house. Kato took his meal into the guesthouse, where he ate it and then made a couple of phone calls to friends. At approximately 10:40 P.M., while he was still on the phone, he thought he heard something or some knocking outside his room, so he nervously went out with a flashlight to investigate. He found nothing, and then, coming around the house, he saw the limo driver. Kato let him through the gates, helped load the bags into the car once O.J. came outside, and watched them drive away at around 11:15. He was awakened at 5:30 the next morning with the news of his friend Nicole's death.

It was unusual to interview two such key witnesses so early in an investigation. Normally the first thing that happens in a case is that a suspect is identified by the police, then arrested and charged with a crime. A defense attorney isn't involved until a client calls and says "I've been arrested, I'm in jail." In this case, that hadn't happened yet. So far, we were ahead of them.

Chapter Two

∞

The primary challenge to the defense is to anticipate the prosecution's case. Since I'm not at all reluctant to admit that I don't know everything, I seek out other professionals who can think like the prosecution with me. When I'm putting together a defense team, I try to find the most credible experts—people who ordinarily and often testify for the prosecution and are or have been employed by government agencies. These people not only gain the respect of a jury, but my getting them keeps the "top of the line" experts out of the hands of the prosecution.

We have to find out what the police know, and do what they're doing as they're doing it. And not only must we do what they're doing, we must do things they *should* be doing but for whatever reason aren't. Most important, they make mistakes, and we have to find out what those mistakes are. *Fast.* So it was on Tuesday, June 14, at ten o'clock at night—one A.M. in the East—that I was on my car phone to New York, tracking down Dr. Michael Baden, the noted pathologist and former chief medical examiner.

I knew that forensic science would play an integral part in this case; the D.A.'s office was already talking about the importance of blood evidence. I had worked often with Dr. Baden, most recently on the Brando case, where he was able to establish the trajectory of the bullet that had killed Drollet, and in doing so refute the prosecutor's case. Baden, who has conducted more than twenty thousand autopsies in his career, had done distinguished pathology investigations into the assassinations of John F. Kennedy, Martin Luther King, Jr., and Malcolm X.

Courtesy of the New York State Police, I finally located Baden in New York, where he is the director of the Forensic Sciences Unit of the New York State Police. He agreed to join me, and then recommended a colleague, Dr. Barbara Wolf, the director of anatomic pathology at Albany Medical Center. Dr. Wolf, a DNA expert, also works with the state police in Albany. Baden also strongly agreed with my idea of contacting Dr. Henry Lee, an esteemed forensic scientist and the director of the State Forensic Science Laboratory in Connecticut.

Although I had never worked with Dr. Lee before, I was familiar with his national reputation as an expert in crime-scene reconstruction. It's said that the instructors at the FBI Academy respect him so much that they rise to their feet whenever he comes into a room. I had seen him testify as an expert witness in both the William Kennedy Smith case in Florida and the federal investigation into the Koresh matter in Waco, Texas. I was confident that Lee wouldn't fall into the trap of exceeding what he knew—that he would go only where the science went. Later on, it turned out that my initial expectations of Henry Lee were a significant underestimation of his great talents. When he simply walked up before the jury on the way to be sworn in, bowed to them respectfully, and said "Good morning," I knew at that moment that this was a special man. In addition to his skills as a criminalist, Henry Lee's intelligence, magnetism, charisma, and ability to relate to the jury surpassed that of any witness I had ever seen.

When I reached Dr. Lee and explained the reason for my late-night call, he agreed to come on board, but cautioned me that since he was a state employee, he first needed to get permission from the governor. Once permission was given—which it immediately was—he, like Baden, would be in Los Angeles within two days.

I then called my friend Bill Pavelic, a retired nineteen-year veteran of the L.A.P.D., with eleven of those years spent as a detective supervisor. Bill is perhaps the most anal-retentive, thorough investigator I have ever seen, and he is passionate about police integrity and behavior. During his time on the force, he received more than two hundred commendations, including ones from the U.S. Justice Department and Los Angeles County District Attorney Gil Garcetti. Pavelic misses nothing. Not only can he find the needle in the haystack, he can tell you who dropped it there and when. If there is a mistake made in police procedure, protocol, or timing, no matter how insignificant it may appear to the layman, he will find it. Most important, Pavelic himself has absolute integrity, as well as an indefatigable work ethic. When he agreed to come on the case, I felt that one of the strongest links in the chain had been forged.

When I finally got home on Tuesday, it was midnight. Linell had waited up, and I told her what was going on—that I was now representing O.J., that we were gearing up for a fight, and my free time, at least for the moment, had just evaporated. We talked about what it would mean for our family and in particular for our two young sons, Brent, who was thirteen at the time, and Grant, who was ten. We had always done a lot of things as a family; the boys were both at an age where they needed more of me, not less. We've been married nearly twenty-six years, and Linell had seen me disappear into all-consuming cases before, but we knew this one would be bigger and that there was no way for me to do it except totally. She knew how I worked, and lucky for me she understood it. For the next eighteen months, she and the boys would collect a sizable stack of IOUs.

Early the next morning—Wednesday, June 15—I called my old friend F. Lee Bailey in Florida. Bailey and I went way back. I trusted and valued his judgment both personally and professionally. We worked together often. I brought him into my cases, he brought me into his. He became godfather to my oldest son, Brent. He allowed me the honor of engraving his name and "of counsel" on my law-practice stationery. We talked frequently on the phone, and when he came to California, he stayed in my home. He was, I believed, as fine a friend and mentor as any man could hope to have.

At Bailey's recommendation, I quickly contacted Pat Mc-Kenna, an affable former Vietnam vet and experienced private investigator based in Palm Beach. Another investigator, Barry Hostetler, came on board at the urging of my old friend Gerry Spence.

Some weeks later, again at Lee Bailey's recommendation, I brought on Howard Harris, a computer expert, and John Mc-Nally, an ex–New York City cop who had worked with Bailey on the Patty Hearst case. The early coup of McNally's police career had been in 1964, when he tracked down fabled jewel thief Jack "Murph the Surf" Murphy, who'd stolen the Star of India from New York's Museum of Natural History.

Thus within two days after O.J.'s phone call, a formidable investigative team was not only on the case but in the field— Pavelic at Los Angeles Airport, McKenna at O'Hare in Chicago, the forensic scientists at the crime scene.

My thought was to get people interviewed at LAX immediately, including baggage handlers, ticket checkers, and security personnel—anyone who would've seen O.J. and could attest to his demeanor at the time he went on the plane. We quickly discovered that American Airlines employees at LAX either couldn't, or wouldn't, talk. Everybody had been instructed that since this was a police investigation the official policy was to be "No comment." In my experience, this was very unusual. Evidently the edict had come down directly from the American Airlines corporate executives, reportedly concerned about the privacy issues involved—who else had been on the plane, for instance, and to what extent American's employees would become witnesses in what was clearly becoming a high-profile case.

In Chicago, Pat McKenna investigated in and around the airport and the hotel where O.J. had stayed, gathering information about which searches the police had already conducted and the areas they were concentrating on, and looking for physical evidence—knives and bloody clothes. Every day we would read lurid stories in the newspapers about what was being uncovered in Chicago, but none of it, ultimately, had anything to do with our case. Bloody clothes were found that were nine months old, rusty knives were dug up in fields or found in ditches. Police investigators had even gone to the extent of actually going through the discarded airline toilet waste and garbage, looking for fabric and knife fragments that might have been disposed of on the plane. No incriminating physical evidence was ever found.

∞

My tendency, when working on a case, is to become completely immersed in it, to the exclusion of anything else going on around me. I don't, as a rule, watch much television; I read the national newspapers on the fly; and if it weren't for my friends in the film industry inviting my wife and me to screenings, I'd probably never see a movie. I do go regularly with my boys to sports events—boxing, hockey, and basketball especially—not just because I enjoy them but because of their escapism quotient. The result is case-induced tunnel vision, and the bigger the case, the less sense I have of the outside world.

This changed significantly when Bill Pavelic contacted Gary Randa, Cathy Randa's adult son, and in essence hired him as our video archivist. Gary's mission was to tape, each and every day, anything on television regarding O.J.'s case. That included news segments in the morning, both local and national, all the talk shows throughout the day, the evening news wrap-ups, and everything on Court TV and CNN. Every few days, the defense team and the investigators would go through the tapes, paying close attention to the "court of public opinion" that was transpiring outside our office door.

The video archive solved the problem of my tunnel vision, providing a way to be both inside the Simpson case and outside, watching and listening to the same information and punditry the public was getting. We paid close attention as rumors circulated, "eyewitnesses" were identified and then discredited, clues surfaced and then were discounted. Our unofficial, and unpaid, consultants soon included everyone from legal and scientific experts all across the country to the citizen on the street—who was also a potential juror. No one was hesitant to critique my performance, offer theories of the crime, or comment on both prosecution and defense strategies. It was invaluable, although I did have to overcome my impulse to talk back to the TV when someone said something particularly inane.

∞

On Wednesday afternoon, I went down to Parker Center, the Los Angeles police department headquarters. The building has surprisingly limited security and open access, and I easily took the elevator to the robbery and homicide division, the L.A.P.D.'s elite corps of detectives. There I met with Captain William Gartland, Lieutenant John Rogers, and detectives Tom Lange and Philip Vannatter to introduce myself as O.J.'s attorney; Detective Mark Fuhrman, who was taken off the investigation early on the first day, was not at that meeting. I wanted to assure the police that I would be personally responsible for making O.J. available. I also wanted to discover whatever I could about the state and stage of their investigation. I told them that I had retained doctors Lee, Baden, and Wolf, explaining that these were the most respected professionals in their fields and that we were offering their services to the police department, to aid in the investigation to any extent that the police would allow. Their response, not surprisingly, was "No, thanks"—they had their own perfectly fine crime lab, their coroner's office always did a great job, and we didn't have to be concerned about that.

When I asked what the time frame of their investigation

was, no one could tell me. "Can you give us an estimate?" I asked. "A couple of weeks? More? I have a client who's going through a difficult time. If you're going to charge him, I need to prepare him for that and have him available to surrender."

But their only comment was, "We have a lot of work to do, and we just got started." Before leaving, I made sure they had my phone numbers, I told them how to locate me day or night, and I assured them that with an hour or so notice O.J. would be available to them at any time.

When I left the building, the press had already assembled. I introduced myself, explaining that I was now representing Mr. Simpson, that we had engaged the services of the best investigators with the intention of finding the killer, and that in the meantime it was our intention to cooperate with the police department in every way possible.

In general, my attitude toward law enforcement has always been one of respect—a respect that I believe has become mutual over the last twenty-five years. I am, as are the lawyers in the district attorney's office, an officer of the court. I'm viewed by them as a vigorous advocate for my client but one who always operates within the boundaries of fairness. I have a reputation as a keen negotiator, attempting to resolve cases without trials but being well prepared when trials are necessary, and I don't believe in cheap shots. It's a waste of time and energy, and it's neither professional nor pragmatic: Once one trial is over, another begins, and we all have to deal with each other in that courtroom every day.

In addition, anybody who practices criminal law has to have one quality in the eyes of police and prosecutors, and that's credibility. I had a good history with the department, and my credibility was respected to such a degree that when the time came, they were prepared on my word alone to allow a voluntary surrender on O.J.'s part, because for the previous twenty-five years, in all cases, I had always kept my word to them.

That said, it's no secret that in recent times the Los Angeles Police Department has had its difficulties, both with procedure and personnel. The overwhelming majority of these cops are honest and hardworking men and women, doing what has become an increasingly difficult job with courage and integrity. They're constantly confronted with horrendous crimes and violence, much of it aimed directly at them, most of it having to do with narcotics. The public and the politicians have responded by leaning on the cops, hard. It's no wonder that crime has come to be viewed as a shell game by the police: Somewhere under those three shells is the pea—the criminal—and we've got to get him, even if it means smashing up all three shells in the process. And the pressure gets even worse in a big case, a media-driven high-profile case, a "sure-thing" case.

A detective's job is, literally, to detect. To solve crime. But once "getting the guy" becomes the goal, then it doesn't matter how it gets done, as long as it gets done. In my opinion, that's not only constitutionally improper, it's strategically foolish as well; because when there's a rush to judgment for whatever reason, evidence is overlooked or mishandled, and serious procedural and investigative mistakes are made.

Immediately after that first June 15 meeting, I faxed a letter to detectives Vannatter and Lange (with copies faxed to the district attorney's office and the county coroner as well), repeating our offer of expert services from doctors Baden and Lee. In addition, I asked that a second autopsy be performed, stating that while I felt it was inappropriate for me to ask this of the Goldman and Brown families at this difficult time, I would appreciate the request for permission being passed along to them. I was quickly informed that the autopsies had been completed, and the bodies were en route to two separate funeral homes.

In that same letter, I also responded to Detective Lange's request that O.J. take a lie-detector test, stating that we were willing that he do so, on the condition that the results be admissible in any potential criminal litigation.

The use of the lie detector, or polygraph, in the criminal justice system is full of inconsistencies. Every law-enforcement agency employs polygraphers; the FBI has done so for at least twenty-five years, and the CIA and military use polygraphs on a regular basis. The L.A.P.D. employs a full-time staff of polygraphers and commonly uses them for internal investigation of police misconduct cases. The test results create charts that can be interpreted and reinterpreted by experts, and challenged on the basis that the operator asked the wrong questions, framed them the wrong way, or misinterpreted the data. Because the results are open to such wide interpretation, prosecutors have traditionally been averse to use polygraphy, especially in the courtroom. In fact, in California, polygraph tests are specifically precluded by law unless both sides stipulate that the results will be admissible.

At that time Marcia Clark, an assistant to William Hodgman (the head of L.A.'s Special Trials Unit), and David Conn had been assigned by the district attorney to prosecute the case. They responded that the D.A.'s office would allow O.J. to be tested, but they would not stipulate that the results would be admissible. I wasn't surprised at their answer, but I wanted it on the record.

∞

When Gil Garcetti, the Los Angeles district attorney, picked Marcia Clark to prosecute this case, it seemed a refreshing choice to me. I had been friends with Harvey Giss, her mentor, and had known Marcia herself for nearly twenty years—from Kleks to Horowitz to Clark, I joked, referring to the name changes reflecting her first and second marriages.

Marcia Clark's reputation as a prosecutor was excellent; she hadn't lost a case in more than ten years, and some of the convictions were high profile, including the Robert Bardo case (Bardo was convicted for stalking and ultimately murdering the young television actress Rebecca Schaeffer) and the Lewis and Oliver case (where two men used a sawed-off shotgun to fire into a Bible class at the Mt. Olive Church of God in South Central L.A., killing two people).

Shortly before my involvement on the Simpson case, my

office had taken on the defense of a young man who'd been initially accused of first-degree murder, as well as aiding and abetting a robbery. Marcia Clark was the prosecutor we dealt with. After she reviewed the facts of the case and spoke with the trial deputy, she and Karen Filipi negotiated the charges to voluntary manslaughter. The client, however, wanted a trial, which ultimately took place a few doors down from the Simpson trial and lasted three weeks. The jury, out five days, eventually acquitted him on the charges of first-degree murder and robbery and "hung" between second-degree and involuntary manslaughter. He was ultimately released after having served a little more than a year in jail. The two cases provided an odd point-counterpoint, involving as they did associates of Marcia and myself, and a potential first-degree conviction. Because of our negotiations, in this and other cases we'd settled, Marcia impressed me as a professional colleague I could talk to, whom I could trust, who was straightforward. I was confident that she would be an honorable adversary in the Simpson case.

We were to find out some weeks later that we had more in common than we knew. In 1989, nine years after Marcia and her first husband, Gaby Horowitz, were divorced, he was shot. Horowitz, a professional backgammon player originally from Israel, was also a gun collector. He was inspecting a Colt .45 of another collector when the gun accidentally discharged while still in its holster, critically wounding Horowitz in the head and leaving him a paraplegic. I happened to represent the owner of the Colt.

Imagine my surprise—and Marcia's—when the tabloids ran a story about how Shapiro defended the man who shot Marcia Clark's husband!

∞

With two people dying in a violent struggle, as Nicole Brown and Ron Goldman had, the murderer had to have sustained some bodily injury also—at the very least some cuts and bruises. Clearly we had to address O.J.'s physical condition and get a record of it immediately. On Wednesday, June 15, I contacted Dr. Rob Huizenga, a Harvard-educated physician, sports-medicine specialist, and the former team doctor for the Los Angeles Raiders, and set up an immediate appointment with him for O.J. I knew Huizenga and his reputation through my own longtime physician and friend Dr. Robert Koblin, and believed that he was exactly the kind of man and doctor to reassure and calm O.J. during a physical examination.

Additionally, his friends were growing concerned about his emotional state. I had arranged that after he was examined by Huizenga, he would then be seen by Dr. Saul Faerstein, a noted forensic psychiatrist whose professional services are often used by the U.S. attorney's office. Nicole's funeral was to be held the next day, there was a wake and a family gathering to attend that evening, and as the hour grew near, O.J. understandably grew more and more depressed.

Where does a man turn when he is faced with two terrible realities: one, the violent death of an ex-spouse; and two, the fact that he is considered the prime suspect in the murder? He'd had no time to grieve, let alone be alert enough to focus on the details that were necessary to both prepare for a court fight and deal with his other obligations, which were significant. His overwhelming concern for his children—the adult ones, Jason and Arnelle, who had dearly loved Nicole, and the little ones, Sydney and Justin, who had lost her—had O.J. in complete turmoil. The questions about what was going to happen to him, what was going to happen to his kids, and what the future had in store for him were all coming up now on a minute-to-minute basis. For years he had provided financial support to his large extended family, supporting his mother, helping his two sisters, and being significantly responsible for the Browns, the parents as well as Nicole's sisters. How would he be able to maintain that? He wasn't sleeping, and in addition to being exhausted, he seemed to be sinking further into shock by the hour.

In fact, while we were at Dr. Huizenga's office, I received a call from the L.A.P.D. "We've just had a very, very distressing report that O.J. has committed suicide."

"That's very interesting," I answered, "because I'm here with his doctor, and we just took his blood pressure. Oh, Dr. Huizenga," I said, loud enough for them to hear, "was he dead or alive when you took his blood pressure?" So much for that rumor.

In the process of the examination, Huizenga found a swollen lymph node in O.J.'s armpit, which gave him reason for concern. He ran some tests and said he wanted a follow-up exam within the next two days. O.J. then left with Bob Kardashian for his first appointment with Dr. Faerstein.

In the meantime, Bill Pavelic was trying to find out who Ron Goldman was and where he fit into the mystery. Was he a boyfriend? Was he a bystander? Aside from Nicole's close friend and Brentwood neighbor Cora Fischman (who cooperated both on the phone and in person), the women who comprised the core of Nicole's group—Faye Resnick, Robin Greer, Candace Garvey (Steve Garvey's wife), Cynthia "CiCi" Shahian (Kardashian's cousin), and Kris Jenner—all simply refused to talk to us. They were in shock, of course, and grieving the death of their friend. And because of their own suspicions, they'd quickly closed ranks against anyone having to do with O.J. Their hostility was tangible.

There was some tension among these women that O.J. told the police had existed before Nicole's death. "They've got some things going on right now. . . . Something's happening because one of the girlfriends is having a big problem with her husband. Everybody was beefing with everybody."

We heard through the grapevine that Cora Fischman had become somewhat paranoid, saying to a friend of hers, "If the murderer's not O.J., then we're all in trouble, because we know too much." When I interviewed Cora, we discovered that Faye Resnick had been staying with Nicole on Bundy, that there had been a drug intervention on the part of Faye's concerned friends, and Resnick had gone into a drug-rehabilitation program—her third—just four days before the murders. In addition, we knew that Ron Goldman had arrived at Nicole's carrying an envelope that, although it was found to contain her mother's glasses left behind at the restaurant, might have been interpreted by an observer as containing something else, possibly drugs.

So initially it appeared that we might have a reasonable basis for exploring a narcotics angle. Bill Pavelic was looking into the record of 911 calls in the area on the night of the murders; there had been reports of prowlers, and we couldn't dismiss the likelihood that if they were borne out, they could have some connection to the crime. At the very least, we had an obligation to investigate further, if only to rule out the possibility. Ultimately, our investigation was to discover much information about Nicole that was of an intimate and possibly inflammatory nature. It was relevant to the case and we chose not to use it as part of the defense. I choose not to use it now.

O.J.'s life, in fact, was completely opposite of what many people believed. Hardly the party-going, run-around single guy, he preferred to be with girlfriend Paula Barbieri and his close friends most evenings, heading to bed surprisingly between eight and nine every night so that he could play his beloved golf at five in the morning.

Nicole, however, liked her tequila now and then, liked to go out with the girls once in a while, dancing at the Roxy, a Hollywood celebrity hangout, or Bar One or the Renaissance in Santa Monica. But they were divorced, and she was a young, attractive woman of comfortable means. A few nights out, in the scheme of things, and in the world they lived in, didn't mean anything particularly negative. Although they had been divorced at the time of her death, there had been attempts at reconciliation, the first at his instigation and the second at hers, in 1993, when O.J. agreed to give it another year. In mid-May of 1994, they finally agreed that they would go their separate ways while doing what was best for their children.

∞

In addition to the press coverage we'd seen already, with everyone from attorneys to entertainment reporters issuing television commentary every night, the tabloid coverage had begun. O.J.'s house on Rockingham looked like a round-the-clock film shoot, with sound trucks, lights, photographers, and reporters, not to mention casual onlookers, tree-climbers, fence-scalers, and autograph hunters. Someone would later take long-lens shots of the children at the funeral. Film crews and reporters were becoming the nearly constant companions of everyone having to do with the case.

I live in a gated community, so at least they weren't camped on my doorstep, but as soon as I drove out through the gate, it was like a military action forming behind me. Keno Jenkins, my longtime driver and security person, has a black Isuzu Trooper identical to mine. At times, just to get to court or my office, I would have our housekeeper drive one car while Keno drove the other, and I would be down on the floor in the back of one of them. Once through the gate, they would each turn in separate directions, to try to throw off the press parade as they played "Find Shapiro." We all got a kick out of it the first couple of times we pulled it off, but very quickly it became tedious and a waste of time.

On Wednesday evening, June 15, I went with O.J. and Bob Kardashian to Laguna Hills for the small, private wake for Nicole at the funeral home; the funeral itself would be held the next day at St. Martin of Tours Catholic Church in Brentwood.

O.J. was distraught and tearful the entire time he was at the wake. People were coming up and hugging him, talking with him, sitting with him, sharing private moments and memories. The casket was open—it would be closed for the funeral the next day—and he kept drifting toward it. After the service, mourners had been invited back to a quiet reception at the Brown home. As we were leaving, O.J. said he wanted to spend some time alone with Nicole. I stood outside the door and watched as he went up, knelt down next to the casket, and spent the next fifteen minutes quietly talking to her.

The Browns live in a lovely home in the upscale Laguna community of Monarch Bay, adjacent to the beach. Juditha and Louis (who with O.J.'s backing had secured a Hertz franchise at the Ritz-Carlton in Laguna Beach) were gracious and welcoming to their guests, in spite of what they were going through. After I paid my condolences, I continued to talk with Juditha.

Even when his marriage to Nicole was troubled and then ultimately failed, O.J. had maintained a very close relationship with Juditha, and she had always been his friend and ally. "I'm so glad O.J. has you on his side," she said to me. "The children need their father."

I asked her, and Nicole's sisters Denise and Tanya as well, about the last time any of them had talked to Nicole. I was trying to narrow down the time of her death. "I talked to her shortly before 11:00 that night," said her mother.

"How do you know that for sure?" I asked.

"Because when we got home from Los Angeles, I looked at the clock," Juditha said. "I had to call her about leaving my glasses at Mezzaluna, but I didn't want to call her too late. I remember that it was just a few minutes before 11:00."

With that information, and knowing that Allan Park had picked up O.J. at Rockingham a few minutes after 11:00, it seemed to me that it was clear that the murders on Bundy had taken place while O.J. was verifiably at home on Rockingham.

I kept checking back with Juditha, to make certain that *she* was certain. Later I was criticized for questioning her and the family so intensely the night before they had to bury their daughter and sister. However, the Browns wanted to answer these questions as much as I needed to ask them. Everybody wanted to find out who had committed these murders.

Much later, it turned out that Juditha was mistaken. We were confident that the phone records would verify her version, but when we saw them during the preliminary hearing, they indicated that the call had actually been made at about 9:45 P.M., not 10:45. So she was off by an hour. But it would be a while

before I would know that. We'd heard that the district attorney's office had some damning evidence: blood, gloves, maybe
a hat. That's okay, I thought. We have the phone call.

Nicole's funeral was held on Thursday morning at St. Martin of Tours Catholic Church in Brentwood, and O.J. of course
attended with his children, the Brown and Simpson families,
and his close friends. But my place that day, I had decided, was
at my office. One of the first calls I made was to Gerald Uelmen, the retiring dean of the law school at the University of
Santa Clara.

Gerry, although he began his career as a successful prosecutor, first came to public attention in 1972 defending Daniel Ells-
berg in the Pentagon Papers case, and his encyclopedic
knowledge of the law had been invaluable on the Christian
Brando case; in fact, he'd successfully argued a motion to prevent Christian's early interview with the police from being used
against him in that trial. Gerry has been rightly called a
"scholar of the state's and nation's higher courts," and I was
glad to hear that he, too, was willing to join our team.

I tracked down Alan Dershowitz in Israel and asked him,
and later his brother Nathan, to come in as consultants on motions and possible appellate issues, which they agreed to do.
The Dershowitzes, based in Cambridge, Massachusetts, where
Alan is a professor at Harvard Law School, had also worked on
the Brando case with me, but I had known Alan as a colleague
and valued his constitutional knowledge for years before that,
often calling him for advice and feedback. Because of his expertise on appeals (which by definition are preceded by a conviction), we nicknamed Alan the "God Forbid!" lawyer.
Passionate to a fault about the Constitution, the appellate process, and his advocacy of his clients, Alan has more brains—
and, at times, less common sense—than almost anyone I know.
Sometimes his passion leads him to take positions that are painful to watch.

One afternoon a few months into the trial, I got a call from
Larry King. "You should come over to the studio tonight,

Bob," he said. "Alan Dershowitz is in town, and he's gonna be on the show, arguing about police brutality with the head of the Police Protective League."

I immediately tracked Alan down and tried to caution him about the need for discretion, that we should avoid slamming the police while O.J.'s case was making headlines every day. "Please tone it down," I asked him. "The lawyers on the team need to be a little more circumspect these days, especially about the L.A.P.D."

Alan assured me he understood. That night, however, I winced as he spoke on Larry's show of police conspiracies, "testi-*lying*," and the way cops are "trained to lie at the police academy."

Clearly, Alan Dershowitz is the man you want on your side where appellate and Constitutional issues are in question, and he was a boon to this case. As the case evolved, he would be the one player who was always on good terms with everyone on the defense team. He wasn't afraid to stand up to O.J. when he was angry, calm him down when things got rough, and play peacemaker when the occasion warranted. And given the opinions and egos on the defense team on any given day, the occasion warranted quite often.

In a high-profile case, the job of a defense attorney expands beyond advocate to include manager and, when appropriate, spokesman on behalf of the client. And from June 13 to the morning of June 17, my job certainly did expand. I was managing a growing team of law professionals, and struggling to manage the information as well. The reporters and TV cameras were everywhere, of course, but O.J. was no stranger to publicity, and with many athletes, entertainers, and public figures as clients, I had dealt with publicity before. I knew that I wasn't the celebrity here, O.J. was. They couldn't get to him, so they came after me and anyone having to do with the case. However, the sheer number of cameras, reporters, and interview requests amazed us all. Wasn't anything else happening in the country? And then came Friday, June 17.

At 8:30 that morning I was on the phone with Michael Nasatir, a noted criminal defense attorney and old college friend, who naturally wanted to know what was going on with the case. What were the police going to do? Was there going to be an arrest?

"I have very little information at this point," I told him. "The unofficial word is that nothing's going to happen for a while." At that point, I had to put him on hold and pick up the other line, to hear the voice of L.A.P.D. Detective Tom Lange.

"We are going to charge O.J. Simpson with two counts of first-degree murder," Lange said. "We want you to surrender him here by ten o'clock."

I took a deep breath. Here it comes, I thought. "I'll contact him immediately and make the arrangements," I said, "and we'll be bringing him in to turn himself in voluntarily." I hung up and switched back to Nasatir.

"Well, I can answer your question right now," I told him. "They're charging him, and I've got to go over and get him ready to surrender immediately." I started to think, This is happening way too fast. What have they got that they should be moving so fast?

Although they could've filed charges at any time, the information we had been getting from the police department and the district attorney was that the investigation was proceeding, they would probably need more time, and they were prepared to take as much as they needed. I thought, in turn, that this would give *us* more time—to prepare with O.J. and to conduct our own investigation. Now that time had run out.

After the funeral the previous day, O.J. had gone into seclusion at Bob Kardashian's. I had never been there before, and so I called Bob to tell him what was going on and to get directions, asking that in the meantime he not tell O.J. anything until I got there.

The directions to Kardashian's were complicated. On the

face of it, he lives only minutes from my neighborhood, but with the hills and the side streets, it was difficult to find. It's a beautifully situated two-story home in the Encino hills, constructed of marble and granite, and when we finally found it, Bob met me at the door, telling me O.J. was still asleep upstairs. He was on some medication, antianxiety or antidepressant, something prescribed by Dr. Faerstein.

Kardashian's house is enormous, perhaps ten thousand square feet, with many rooms and long hallways. He led me to the guest room where O.J. had been staying. When I woke him up, O.J. was groggy and somewhat confused as to why I was there. When he learned the reason, he was stunned. I immediately called Dr. Faerstein and phoned Dr. Huizenga as well. There had been no time to deal with O.J.'s swollen lymph node, which could have been a precursor to cancer, and it was imperative also that Huizenga take our own set of forensic samples—skin, blood, hair—for our own analysis and comparison. I knew that once O.J. was actually in jail we probably wouldn't have the opportunity to do it. I also wanted Faerstein and Huizenga available for O.J.'s support when he surrendered. In addition, I wanted him reexamined by Baden and Lee, with more photographs. These photographs wouldn't be for public consumption; they'd be offered as defense evidence.

As everyone converged on Bob Kardashian's house, the day began to take on a tone of controlled chaos. Not frantic or hysterical—there was too much to do, and too much at stake, for hysteria. Rather, it was tense but controlled, like a war room might have been, or a hostage negotiation.

Kardashian, of course, was there, as was Kardashian's girlfriend, Denice Shakarian Halicki, Cathy Randa, Paula Barbieri, and A.C. Cowlings, O.J.'s old friend. I had known Paula for some time; she had once dated another client of mine. A sweet-natured and quite beautiful young woman, whose emotional support was invaluable to O.J., she was primarily concerned that those around him were doing what was necessary to protect him. I had known A.C. as well, running into him over the years. He had grown up with O.J. in the Portrero Hill Housing projects in San Francisco and played football with him at both USC and Buffalo. He was his oldest, closest, and most loyal friend. It seemed to be the kind of fierce, wordless friendship in which one man knows what the other is about to say or do before he says or does it.

Los Angeles, for all its sprawl and speed, can often seem like any other town: a series of neighborhoods in which the same people can run into each other for years and in which people's lives overlap, in joy and tragedy, just as they do all across the country. On Friday, June 17, many of those lives were colliding under Bob Kardashian's roof. And each person thought that what he or she had to do was the most important.

O.J. made endless phone calls; he needed to put his affairs in order, he wanted to talk to his kids, to his mother. By 9:30, Huizenga and his nurses were taking blood from both of O.J.'s arms simultaneously. Henry Lee, who needed body samples that would address his investigation, was pulling out O.J.'s hair and scraping his skin. Michael Baden, in the process of a painstaking pathological examination, was taking pictures of his body. Paula was in and out of the room, talking quietly to O.J., trying to comfort him.

I called Marcia Clark. "We're not going to make it to the Parker Center by ten."

She said, "Bob, you've got to make it by ten."

"Look," I said, "we know you're going to lock the man up. I thought we'd have another couple of days before this would happen. He's talking to his personal attorney, there's the matter of his two small children. He has to get his affairs in order, talk with the rest of his family, Jason and Arnelle, and his mother. There are doctors here examining him. Marcia, let me call Parker Center and see if we can stretch this a little."

She agreed that I could call the police and ask for some leeway. They gave us until eleven o'clock. By eleven, although we were getting close, we still weren't ready to leave, and everyone's nerves were getting a little raw. At the center of it all was O.J. He had written and sealed some letters, addressed to family and friends. Now he was sitting in his underwear, methodically arranging custody of his children and power of attorney over his personal and business affairs while nurses drew blood out of his arms and scientists pulled hairs out of his head.

And then, as we came down to the wire, he walked into another room with A.C. to talk privately. All through the previous days, A.C. had been a constant presence, solid as a rock. We didn't worry about O.J. as long as he was with his friend, who seemed to have grown bigger and stronger as O.J. became quieter and more passive.

After they'd gone, Michael Baden and I spoke quietly to Dr. Faerstein, who was very concerned about O.J.'s state of mind. I was genuinely concerned about the potential for suicide. For a man who defined himself in physical expression and motion, there was a curious stillness to O.J., a leaden presence. His skin was ashen and his eyes seemed somehow flattened out in his head. Michael Baden had observed all through the week that although O.J.'s weight had remained the same, his body seemed to have shrunk somehow. Perhaps it would be a good idea, Baden suggested, if Faerstein called the doctor at the jail, to let him know what was going on and make sure that O.J. was put on suicide watch once he got there.

I made another call to the police and the district attorney's office, trying to negotiate more time for O.J.'s surrender. But finally, when it was close to one o'clock, Detective Lange announced, "No more time. We're coming to arrest him."

I said, "Look, we're all driving down to Parker Center together, in two cars—his doctors, me, A.C., my driver, Bob Kardashian. Just give us a little more time."

"No go," he said. "We're on our way to you now."

"Wait, wait, just talk to his doctor," I said. I put Dr. Faerstein on the line, and he tried to talk to them about O.J.'s condition and his professional concerns about a possible suicide attempt. But Faerstein had no success. "The commander said this has gone past the deadline," Lange told him. "We have a warrant. What's your location?"

Defeated, Faerstein just looked at me. "They want to know where we are," he said. "They have a warrant."

I passed the phone to Kardashian. "We don't have a choice, there's a warrant for his arrest. We have to give him up, now," I told him. "Tell them where we are."

In order not to panic O.J., we decided among ourselves not to go downstairs and tell him and A.C. that the police were on their way. We would wait, we decided, until they got here. Fifteen minutes, twenty minutes. It was grim.

When the two police cars finally arrived, Kardashian went down and opened the front door to let the four officers in, showing them where O.J. was waiting for them. Only he wasn't. And neither was A.C. My heart just fell. O.J., I thought, what have you done?

Kardashian mentioned the letters O.J. had written. We quickly found them and opened the one addressed "To my friends." It was handwritten, and quite long. We read it over each other's shoulders.

> *To whom it may concern: First, everyone understand, I have nothing to do with Nicole's murder. I loved her. I always have and I always will. If we had a problem, it's because I loved her so much.*
>
> *Recently we came to the understanding that for now we were not right for each other, at least for now. Despite our love we were different and that's why we mutually agreed to go our separate ways. It was tough splitting for a second time but we both knew it was for the best.*
>
> *Inside I had no doubt that in the future we would be close friends or more. Unlike what has been written in the press, Nicole and I had a great relationship for most of our lives together. Like all long-term relationships, we had a few downs and ups. I took the heat New Year's 1989 because that's what I was supposed to do. I did not plead no contest for any other reason but to protect our privacy and was advised it would end the press hype.*
>
> *I don't want to belabor knocking the press, but I can't believe*

what is being said. Most of it is totally made up. I know you have a job to do, but as a last wish, please, please, please, leave my children in peace. Their lives will be tough enough.

I want to send my love and thanks to all my friends. I'm sorry I can't name every one of you. Especially A.C., man thanks for being in my life. The support and friendship I received from so many, Wayne Hughes, Louis Marks, Frank Olsen, Mark Packer, Bender, Bobby Kardashian.

I wish we had spent more time together in recent years. My golfing buddies, Haas, Alan Austin, Mike, Craig, Bender, Wiler, Sandy, Jay, Donnie, thanks for all the fun. All my teammates over the years. Reggie, you were the soul of my pro career; Ahmad, I never stopped being proud of you; Marcus, you got a great lady in Catherine, don't mess it up. Bobby Chandler, thanks for always being there. Skip and Cathy, I love you guys, without you I never would have made it through this far. Marguerite, thanks for the early years. We had some fun. Paula, what can I say? You are special. I'm sorry I'm not going to—we're not going to have our chance. God brought you to me, I now see as I leave you'll be in my thoughts.

I think of my life and feel I've done most of the right things, so why do I end up like this. I can't go on. No matter what the outcome people will look and point. I can't take that. I can't subject my children to that. This way they can move on and go on with their lives. Please, if I've done anything worthwhile in my life, let my kids live in peace from you, the press.

I've had a good life. I'm proud of how I lived. My mama taught me to do unto others. I treated people the way I wanted to be treated. I've always tried to be up and helpful. So why is this happening? I'm sorry for the Goldman family. I know how much it hurts.

Nicole and I had a good life together. All this press talk about a rocky relationship was no more than what every long-term relationship experiences. All her friends will confirm that I have been totally loving and understanding of what she's been going through. At times I have felt like a battered husband or boyfriend but I loved her. And I would take whatever it took to make it work.

Don't feel sorry for me. I've had a great life, great friends. Please think of the real O.J. and not this lost person.

Thanks for making my life special. I hope I helped yours.

Peace and love, O.J.

In a gesture that seemed oddly childlike, he had drawn a smiley face inside the *O*. Stunned, I looked at Dr. Faerstein. "What do you think this means?" I asked, almost not wanting to hear his answer. He just shook his head. I don't think there was anyone in that room who didn't believe, at that moment, that O.J. had gone off to kill himself.

It was now nearly two—and the police declared the Kardashian house a crime scene. They detained all of us under house arrest and took a statement from every person. As the long afternoon wore on, the tension and fear factor increased.

At about three, Gil Garcetti called, asking to speak to me. When I put the phone to my ear, there was no doubt that the district attorney was livid.

"I'm here with Suzanne Childs [his press secretary] and we're at a loss to understand this, Bob," he said, his voice barely controlled. "Can you explain to me how a murder suspect just disappears from a house full of people?"

I knew Garcetti reasonably well; in fact, not only had I supported his reelection campaign and done some major fund-raising for him, I had been named to the board of advisors of the District Attorney's Association. He'd come to my fiftieth birthday party. He had trusted me. Now, it was clear, he believed that his trust had been badly misplaced. I could only imagine, between the press and the police chief's office, the kind of heat he was getting at this moment—heat that he was ready to redirect towards me.

"Gil, look," I said, trying to control my own fears about O.J. and calm Garcetti's anger at the same time, "I gave my word that he would surrender on his own, and that's still my intention. Don't forget I promised to bring Erik Menendez in, and I did, all the way from Israel. If O.J.'s alive, and we're hoping that he is, I'll do everything I can to get him there."

In the meantime my wife, who hadn't heard from me all day, had grown more and more worried, and she finally beeped my driver, Keno, who called me to the phone.

"What on earth is going on there?" Linell asked. "We're

watching TV, and they're reporting that he's disappeared or something."

"You know as much as I do," I told her. "We were preparing to surrender him, and then . . . and there's this letter. It's awful, Linell. We're pretty sure that he's gone off to kill himself."

"Everyone's calling here looking for you," she said, "and I was so worried. Nobody knew where you were, and when I didn't hear anything, we began to think that maybe you'd gone with him. And now there's all this speculating on television."

She told me that David Gascon, the L.A.P.D. commander, had appeared on TV, obviously furious, and made a statement to the effect that anyone who was involved in O.J.'s disappearance was now involved in a felony and would be dealt with as a felon. Gascon's anger didn't dissipate over time. A year and a half later, when Michael Nasatir and I were at a Kings hockey game, we ran into him, and it was apparent, although he was cordial, that he was still smoldering over the fact that O.J. hadn't been surrendered as we had promised—thus making the L.A.P.D. look foolish.

In the meantime, Linell had more information for me. "Lee Bailey called," she said, "and asked that you call him back immediately."

When I got Bailey on the phone, he said, "Bob, you have to respond to this somehow. They're on the air, out-and-out accusing you, claiming that you're involved somehow, that you're deliberately not surrendering him."

"Lee, wait," I said, "that's totally ridiculous. I mean, we've got this suicidal letter here, and—"

"No, no, no," he interrupted. "You've got to speak up, and do it now. Before it gets worse."

I told Kardashian what was going on outside the walls of his house. And then I called up my office and spoke with Bonnie, asking her to please do whatever it took to set up a large conference area somewhere in the building and to notify the press that we would be there at 5:00 P.M. to make a statement.

On the way over in the car, Kardashian and I discussed O.J.'s letter, which I thought he should read aloud at the press conference. "People have to hear his own words, so they can understand what's going on," I said. "So they'll know what we know."

"Bob, I can't do that," Kardashian said. "In front of a room full of reporters? I don't think I'll be able to get through it."

As I tried to figure out a way to help him, I suddenly remembered a conversation I'd once had with Jack Nicholson. I'd met him while I was working on the Brando case and asked him about talking in front of a camera, about how to be effective and not self-conscious. He told me, "The best help I ever got was from John Wayne. Years ago I was riding with him in an elevator at the studio and asked what kind of advice he might give to a young actor. He just said, 'Remember two things: Speak low, and speak slow.'" This was what I told Bob Kardashian.

When we got to the conference room—it was actually the former lobby of a bank in our office building—it was a mob scene. I had spoken at press conferences before, but nothing like this. The camera lights were blinding, it was hot, and it was noisy. But the room grew stone-cold silent when I walked up to the microphone. "O.J.," I said, "wherever you are, for the sake of your family, for the sake of your children, please surrender immediately. Surrender to any law-enforcement official at any police station, but please do it immediately."

I then detailed the events of the day, and Bob Kardashian quietly and slowly read O.J.'s letter. His fingers gripping the paper, he read it well. He told me later that his heart was about to come out of his throat.

Afterward, I faced the reporters and answered questions for about forty-five minutes. Then we all went upstairs to my office, frustrated and sad. Where was O.J.? Kardashian speculated that perhaps he was headed for the Coliseum or USC, to kill himself there as some type of symbolism. Or maybe he was going to Nicole's grave. After a few desultory minutes of conversation, Keno drove Bob Kardashian home, everyone else drifted off, and I sat at my desk alone, trying to make sense of it all.

In four days I had gone from a cheerful party at the House of Blues to a murder investigation to a client I believed at this very moment was committing suicide. Perhaps he was dead already. To top it off, the police were all but calling me a felon. It was some small comfort the next day to read in the *Los Angeles Times* that we had conducted "the most captivating live press conference ever" in front of approximately ninety-five million TV viewers. I felt many emotions as I stood in front of those cameras, but "captivating" wasn't on the list. I was hoping only that O.J. was alive—hoping that he had been alive to hear me and Kardashian and that he would stay alive and come in on his own.

An hour later, I was still sitting numbly at my desk. A little before seven, Peter Weil, one of my law partners, dropped by the office. He had his son with him. "Boy, this has been a rough day for you," Peter said.

"You have no idea," I said.

"Are you going home soon?" he asked.

I shook my head. "No, I have to wait. The press is still camped outside, I don't want to leave until they've thinned out a little. One press conference a day is plenty."

"Bob, I have an idea," Peter said. "I'll bring my car to the side entrance, and we'll sneak you out that way. They won't be watching that door—security closes it at six—and they're not looking for my car, either."

His plan worked. On the drive home, I tried to lift my spirits by talking with Peter's son, Adam, who was not quite nine. I love my own boys so absolutely. What they think and what they care about is tremendously important to me, and so it was a comfort to fall into easy conversation with young Adam. Very quickly I discovered that he was an avid baseball fan.

When we got to my house, I asked them if they would please wait a couple of minutes while I ran inside. I promised I'd be right back out. When I came through the front door,

Linell was standing there. "Bob, what on earth is going on? Where are you going?"

"Just a minute," I said, and went into my study.

I have a lot of baseball memorabilia that I've collected over the years, both from the professional players I've represented and from the ones I've been a fan of. After looking it all over for a couple of seconds, I grabbed a signed baseball, took it back outside, and gave it to Adam. He looked at it.

"Orel Hershiser!" he exclaimed. There, I thought, as Peter and Adam drove away, I feel a little better.

"Well, it's just a matter of time," I said to Linell as I walked back into the house. "O.J.'s killed himself, I know it. It's just a question of when they find him."

She looked at me in shock. "Are you crazy?" she asked. "Where have you been? He's on television, Bob. He's been driving up and down the freeway for hours with Al Cowlings. Complete with news helicopters, and some kind of police escort, and people cheering him on the overpasses, you can't believe it. Come in here, you've got to take a look at this!"

I stood in front of the television in disbelief. There he was in the white Bronco, with A.C. driving. He had a gun, someone had reported, and a cell phone. His former football buddies Vince Evans and Walter Payton were pleading with him to surrender. The conversations were being picked up and broadcast on radio and television, and all the while people were following him in their cars, or standing on the sidelines cheering, like he was running down a football field. "I can't believe this," I said. "There's just no way this can be happening."

Later there was much made of the fact that he also had a great deal of cash, his passport, and a beard-and-mustache disguise with him in the car. The theory was he was heading for Mexico, or even farther. But through what airport, over what national border, could this man reasonably have gone? The police were watching him constantly, and so was the press, and he was aware of that. For four days his image had been plastered on the front of every newspaper and broadcast on every television news report.

The explanation was simple: The mustache-and-beard disguise had been ordered by him some weeks before (using his own name and address, the police easily discovered, which hardly pointed to subterfuge) so that he could take his children on a planned trip to an amusement park without being recognized; the sizable amount of cash and passport were always with him, as was the cell phone, when it wasn't in one of his cars. These items were all carried in the black leather bag he was known to have with him constantly, not unlike other business people with their bulging computer cases. He flew back and forth across the country quite often, and on short notice, on business for Hertz or the NBC network, for whom he was a sports commentator. The cash was his "pocket money" used for golf, gambling, tipping, et cetera; in fact, Faye Resnick, in her book, noted that both O.J. and Nicole were known to carry large amounts of cash, into the thousands, all the time, and they often paid for things, even big-ticket items, with cash rather than with their credit cards. In this instance, it was evidently O.J.'s intention that after his suicide the cash go immediately to his small children as a stopgap support measure until the larger legal matters were handled on their behalf.

Linell and I were transfixed in front of the television. All over the country people had done what I just did: walked into the house after a long day, to be greeted by a televised three-ring circus, a weird national spectacle, at the center of which was my client. Larry King had tracked down Michael Baden in Los Angeles, and now Baden was providing mile-by-mile commentary for CNN. Network coverage of the NBA playoffs had been temporarily interrupted for the breaking O.J. news, and when coverage was resumed, a window in the upper right side of the TV screen monitored the Bronco's strange ride.

"My God," I said to my wife, "I hope the police don't decide to start shooting at that car." And then we heard he was heading home, back to Brentwood.

"You'd better get over to Rockingham," Linell said.

I ran out and got into my car, grabbed the car phone, and punched in 911 as I took off. "I need to talk to the L.A.P.D.," I snapped.

"Is this an emergency?" the operator asked.

"Yes, it's an emergency!" I said. "I'm Robert Shapiro, O.J. Simpson's lawyer, and I have to get to him, to his house in Brentwood. I know the police have blocked off some streets, and what with the traffic and the people, I'm going to need some help to get there."

In a minute or two, the police were on the line. "Where are you, Mr. Shapiro?" they asked.

"Beverly Glen and Sunset," I said.

"Just keep going that direction." They took the description of my car, and within two or three more minutes a motorcycle cop pulled up, motioned me to follow him, and turned on his flashing lights and siren. Falling in behind him, I took off on what would normally have been about a twenty-minute drive. This time, weaving in and out of traffic on Sunset, mostly on the wrong side of the street, the trip took all of five minutes.

When I turned onto Rockingham, the street was cordoned off and lined with people. Someone recognized me, presumably from the televised news conference earlier that afternoon, and a voice shouted out, "It's Shapiro, it's Shapiro!" People actually started cheering. All I could think was, Where the hell is O.J.?

The police let me drive a little farther down the street, near the front gate. The captain and the commander came over and asked me to stay back—they had a SWAT team lined up there. O.J. was in the house with A.C., Kardashian, and Jason, his son. Eunice Simpson, O.J.'s mother, had been checked into the hospital in Oakland. No one knew for sure whether it was a heart attack or an understandable physical reaction to the emotional roller coaster of this day. I could hear the voices squawking on the police radio. "He's coming out, he's coming out. He's in the police car."

When the squad car rolled back down the drive, I could see

O.J. inside. He turned and saw me and nodded almost imperceptibly. I nodded back, and then the car drove away. Later O.J. would say that as A.C. had pulled the Bronco into the driveway, he was still holding the gun to his head, not yet ready to abandon the idea of suicide. When his son Jason ran up to the driver's-side door, Cowlings, who knew that the situation was still delicate and O.J.'s behavior unpredictable, instinctively shoved Jason out of the way, both to protect him and to try to keep things stabilized. When O.J. heard Jason cry "Dad! Dad!" he suddenly realized that for his children's sake, suicide was not an option for him. It's entirely possible that Jason saved his life.

Michael Baden, who'd hitched a ride to Rockingham on a TV camera-crew truck, joined me on the street. As we glumly watched the police car pull away from Rockingham, a good strong wind could have blown me over. I hadn't eaten anything all day and had only a vague recollection of grabbing a soda at Kardashian's. All I could think of was the strange ride O.J. had taken and the police caravan that hadn't followed him as much as escorted him.

I offered Baden a ride back to his hotel, and as we slowly walked back to my car, some reporters stopped me and asked for my comments.

"I want to personally congratulate Chief Willie Williams and the entire staff of Los Angeles police officers who were able to resolve one of the most incredible situations in a very, very peaceful manner," I said, and I meant every word. "I can't express the fear I had that this matter would not end the way it did. Also at this point I ask all members of the public to please reserve any judgment on this case until the evidence is reviewed in a court of law."

As I got into the car, a man walked by with two children. I didn't recognize him (because, as my wife says, I never recognize anybody), so for a second or two I didn't have any context for what he said to me.

"When you see O.J., tell him good luck from Kurt and Goldie." It was actor Kurt Russell. Once again I was reminded that Los Angeles is a company town.

Chapter Three

My legal assistant, Bonnie Barron, has run my law office exceptionally well for five years. In addition, I have two young associates, Karen Filipi and Sara Caplan, both superb attorneys and trusted colleagues. It was not until after the Simpson trial was over, in October of 1995, that I officially became a partner in one of Los Angeles's leading law firms—Christensen, White, Miller, Fink, Jacobs, Glaser and Shapiro—and had access to its support staff. Until then, although my offices were in the same physical location as the firm, I maintained my own practice and my own staff, four people in all.

After the Bronco chase and the press conference, it became obvious that this case would require much, much more staff and support than we had. Camera trucks took up residence in the parking lot and reporters arrived in the reception area and insisted on seeing me. Access to the nineteenth floor, where my office was located, was quickly restricted by building security. The mail began to pile up, hundreds of pieces each day. Initially it was from professionals—private investigators, lawyers, scientists, forensic specialists—all offering their services, but within days, envelopes began to come in addressed to O.J. from supporters, detractors, football fans, unrequited lovers. Death threats, marriage proposals, single dollar bills falling out of envelopes. We were in danger of being buried by the avalanche. Help arrived when Gerry Uelmen contacted a friend of his, Stan Goldman, a professor at Loyola, who brought in student volunteers from the law school to help us with the mail. Each piece had to be opened, logged, read, and screened for threats or possible clues.

The telephone rang constantly, with messages coming in faster than they could be logged. Quickly, new phone lines were added, but that only increased the noise factor. The first time O.J. called collect from the jail, his voice was low, almost inaudible. Convinced it was yet another crank call, Bonnie adamantly refused to accept it. A minute later he called back and again gave his name, this time very slowly and deliberately. This time the call was accepted, with apologies.

By the end of the first week, Bonnie and some of the others (ultimately there were more than twenty) were ducking out of the office every couple of hours, forwarding the telephone calls to the firm's receptionist before they left, then heading for the parking lot to smoke cigarettes or have a good cry. Everyone involved was being contacted for press interviews or being followed by tabloid reporters. "Nobody dares to ask me for an interview," Bonnie boasted with typical determination. "I'm too rude."

Given what she was fending off, she wasn't as rude as she was probably entitled to be. Within a couple of weeks, she had recruited her adult daughter, Erika, to help with the phones, and her friend Stephanie Pion to work as assistant to the four private investigators, coordinating their telephone messages, mail, and their file memos to the attorneys. At around the same time, Petra Brando, Marlon's daughter (who was scheduled to begin law school in the fall), started coming in and archiving the print material—page after page of magazine and newspaper articles, as well as analytical pieces in law journals. This, in addition to Gary Randa's video files, kept us all in touch with the outside world, which was important, given that none of us were actually living in it.

There were days that it seemed less like a law office than the fabled mail room at the William Morris Agency, or some kind of surreal factory assembly line. It was hard to think, let alone find the focus and concentration that we all needed. The voice-mail system's capacity was fifty messages, and we easily reached that every twenty minutes, at which point the "mailbox" would simply shut down and take no more messages. The calls were coming in at such a rate that no one could ever get a line for outgoing calls, so we had to have new lines installed for our own use. And when we announced an 800 number, along with a $500,000 reward for information leading to the arrest of the murderer(s), fiber-optic hell broke loose: within the first two weeks, Pacific Bell's voice-mail system had recorded and logged 250,000 calls—one a minute—which we then had to log and store on cassette tapes as part of the investigation. Callers who couldn't get through on the 800 number reverted to calling the office number. Every hour or so Bonnie had to "dump" the voice mail and then record the messages in her computer, deciding which ones were genuine and which ones were cranks, and pass them along to Bill Pavelic. We couldn't possibly deal with every call, but it was difficult to dismiss the possibility that among the callers who received radio signals in their fillings or saw the killer's name in their tea leaves might be the one solid lead we needed.

Immediately after O.J.'s surrender on June 17, I heard from many of his closest friends, all asking questions about the legal procedures to come and wanting to know how they could help. They were especially anxious to stay in touch with O.J., to do whatever he needed to keep his spirits up. So I arranged for a number of them to come into my office on the following Sunday.

Skip Taft and Bob Kardashian were in the group, of course, as was A.C. Cowlings. Others included football great Marcus Allen and his wife, Catherine; Raider quarterback Vince Evans;

O.J.'s golfing buddies Alan Austin, Craig Baumgarten, and Bob Hoskins; clothing entrepreneur Alan Schwartz; talent agent Joe Kolkowicz; and businessman Wayne Hughes (the founder of a public-storage company, upon whom O.J. had long relied for financial advice). Bill Pavelic came also; he needed to get to know these people and the roles each of them played in O.J.'s life.

Once everyone was assembled, we set up a conference call with O.J. As his familiar voice came over the speaker phone, the emotion in the room immediately ran high. Marcus Allen was the first to speak.

"Hey, Juice," he said, fighting back tears. "Hey, man, how ya doing?"

"I'm doing okay, Marcus," said O.J. quietly. "I'm doing okay."

As he had done with the police, he quickly apologized for worrying everyone during Friday's Bronco ride. One by one, their voices cracking, each person spoke to him, telling him how much they cared for him, encouraging him to be strong, vowing to do whatever they could to get him through this ordeal. It was clear that he was moved, not just by what they said but by the realization that these people had all come together solely for his sake.

Loyalty is the one human quality I value more than any other, and as I listened, it struck me that these friendships were mostly all long-standing ones, among self-made men with drive and talent, who had worked hard, stayed close to each other through their struggles, and built solid, successful lives. Jocks and businessmen alike were unashamed to cry, not afraid to use words like "love" to another man, knowing that's what he needed to hear. I could easily identify with them, because my friends were cut from the same cloth. Surely, I thought, this speaks to the quality of O.J.'s character. These people had known him well, for many years, and they believed him.

Since each of them had been in contact with O.J. immediately around the time of the murders and therefore could speak to his demeanor, we were successful in getting them on the court-approved visitor's list of material witnesses at the county jail. Nicole Pulvers, a young lawyer who had been working for Bob Kardashian, was designated as the attorney who would be present for these visits, as the court required.

Sadly, some of these friendships would dissolve in the difficult months to come, as tension, doubt, and the glare of the media caused some to lose faith. Alan Austin became disillusioned and gradually separated himself, as did Alan Schwartz. Rumors were flying about there having been a relationship between Marcus Allen and Nicole, which Marcus vehemently denied and which caused great heartache to his wife. We tried to subpoena him in Missouri, but he was successful in fighting it. And within a few weeks, Wayne Hughes and I would come to loggerheads about O.J.'s defense; he wanted to have a stronger voice in directing it, and I couldn't allow that.

Almost immediately after O.J.'s arrest, Gil Garcetti went on an unprecedented media "tour," hitting the local airwaves as well as the national ones, with appearances on *Nightline* and *This Week with David Brinkley*. He freely discussed the charges of first-degree murder and offered his personal opinion that not only was O.J. guilty but in all likelihood he would use a "Menendez-type" defense (in which the Menendez brothers admitted that, yes, they killed their parents, but years of abuse had driven them to it).

I had been practicing criminal law for twenty-five years, and many of my cases had been high profile. It was only natural that I had accumulated some expertise in dealing with the press, believing as I did that wealth and fame not only didn't protect or insulate people accused of crime, it often made their situation worse. In fact, in a paper written for a law journal two years before, I had said that immediately after a celebrity arrest, a D.A. and chief of police can almost inevitably be counted on to go to the press, announce that they have solved the crime, congratulate each other on doing such a wonderful job, and take credit for quick and fast action in their crime-solving ability and pursuit of justice. Even knowing this, Gil Garcetti's statements completely surprised me. He might've been angry that O.J. hadn't surrendered in a timely manner; maybe he thought the press coverage of the Bronco ride and subsequent arrest was too sympathetic. Whatever his reason, as I saw his quotes picked up by news stations and newsmagazines across the country, I thought, This is going too far.

The district attorney position in Los Angeles is a political one; candidates run for election every four years. Historically, incumbents pay the price for losing high-profile criminal cases. For instance, the renowned McMartin Pre-School molestation case (which dragged on for an unprecedented six years) made Robert Philobosian vulnerable to Ira Reiner. After the acquittal of the McMartin defendants and the defendants in the first Rodney King trial, Reiner gave way to Gil Garcetti. Now, in the wake of the Menendez hung jury and the Reginald Denny trial, Garcetti needed O.J.'s case as political damage control. The question, then, was not whether an indictment would be returned, the question was how soon.

There are two ways for a felony charge to be brought against someone in the state of California. One way is for the police, after an investigation, to submit charges to the district attorney, who then simply signs the complaint, has an arrest warrant issued, and charges someone with that felony, at which point a preliminary hearing takes place. At a preliminary hearing the prosecution presents witnesses under oath, and the rules of evidence are greatly relaxed; for instance, hearsay evidence is admissible. Defense cross-examination is allowed but generally very restricted. The burden on the prosecution is light; they only have to show that a crime has been committed and that there is a strong likelihood that the person charged is guilty.

The second way for a felony charge to be brought is for the prosecutor to bring a case before the grand jury. The proceedings are secret, and there are no rules of evidence, no judge, no cross-examination. Only the prosecution is present; the defendant and defense counsel are not. If sixteen members of that jury vote for an indictment, a person is then charged criminally, and the matter goes directly to trial.

The term "grand jury investigation" is a misnomer. Although legally empowered with the ability to begin investigations on their own, grand juries in California—and indeed, in most American jurisdictions—are a powerful tool in the prosecution's arsenal. Traditionally a body that meets in secret to investigate corruption or allegations with political overtones, a grand jury is made up of citizens (the number depends on the size of the county's population; there were twenty-three people hearing the Simpson case) chosen after being nominated by judges. They serve for a term, rather than for a case—a period of one year (in California; eighteen months in most other jurisdictions)—and have the power to subpoena, investigate, and indict; they can charge an individual with a crime (called a "true bill") or reject charges (called a "not-true bill").

Grand juries are a potent prosecution tool because they compel witnesses to come forward who might otherwise be reluctant to do so. They're a political tool as well, allowing the district attorney to step back from filing charges independently, letting the grand jury do it instead—which is especially important in politically sensitive cases or instances where the potential defendant is either popular or powerful. Within hours of O.J.'s arrest, we knew that Garcetti was going to the grand jury.

After the district attorney's TV blitz, I quickly called Gerald Uelmen and Alan Dershowitz, and they agreed with me that he had gone over the line. Making out-of-court statements that speculate on guilty pleas and mental defenses raise more than a few serious questions; and when the head of the largest district attorney's office in the country announces categorically, just days after a murder, that the case is solved—before any meaningful forensic examinations have taken place, before any DNA analysis—it tilts the strategic weight heavily to the prosecution's side.

"An independent review from the grand jury is out of the question now," I told Dershowitz and Uelmen. "I think we should consider filing a motion to disqualify the grand jury, shut it down, based on prosecutorial misconduct."

Their reaction was hardly a vote of confidence. Gerry said we had *no* chance for the motion to prevail; Alan, ever the optimist, thought it was worth giving it a try but acknowledged that our chances weren't great. Nevertheless, with Sara Caplan's assistance, we started looking for precedents. Yet we couldn't find a single case—in the entire country—that had ever managed to stop a grand jury before deliberation.

"I want to pursue it anyway," I insisted. "Garcetti's gone too far, he's writing 'case closed' on this before we've even begun, and he's doing it in public." In fact, I believed that when Garcetti opened up on us with his public-relations big guns, he also opened up a hole big enough to drive the Constitution through.

For days, Uelmen, Dershowitz, Sara and I prepared separate drafts on how to approach this; the ultimate motion would incorporate everyone's thoughts and research, but the thrust of the argument remained prosecutorial misconduct. And while we were working—fully aware that the grand jury was hearing secret testimony at the same time—the 911 tapes were released.

In response to a demand from news organizations citing California's Public Records Act, L.A. city attorney James Hahn had released tape-recordings of phone calls that Nicole Brown Simpson had made in 1993 to the 911 police emergency number. They were being played on radio and television broadcasts, and the transcript of the tapes was being read, not just in Los Angeles but all across the country.

I had an immediate visceral reaction to the tapes, and not just because they related to O.J. The previous year, I had represented Tina Sinatra in her action against James Farentino, her former companion. After their five-year relationship ended, Farentino had begun harassing Tina, leaving frightening messages, up to fifty or sixty a day at one point, on her phone and fax machines. Although he never physically abused her, the angry messages included threats of physical violence or death to her and members of her family, as well as destruction of property. Tina never took the threats lightly; Farentino was known to have a temper, and a recurring battle with alcohol, which she knew exacerbated his behavior. Caught between her compassion for him, and her growing fears for her own safety, Tina waited for months before telling anyone what was going on. "I knew it was out of control," she said, "but I was embarrassed, and scared for him."

When she finally reported the matter to the police, they were sympathetic, but because the couple was not living together, and because there were never any physical acts of violence, there was very little they could do. Tina obtained a restraining order that forbade Farentino to contact her, but as most victims discover, weaknesses in enforcement can make a restraining order an empty remedy. "We can't make an arrest until someone is hurt" is a frequent response. And besides, how do you restrain a fax machine? That's when Tina came to me, completely stressed out, angry, and frightened. She needed to find a way to stop Farentino before his behavior grew worse, which she absolutely believed would happen.

Bill Pavelic began an investigation that traced the pattern of phone and fax messages, establishing clearly that they were coming from Farentino. We then went to Los Angeles city attorney James Hahn, who has been very active in pursuing victims' rights, and presented him with our information. The constantly escalating threats and Farentino's refusal to abide by the restraining order were sufficient to bring the case into the realm of the state's stalking laws. At that time, stalking was a misdemeanor in California; now it's a felony.

Farentino was arrested and charged with twenty-four misdemeanor counts of stalking. He ultimately pleaded no contest to one count and was sentenced to thirty-six months probation and a regimen of psychiatric and alcohol counseling. The legal remedy and the subsequent treatment were successful; both parties have now gone on with their lives. However, when I heard the sound of Nicole's voice on the 911 tapes, I heard the same fear that Tina had experienced. Indeed, anyone who heard the tapes—and much of the world did—would never be able to forget the sound of the frightened woman and the enraged man.

The police department blamed the district attorney's office for releasing the tapes; Garcetti's office blamed the city attorney. I didn't care at that point whose fault it was, I only knew that the tapes should never have been released at all. How could a jury be impaneled after this? How could O.J. ever get a fair trial?

Chief of Police Willie Williams quickly agreed to impose a gag order on his department, and Garcetti pledged that no matter what pressures the press brought to bear, absolutely nothing more would be released by his office or the L.A.P.D. He said he disagreed with Hahn's release of the tapes and claimed that in spite of the publicity, he had no doubt about the possibility of an impartial jury and a fair trial for O.J. "I'm confident," he said, "that we can find twelve jurors who know very little about this." And where will you find them? I wondered. Living in caves?

That same week, *Time* and *Newsweek* ran identical covers of the police photograph that had been taken when O.J. was arrested after the Bronco chase. But *Time* had tinkered with their version, making O.J.'s skin tone darker than it actually is, much darker than the original photo itself. This is getting out of hand, I thought angrily. This isn't a courtroom sketch artist's rendering they're fooling with here, it's a *real photograph*. What were the editors thinking? Why make a black man look blacker than he is?

There was an immediate, and negative, public response to the photo "enhancement" and a subsequent apology from *Time*'s editors, but I guessed that the people who read the apology were a tiny fraction of those who had seen the magazine cover.

Finally, at 8:30 on June 24—exactly one week after the Bronco ride—Gerry Uelmen and I were ready to file our motion to stop the grand jury. On the way to court, Uelmen looked at me and said, "Bob, we're right to file this, but you know we're going to lose."

"I think we're going to win," I said. "Because we're right." If we won, it would be an unprecedented legal victory; if we lost, at the very least it would be the beginning of what lawyers call "building the record," forming the basis for an appeal in case of a conviction.

We filed our motion with Superior Court Judge Lance A. Ito (who at that time was the assistant supervising judge of the criminal division but had not yet been assigned to hear this case). Our brief requested that he question each of the twenty-three grand jurors to determine if they'd heard either Garcetti's statements or the 911 tapes and might possibly be influenced by them. We also brought up the fact that a day or two earlier Marcia Clark had publicly concluded that O.J. was the "sole murderer."

"The district attorney's office has improperly released, and massive publicity has been given by the media to, inadmissible evidence in this case, the best example of which was the massive airing . . . of the 911 tapes," we argued.

"Before any charges were brought or conclusive tests could be run, the public was made aware of bloodstains on driveways, matching blood types, bloody gloves, and the alleged weapon," read our motion. Uelmen stated that the "barrage of publicity" had been "unprecedented."

While we were presenting our motion before Judge Ito, Judge Cecil Mills, the supervising judge of the Superior Court (for both civil and criminal court), was interviewing the grand jurors, reportedly in response to a request from Gil Garcetti, perhaps motivated by the copy of our motion in his hand. What Mills was hearing from the jurors disturbed him, and at 10:30 that morning, he issued his ruling.

"Having made the inquiry, the court finds that as an unanticipated result of the unique circumstances of this matter pending before the 1993–1994 grand jury, some jurors have become aware of potentially prejudicial matters not officially presented to them by the district attorney," he said. He was thus dismissing the grand jury "to preclude any unintended consideration of prejudicial matter and protect the due process rights of Mr. Simpson and the integrity of the grand jury process."

We had won it! We had gotten a grand jury dismissed before they'd ruled, and we had created legal precedent at the same time. And a good thing, too: At the point at which they were stopped, the jurors had heard all the testimony and were on the verge of taking a vote. One dismissed grand juror was quoted as saying, "Almost everything that the jury knows has been reported in the paper. I would say if you read the papers, you know everything the grand jury knows." Included in our motion was a request for the transcript of the grand jury proceedings, which would normally have been kept secret. The transcript would give us a good preview of the prosecution witness lineup.

I felt like we had been taking a beating for days, and now the momentum had finally, finally shifted in our favor. Now the district attorney would either have to impanel a new grand jury or schedule a preliminary hearing. In fact, California law entitles people in custody to preliminary hearings within ten days of being charged.

Rarely, however, can anyone meet that deadline. Courts are crowded, lawyers need time to prepare, and a "waiver of time" is routinely granted to the defense to allow additional preparation time. We heard reports that just after the grand jury was dismissed, Garcetti held a meeting of his assistant district attorneys in which he asked how many of them had ever tried a preliminary hearing with me. Almost all the hands went up. When he facetiously countered with, "And how many of those hearings started on time?" most of the hands went down. So the prosecution's office thought they were safe in assuming that with a high-profile double homicide, and a defendant possibly facing the death penalty, we would be in dire need of a waiver of time before beginning a preliminary hearing. And I knew that if we asked for it, we could get it. Which would, in turn, give *them* more time. I decided not to ask for it.

We were ready to go, and they were not.

Chapter Four

As he became more involved in the decision making—and more knowledgeable about the judicial process—O.J. began adjusting his hope of being home in time to go trick-or-treating with his kids for Halloween. Maybe Thanksgiving made more sense. Christmas at the latest. We couldn't have imagined that it *would* be Halloween—a year later.

In my opinion, we were ready to go ahead with a preliminary hearing the following week. The prosecution didn't expect us to be prepared so soon—I'm sure they believed we would ask for a waiver of time. Putting the pressure on them, and ourselves, was a risk. But it was one I wanted to take.

Getting ready for a preliminary in such a short time required an effort that, as always, paralleled the prosecution's. My associates, Sara Caplan and Karen Filipi, put in extraordinarily long days, checking and cross-checking motions, witness statements, and reports and memos from the investigators. Since Karen had recently left the district attorney's office, she was very familiar with their procedures, and Sara, a Phi Beta Kappa graduate, was as diligent as she was smart. I knew they wouldn't miss anything.

The clerical work alone was daunting: There were fourteen people on our document-distribution list, so every memo, every motion, every piece of paper was duplicated fourteen times and distributed. We'd experienced a lot of document bootlegging during the Brando trial, so the duplication process had to be monitored very closely. If the originals were taken out of the office to a copy service, someone from the office would stand beside the machine and watch every piece of paper that went in and every piece of paper that came out. When paper jams stopped the photocopiers, Bonnie took the crumpled paper home and destroyed it there. She kept a close eye on the gentle-manly Dean Uelmen as he sat in the research library poring over law books, drafting motions, and writing in longhand on yellow legal pads. Not one of his discarded yellow sheets was ever allowed to sit in a trash can or on a tabletop.

Barbara Wolf devised a complex computerized tracking sys-tem for the forensic evidence—blood, hair, body fluids, fabric, clothing items—that had been gathered at the crime scene and was going out to labs for analysis. As part of discovery—the mandated exchange of information between the prosecution and the defense—we would receive memos or lists of items, their destinations, and all ultimate test results. Wolf and Baden would then chart everything. The list, which was originally numbered 1 through 60, was close to 400 by the end of the trial.

Knowing that the tabloids would go through people's gar-bage, I got a paper shredder for the office and home, and Bob Kardashian and Skip Taft each got one as well. In addition, we began to pay extra careful attention to the messages coming in on the phone lines, as Bonnie screened them and passed them on to Bill Pavelic.

∞

There are two different strategies a district attorney can use at a preliminary hearing. One is the bare-bones approach: present-ing a small amount of evidence to get by the "probable cause" burden set by law, which is quite minimal. In the second ap-proach, all, or nearly all, of the evidence is laid out, in a process that almost resembles a dress rehearsal for the trial itself. This is often done with high-profile cases, so that the prosecution can publicly demonstrate the strength of its case and at the same time counter any possible cynical public opinion.

If the bare-bones approach to a preliminary was used against Simpson, the public might wonder where all the evidence was. And if we had gone from a secret grand jury hearing directly to an indictment, the defense wouldn't have been able to see the prosecution's cards. However, with the kind of preliminary hearing I suspected we were about to get, I'd not only be able to see what they were holding, I might even be able to raise the bet.

From the defense standpoint, a preliminary hearing can work in two ways: first, as a discovery tool, to find out about the prosecution's case; second, as a way to lay the groundwork for the trial itself. In essence, a preliminary can serve as a small-scale trial, and in the O.J. Simpson case, that's exactly what happened. What is normally a perfunctory stage in a case very quickly became an essential part—if not *the* essential part—of the Simpson defense strategy. And within two weeks of O.J.'s arrest, we had laid the groundwork for the trial that we knew was coming.

From the very beginning, we believed the scientific evidence would be the strongest part of the D.A.'s case, and we would most likely have to embrace the science rather than attack it. DNA is accepted as legitimate in the scientific community; and generally, whatever is accepted in the scientific community is accepted by the public at large, even though very few people have any real understanding of it, including lawyers who practice in the criminal courts on a daily basis. Since 1987, DNA evidence has been admissible in most U.S. courts, although Washington, Arizona, Vermont, and Massachusetts have ruled it inadmissible for the time being. So far, however, it's been used in more than twenty thousand cases.

Contained within our chromosomes—and identifiable in blood, blood stains, hair, semen, body fluids, and skin tissue—DNA (deoxyribonucleic acid) is often referred to as the "building block" or "genetic fingerprint" of human beings. More than 99 percent of human DNA is identical among individuals. It is the less than 1 percent remaining that gives individuals (with the exception of identical twins) unique characteristics and can make DNA a vital piece of evidence in a criminal case. Properly collected dried blood or semen stains, tissue fragments, or chemically preserved whole blood can link a suspect to a scene or victim, a weapon to a victim, or a victim to a particular location. A defendant's blood type is cross-matched with blood or tissue samples found at a crime scene, to see if there is a match. Then lab technicians run a set of statistics that point to how likely—or not—it is that the match might be the result of a false positive.

Initially, forensic DNA typing is performed through a process termed restriction fragment length polymorphism, or RFLP. Using a technique called autoradiography, in which a radiograph resulting from the exposure of X-ray film corresponds to fragments of DNA labeled with a radioactive probe, RFLP detects DNA sequences repeated a variable number of times among different individuals. The technician then compares the autoradiogram with a sample obtained from a suspect.

However, if forensic specimens have deteriorated or degraded, there may not be an amount of DNA sufficient to do RFLP testing. When that's the case, the next step is polymerase chain reaction (PCR) technology, which allows as little as one to two nanograms of DNA to be amplified hundreds of thousands of times, in a process popularly called "molecular Xeroxing." RFLP is considered to be more specifically "discriminatory"—that is, precise; PCR is faster and can be applied to smaller samples, or to those in poor condition.

Over the years, there has been a great debate about the admissibility of DNA evidence. With all science there are pitfalls, and DNA typing, for all its scientific reliability, is not immune. There are three billion chemical units to each human being's heredity. DNA only tests for six of them. Another argument says that DNA statistics can be so overwhelming to a jury that they effectively cancel the importance of other evidence, predisposing a jury to a prosecution's argument. In addition, if specimens for analysis are not properly collected and preserved, their biological activity may be lost. Yet another argument debates the reliability of "population genetics," which places individuals and their DNA characteristics in relation to ethnic groups. Additionally, there is subjectivity inherent in interpreting the results of DNA typing; that is, one forensic scientist may interpret a test differently than another. And as with all forensic evidence, DNA evidence doesn't exist in a vacuum; it must be interpreted in light of other information and other evidence. For example, although DNA collected at a particular scene may link an individual to that scene, it doesn't tell us when that DNA was left there. Furthermore, although RFLP had been admitted in trials all over the country, PCR had never been admitted in California by any appellate court.

I believed that the defense strategy should focus on the collection and contamination of the evidence, not on the scientific analysis itself. I needed experts not to debunk the science (as was often the case in the early use of DNA evidence) but to find the inevitable human errors and counter them with expertise.

I had never worked on a case before where DNA was involved, and knew little about it. However, I knew enough to realize that the immediate challenge was not only educating myself in the science but learning how to make it understandable to a jury. With the advice and recommendations of Michael Baden and Barbara Wolf, I put together a reading list, preparing my crash course on DNA. I wasn't fool enough to anoint myself an instant DNA expert. I had to go elsewhere for that.

Although I'd not met them, I had seen DNA experts Barry Scheck and Peter Neufeld on TV commenting on the Simpson case, speculating on the role that DNA analysis would play in the prosecution's argument. Few defense attorneys had combined national reputations in the field of DNA with acknowledged expertise as trial lawyers, but Scheck and Neufeld were at the top of the field. In addition, they were noted for setting up Yeshiva University's Innocence Project, the purpose of which is to use DNA to prove innocence on behalf of people already convicted of crimes.

Michael Baden, when he'd served on New York governor Mario Cuomo's commission on the use of DNA in criminal trials, found Scheck and Neufeld lined up on the other side of the conference table. He was representing the police-and-prosecution side of the argument; they were representing the defense side. Baden told me he thought they were brilliant; "very effective curmudgeons" is how he described them. In asking them to come onto this case, I knew I'd be presenting them with a dilemma: In order to counter the prosecution's use of DNA, I needed them to point out weaknesses of the science they'd worked so hard to establish as an evidentiary tool. Nevertheless, they agreed to join us. It wasn't long before the office staff had dubbed the two New Yorkers Simon and Garfunkel.

A few days after the Bronco chase, Baden, Wolf, and Lee met with Dr. Lakshmanan Sathyavagiswaran, the Los Angeles County coroner, to examine the forensic evidence from the autopsies. Baden and Lakshmanan had known each other for some time. Baden, who years before had hired Lakshmanan at the New York City Medical Examiner's Office, called him Lucky.

The district attorney had insisted that everything we do be videotaped, but I appealed to the judge that such action was not only unnecessary, it was unprecedented. Even without the video cameras, Dr. Lakshmanan was exceedingly guarded in his conversations with us. Although he and Baden had great respect and admiration for each other, there was no mistaking the battle line down the middle of the room. Baden, for instance, was later to testify that although he was "allowed" to examine evidence, he wasn't allowed to photograph it; and the normally imperturbable Dr. Lee testified that "they wouldn't even give me a microscope!"

As they examined the evidence, our scientists found numerous errors had been made. For example, they pointed out a very obvious brain contusion sustained by Nicole that Dr. Irwin Golden, the deputy medical examiner who had actually performed the procedures, had completely missed. In addition, he had discarded her stomach contents without performing the kind of analysis that would have helped narrow the time of death, and he hadn't swabbed either Nicole or Ron Goldman for semen samples, a standard procedure in murder investigations. What else, we wondered, had he missed—or done wrong?

∞

Getting the grand jury dismissed didn't stop—or negate—the effects of Garcetti's comments about Menendez, and Clark's comments about O.J. being the sole killer. They had been repeated and reprinted everywhere. Our potential jurors were out there listening and reading; they had some information already and would gain even more with the televised preliminary hearing, so it was imperative that our reasonable-doubt counterattack begin there. (Later, the answers we received on the first round of jury questionnaires indicated that the majority of the pool had seen at least portions of the preliminary and had *already* formed opinions!) The preliminary hearing would be, in essence, nothing less than a battle for the hearts and minds of the jury pool.

In addition to DNA, the issue I was most focused on was the search-and-seizure procedures of the investigating police officers. Armed with the L.A.P.D. procedures manual and his own extensive experience, Bill Pavelic began a log that cross-referenced official procedure with what the police investigators had actually done at the crime scene. Very quickly, he came up with a damning list: they had failed to notify the coroner in the prescribed time; they had failed to complete individual chronology reports; they prepared erroneous property reports; they misrepresented the facts in the search warrant affidavit on the first day of the investigation; they carried forensic evidence from Bundy to Rockingham, rather than taking it to a lab; they didn't secure evidence (Nicole's home, O.J.'s car) in a timely manner; they used the crime scene at Bundy as a staging area for their investigation, using the phone inside the house to make their calls, and the furniture inside to sit on while they talked, rather than cordoning it off completely; and finally, of the chronology reports that were completed, not one was contemporaneous. No one, it seemed, made notes while they looked at their watches. No one had even *looked* at their watches.

Pavelic was irate. As a senior police detective, he had actually been responsible for auditing the department's "murder books," the step-by-step records investigating officers complete for each case. He well knew what an acceptable level of procedural error should be; in this case, they were way over their limit. "I've never seen a police investigation so screwed up in the infancy stage," he told me. "If there's an anatomy of how *not* to do an investigation, this might be it."

The police report on the way evidence was gathered was written by detectives Tom Lange and Philip Vannatter. A common technique to avoid inconsistencies is to have one officer write a summary report, based on individual reports; but the proper procedure is that anyone who does anything substantial is responsible for recording that aspect of the investigation. Mark Fuhrman, who we later discovered had played a key role in the early stage of the investigation, never wrote a single report. The police might argue that Fuhrman had been taken off the case within the first hour, once the elite Robbery-Homicide division came on the scene; however, I would argue that finding a key piece of evidence—the gloves—would certainly qualify as "something substantial" and require a written report, however brief, from Fuhrman. So why didn't he write one?

We knew that four detectives (Lange, Vannatter, Fuhrman, and Phillips) left the crime scene on Bundy at a little before 5:00 A.M. after only a minimal, almost perfunctory investigation, and then went to O.J.'s house at Rockingham—either because they believed that someone there was in imminent danger (according to Fuhrman) or to notify O.J. Simpson of his ex-wife's death and the needs of his small children (according to Vannatter). Fuhrman testified that he was the first detective at the Bundy crime scene and, because he knew the way to Rockingham, was asked to show Vannatter how to get there. Vannatter, however, testified that he knew the area well and would have had no trouble whatsoever in getting to Rockingham on his own.

While a personal notification is always appropriate, it was implausible to me that with the entire department brass available, the only four homicide detectives on a case would leave a crime scene—and let another ten hours pass before the coroner was called to that scene, which is a violation of state law. Why didn't two detectives go to Rockingham and two stay at Bundy? Why was the department criminalist, Dennis Fung, dispatched to Rockingham first (where no crime was known to have taken place) as opposed to Bundy (where evidence of a double homicide was everywhere)?

If, as Vannatter testified, O.J. was not then a suspect, why, when no one answered the telephone or the bell at the gate after ten or fifteen minutes, didn't they say "Let's go back to Bundy and continue the investigation"? Instead, Fuhrman testified that he decided to take a walk around the corner and coincidentally saw the Bronco, parked at what he thought was an odd or inappropriate angle. On further inspection, he said, he saw blood—a minuscule blood spot on the driver's door near the handle, as well as faint blood smears on the bottom of the door. Now, he decided, it was an emergency, so he scaled the fence, opened the gate for the others, and they all proceeded to inspect the property for hours without a warrant. They discovered O.J.'s daughter, Arnelle, and Kato Kaelin, in their separate quarters outside the main house. The detectives woke them up, questioned them, and told Arnelle she had to let them into the house "so they could search the premises." It's here where the notification explanation quite obviously falls apart.

If, however, the other explanation prevailed—and they believed an additional crime might have been committed or was possibly being committed that moment at Rockingham, placing its inhabitants in danger—why did they go there without calling for backup, without bullet-proof vests, without drawn weapons? Why, if they believed that criminals might have been lurking and house occupants might have been in danger, did they ask Arnelle Simpson, a young woman, to go back into the house first, alone? Once in the house, why didn't the detectives themselves immediately go upstairs? There were any number of rooms and closets where someone could have been hiding.

Warrants are available twenty-four hours a day, and at night they are frequently granted over the telephone; in fact, judges are assigned to night duty for that specific purpose. But not until six hours after arriving at Rockingham did the police finally obtain a search warrant, one based primarily on their contention that Mr. Simpson had "suddenly" gone on an "unexpected" trip—when in fact they'd been told quite clearly by Arnelle and Cathy Randa that his trip had been planned for some time. In fact, they'd spoken to O.J. in Chicago at that point. They knew where he was; they knew the Chicago police would have assisted in keeping him from fleeing, or escorted him back to Los Angeles.

And when Fuhrman found that leather glove at Rockingham, wouldn't that have been an occasion to share his finding as soon as possible with all the other detectives? An officer who had just come from a crime scene where one glove was discovered and then found what looked like its match in a second location—wouldn't he have wanted his colleagues to know this immediately? Why instead did he approach the detectives one by one and take them individually to the place where the glove lay? His behavior didn't pass the common-sense test.

In addition, although Vannatter testified that O.J.'s Bronco (which had been parked on the street) had been secured by the police at 7:00 A.M., our own investigation revealed coffee stains on the hood of the car as a result of the press gathering around and leaving their cups on it. Not only had the car not been correctly secured, it apparently took on the public-access status of a park bench. We even had a video of someone—not a police officer—touching the door handle on the driver's side as the car was being towed to Viertel's, the police-authorized towing service. An employee from the towing service, John Meraz, was later to testify that not only did other employees get in and out of the Bronco (in an odd sort of curiosity-seeking behavior), but he himself took credit-card receipts from it, receipts that had been signed by both O.J. and Nicole. The lax security conditions and easy access to the Bronco lasted for nearly three months.

So what was their story? Did four homicide detectives leave a crime scene to notify an ex-spouse (who was not, in fact, the next of kin to the murdered woman) of those murders? Did they rush to Rockingham to save its inhabitants from harm? Or did they rush to judgment, deciding among themselves in those early dawn hours that O.J. Simpson was the primary suspect and therefore it didn't matter which came first, the evidence or the warrants? It was the old police shell game: The pea's under here; we know it, and it doesn't matter how we get it.

Ironically, if the detectives had said from the very beginning that they believed O.J. was a suspect and they were in hot pursuit, such an opinion would've been sufficient to allow their entry onto the property without a warrant. Instead, unwittingly or not, they built a web of lies, with Mark Fuhrman at its center. And then they got caught in it.

∞

The criminal process is divided into two general areas: factual issues and legal issues. Factual issues are determined by a "trier of fact," which can be either a judge or jury. Legal issues are determined only by a judge. These are not "technicalities" or "loopholes." They are constitutional rights.

Prior to the preliminary hearing, Gerry Uelmen, Sara Caplan, and I prepared and filed a motion on Wednesday, June

24, stating that the thirty-four items of evidence taken from Rockingham were gathered in violation of O.J.'s Fourth Amendment right of protection against illegal search and sei-zure, and therefore should be inadmissible. In raising the admis-sibility of the evidence, we were challenging the validity of the warrants but not the credibility of the officers; that would be saved until later. Los Angeles municipal judge Kathleen Ken-nedy-Powell stated that she would hear defense and prosecution arguments and rule on the motion the following week.

The law in California allows us to raise search-and-seizure issues only once; thus if we raise them at a preliminary hearing in municipal court, we can't raise them again in superior court. So caution—and strategic planning—generally dictate that mo-tions be made later rather than sooner. And the reality is that judges generally apply a lighter constitutional standard as evi-dence becomes more important to the prosecution's case and thus harder to exclude. For example, if under the same set of circumstances either a small amount of marijuana is found or a murder weapon is found, a judge might be inclined to grant the defense an illegal search motion for the marijuana (therefore not allowing it into evidence), but he wouldn't be likely to do the same for a murder weapon, given the negative consequences to the prosecution.

I decided to hold off litigating the credibility of the search warrants themselves until we got to superior court, to the trial. This turned out to be the right decision, because even though Judge Ito ultimately upheld the warrants, he also found that Detective Vannatter had exercised a "reckless disregard for the truth" when he procured them. That's harsh on-the-record lan-guage, and it certainly went to the credibility of one of the lead detectives in this investigation.

∞

On Sunday, June 26, the weekend between the grand jury and the preliminary hearings, I called a last-minute summit meeting of friends and colleagues in my legal community who specialized in strategy, trial law, and appellate law. These were lawyers whose reputations were excellent, whose peer group held them in the highest esteem, and whose advice and counsel I greatly valued. They willingly came, with very little notice and no compensation, knowing that this wasn't an "audition" for a position on the defense team but a brainstorming session for my benefit—and, by extension, for my client's. Forty were invited; thirty-nine attended. Only Barry Tarlow, a gifted trial and appellate lawyer, was missing—because he mistakenly did not get the message.

The group included my associates Sara Caplan and Karen Filipi; Don Ré, one of the lawyers instrumental in the DeLorean case; Mona Soo Hoo, who had worked with Ré and prepared all the DeLorean motions; Alvin Michaelson and Janet Levine, two estimable trial lawyers; Marshall Grossman, a civil trial lawyer; Larry Feldman, a personal-injury specialist who had successfully represented the young boy who accused Michael Jackson of molestation; Michael Nasatir and Richard Hirsch, college classmates of mine and former federal prosecutors; Jay Jaffe, a USC graduate and authority on criminal law, as well as an expert in capital punishment; Dennis Fischer and Charles Lindner, the appellate specialists we would later bring in to help us with writs on motions that had been denied by Judge Lance Ito; Tony Glassman, a First Amendment specialist; Terry Christensen and Patty Glaser, superb trial lawyers who were later to become my partners; Richard Sherman, a trial lawyer who had been Gerry Spence's protégé; and Roger Cossack, a former U.S. attorney and now host of CNN's *Burden of Proof.*

All through that day, this summit made a 360-degree examination of every aspect of the case any of us could imagine. We made lists, invented hypotheticals, shared opinions, experiences, and lists of potential expert witnesses. We compared notes on jury consultants: Who had everyone used? Of those, which ones had been effective? Which ones had been less so? What kind of courtroom style and expertise would be required at the trial, and what kind of technology? We talked about graphic artists and the preparation of demonstrative evidence, such as computerized graphics of timelines and charts of medical evidence. What lawyers should possibly be at the defense table with me? Who would be more effective working in the background?

With Marcia Clark representing the prosecution, I felt strongly that a woman as defense co-counsel would strengthen the case. I've always enjoyed working with women lawyers, and have worked with some brilliant ones. Call it instinct, women's intuition, the ability to relate to female jurors—I've found all these qualities to be advantageous.

In addition, since the D.A. had chosen to prosecute the case in downtown Los Angeles, we knew that a mixed-race jury was a given. And although African Americans make up a relatively small percentage of the voter registration, when it comes to jury service, the downtown panels generally include a higher proportion of black jurors. Bringing in an African-American woman lawyer might serve to psychologically balance the fact that O.J. had been married to a white woman. It might also give me greater insight into the thinking of African-American women jurors, and women in general, on the allegations of past spouse abuse, which the district attorney was clearly going to use to establish motive. But would it be perceived positively or would it simply look like tokenism? Would it put undue emphasis on race as a factor in the case, or would it provide a common-sense depth and balance that we might otherwise be lacking?

From ten o'clock that morning into the evening, we wrestled with these questions and many more besides. When the session was over, I came away with a legal pad full of notes, names, phone numbers, legal citations, and precedents, as well as a defense strategy that I believed would be unbeatable.

∞

The preliminary hearing, which was to last six days, began on Thursday, June 30, with Judge Kennedy-Powell presiding. Bob

Kardashian, Skip Taft, Gerry Uelmen, Sara Caplan, and Karen Filipi accompanied me to court; Marcia Clark was now joined at the table by her boss in the D.A.'s office, Bill Hodgman. David Conn, the original co-lead prosecutor, had been taken off the case when his statement regarding the release of the 911 tapes contradicted that of Chief Willie Williams.

Later there would be some press speculation that Clark had been paired with Hodgman because he was gentlemanly and fatherly with witnesses and might "soften" her image. But Hodgman was hardly window dressing; in his distinguished career, he had prosecuted over forty murder cases, and he most recently had won the conviction of savings-and-loan magnate Charles Keating. Lance Ito had been the presiding judge in the Keating case. I knew that Bill Hodgman's gentlemanly demeanor blunted neither his intelligence nor his intention to fight this case down to the wire.

During the six-day preliminary, twenty-one witnesses would testify. Marcia Clark and I spent the morning of the first day splitting hairs. At first they were literal ones. She wanted one hundred hairs removed from O.J.'s head for forensic testing, in order to compare them to hairs found inside a navy-blue watch cap seized by police at Bundy. I countered that Dr. Lee had advised us that three hairs would be sufficient. Judge Kennedy-Powell ultimately ruled that the prosecution could have up to one hundred.

It was during my cross-examination of Michelle Kestler, the assistant director of the L.A.P.D. crime lab, that the question first came up of splitting or sharing forensic evidence for DNA testing. What had been tested so far? What remained to be tested? Would there be enough left, after the prosecution's tests had been done, for the defense to run its own DNA tests? As I proceeded to question Kestler item by item—there were sixty—Marcia Clark began her pattern of objections. Some were sustained, some overruled, but the net effect was to establish in a very real way the adversarial nature of our relationship in that courtroom.

Clark: "This is going to take all day in the manner in which counsel is proceeding."

Shapiro: "Your Honor, with all due respect, I am representing a man who is charged with two counts of first-degree murder and may be facing the death penalty."

Clark: "I'm trying to assist counsel in being more efficient and more effective."

Shapiro: "We certainly appreciate that. . . . If we don't have any further interruptions or suggestions as to how we should present our case, perhaps we can finish this."

∞

Two witnesses at the preliminary hearing were called regarding the murder weapon—or rather, speculation about the weapon, which had not been found. The police had been contacted by Allen Wattenberg, the owner of a cutlery store in downtown Los Angeles, who told them that O.J. had come in about six weeks before the murders and purchased a large stiletto knife from a store clerk, Jose Camacho. Upon hearing this, detectives Lange and Vannatter went to the store, purchased a similar knife, and brought it to the coroner for comparison with the sizes of the wounds, at which point, it seems, they all concluded that the knife O.J. had purchased had been the murder weapon.

During his testimony, Camacho revealed that he'd been paid $12,500 by the *National Enquirer* for his story. (The TV tabloid show *Hard Copy* had only offered him "peanuts," Camacho said.) The appearance of seeking notoriety can impeach a witness's credibility—that is, make it look like he has his own agenda for testifying. Although he should have been told by the prosecutor's office not to discuss anything with reporters, he testified that when he asked someone who was in charge of witnesses in the D.A.'s office if he could talk to the tabloids, she told him that talking to the press was up to him. This wouldn't be our last experience with potential witnesses jumping on the cash-for-trash bandwagon. When payments are made for information that becomes testimony, questions are raised not just about a witness's credibility but about his agenda or possible bias. Some people will say anything for money.

The actual knife that O.J. bought was found exactly where we believed it would be. In his master bedroom, there is a dressing table with a three-panel mirror on top of it. The side panels open, revealing storage areas. That's where he had put the knife—which was in fact the smaller of the two versions the store clerk had described. And it had never been used at all, for anything. We filed a motion to have a Special Master appointed to go retrieve the knife from its location.

"Special Master" is a term used to describe a lawyer or judge appointed to supervise a sensitive search warrant; for example, one for an attorney's office, where the police might come upon confidential information that is either irrelevant or beyond the scope of the search at hand. A Special Master is independent of the court and the prosecutor-police, and sworn to ignore items not related specifically to the warrant. If there's a dispute or question about an item, the Special Master brings it back for a hearing with an outside judge, so there won't be any chance of tainting the evidence.

We were not obligated to turn over or notify the prosecution and court of evidence that was exculpatory—that is, favorable to the defense—which the pristine knife certainly was. But my thinking was that had we waited until the trial (which at that point looked like it would occur in August of 1994 but would in reality not begin until January 1995) and then argued that this knife had been seized by Mr. Simpson's lawyers and kept since June of 1994, it would put the lawyers' credibility in question and raise a great deal of suspicion as well. Why, the question would be, did the defense hide that until now?

Gerry Uelmen and I met with Judge Ito in his chambers and asked him in his administrative role to appoint a Special Master to retrieve the knife and turn it over to the court for safekeeping. Ito then contacted retired judge Delbert Wong, explained the situation to him, and asked him to serve as Special Master. Wong agreed, and the next morning, accompanied by Bob Kar-

dashian, he went to Rockingham, took copious notes, and removed the knife from its hiding place. The knife was returned
in a manila envelope, under seal, to Ito. It was our intention
that it remain in the custody of the court until and unless it was
needed in the trial itself.

In a particularly dramatic moment at the preliminary hearing, I took a risk and broke my own rule of never asking a
question I didn't know the answer to. We wanted to establish
that the knife O.J. had purchased had been put in a safe storage
place and never removed, by O.J. or anyone else. I asked the
searching officer if he or the others had thought to look in the
mirrored cabinet. When he answered that he had not, I looked
at O.J. with relief.

The "mystery envelope" containing the knife took on a dis-
proportionate importance when Judge Mills walked into the
courtroom with it and called Judge Kennedy-Powell off the
bench (in front of the TV cameras). She returned to the bench
with the envelope and announced that she was going to open
it. I immediately objected. Judge Kennedy-Powell ruled that
the envelope would stay sealed until defense and prosecution
had time to submit briefs on why—or why not—the envelope
and its contents should become evidence.

It turned out that immediately after Judge Ito had taken the
envelope under seal, he went out of town on a planned long
weekend. When Judge Cecil Mills heard about the envelope, he
had a different opinion about our use of the Special Master
and whether evidence like this should be withheld from the
prosecution. So he gave it to Kennedy-Powell with the idea that
once the prosecution became aware of it, they would insist that
it be entered into evidence.

While speculation mounted that the envelope contained the
actual knife that O.J. had purchased, the prosecution never
again talked about it, its purchase, or their theory that it had
been the murder weapon. It wasn't. Dr. Lee's forensic tests
revealed that the knife had never been used by anyone for any

purpose, and it was in the exact same condition it had been in when purchased.

Although we were still at the beginning of what we both knew would be a lengthy process, I began to sense that in spite of our previous working relationship, I was getting under Marcia Clark's skin. No matter what I said or did, she would come right back at me—that is, it seemed, at *me*, not at what had just occurred procedurally. When she countered our manila envelope with one of her own, ostensibly containing the records of Juditha Brown's telephone conversation with Nicole, she seemed to present it with a "take that!" gesture. As was noted in *Newsweek* at one point, "Lead prosecutor Marcia Clark never lost an opportunity to retail her material with theatrical flair."

Just as the preliminary got under way, the Fourth of July holiday weekend arrived, and court was recessed. Normally Linell and I take the two boys to the beach for fireworks, but this year she took the boys, and I stayed home working. Miraculously, the phone didn't ring. It was strange not having anyone around, but the peace and serenity of being by myself there was something I hadn't experienced in a long time. It lasted exactly two days. On Monday, we all trooped back into the office.

As I was leaving Drai's one evening prior to the preliminary, I met a woman named Jackie Kallen, the only female boxing manager in the world. I knew the name, and I knew she was managing world champions. You might expect a woman in the fight business to be the prototype of a tough broad, but Jackie Kallen, lovely in both dress and appearance, is tough where it counts: in her brain.

"I manage James Toney, the middleweight champ," she said. "We're in town for a couple of weeks training for his Las Vegas championship fight with Prince Charles Williams. I understand you like to box. Would you like to come by the gym? If you want, you can even work out with him a round or two."

Astonished at the chance not only to meet Toney but to spar with him, I eagerly made a date for the following Sunday. It was to be a private session; Toney's training time in the gym was closed except to his family and close friends, and I didn't tell anybody except my family what I was going to do.

The gym was in an old office building. The boxing ring was in a far corner, along with two speed bags, a couple of double-ended bags, an area for jumping rope, and a bathroom that was there long before World War II. Toney was in the ring with his sparring partner, who was about three inches taller and out-weighed him by twenty pounds. Toney himself, although he fought at 165, looked more like 190, even though he was only two weeks away from the championship fight. Working inside, he was deliberately absorbing blows to toughen himself up. With Grant lingering somewhat shyly behind us, Linell and I greeted Jackie, who introduced us to the manager of the gym, the trainer, and James Toney's mother, who seemed almost too young to be the mother of the man in the ring.

While in a clinch, Toney leaned out and said, "Is that pussy lawyer here? I hate goddamn lawyers. I'm gonna kick the shit out of him. Can't wait to get him in here."

Jackie turned to me and said, "Don't worry about it, he's just trying to make you nervous. He's just talking shit; that's the way some fighters are." "Nervous" is hardly sufficient to describe the way I felt. It didn't help when I heard the *smack* that accompanied the clean right that Toney fired at his sparring partner, rearranging the guy's nose.

After I changed, my hands were wrapped for the first time by a professional trainer—Jackie herself. Afterward, she introduced me to another trainer, who looked at me dubiously and said, "Let's work out for a few minutes and warm up." He seemed relieved to see that I'd had some professional training and basic boxing skills. After he'd given me a few pointers, he told me that the most important thing to do was relax.

"Get that pussy up here!" I heard Toney yell. Jackie looked at me and said, "You know, I'm not sure this is such a good idea. James is two weeks away from a major fight, and he's pretty unpredictable. I've got a couple of other great fighters here who'll give you a good workout. Why don't I put you in the ring with one of them?"

"I came to fight the champ," I said, my own words ringing inside my head, "and I'm going to do the best I can."

Toney's mother took Linell aside and softly said, "He's my son and I love him, but he has a hot temper. No one knows what can set him off. Tell your husband not to do it."

"Bob is going to do what he's going to do," said my wife, "and nothing I say will change his mind."

Through the ropes and into the ring I went. Toney would tell me later that he was amazed not to see any signs of fear whatsoever. Quite honestly once I was in, I didn't feel afraid. I was just ready to give it everything I had, to do the best I could—hoping he would hold back. Clearly I wouldn't have had a chance if he was fighting seriously. For amateurs, sparring isn't fighting—it's a way to sharpen your skills, to get a good workout. The general rule is, you get hit with as much force as you hit your opponent. For pros, it's different. Boxing is their livelihood; there are championships at stake. And when they spar, the sparring partner always comes in second.

I went to my corner, where grease was smeared on my face, and then walked into the center of the ring, where Toney was waiting. We touched gloves, and after that, he was pure speed. My first couple of jabs hit the air; he was giving me the opportunity to connect and I couldn't do it. He had that lightning footwork, that boxer's dance, backing up instantaneously every time he saw a muscle tighten. He slowed down a bit, allowing me to get my rhythm. I was able to throw a few jabs, but every one met a quick response. Although I'd trained for as long as twelve rounds before, I had never sparred more than four, and the tension in my body after the first thirty-second flurry felt like it was going to burn me out. I could hear my corner yelling "Take a breath! Relax! Relax!"

I went for a second wind, got into a clinch, didn't like the body punches that resulted, and then went toe-to-toe, each time trading punches as Toney bobbed and weaved. It was the longest three minutes I'd ever spent. I felt like I was in a world championship match all by myself. When it was over, Toney said, "One more round." I went back to my corner, where they poured cold water on my head. Invigorated, I thought, well, sure, okay, another round.

As I got up, still facing the trainer in my corner, Toney snuck up behind me and threw a half-punch to my jaw, like a little kid taunting and teasing but thinking himself pretty damned amusing. I came back at him immediately, throwing three or four fast punches that danced us to the center of the ring. He got me into a clinch, doing what fighters call "leaning on you." I weighed in at 165, the super-middleweight limit, and Toney outweighed me by what felt like a good twenty pounds. I got lucky and landed a great uppercut, and then thought: "Oh, my God, *now* what'll he do?" Because if he hit me in kind, I'd have been knocked through the ropes. Instead, he got me into another clinch and then bit me on the shoulder. Top dog, the gesture said. I'm in control here.

After we'd finished, we embraced, as fighters do. Jackie took pictures of me and James Toney and my son Grant. I couldn't stop grinning. It had been the most exhilarating six minutes of my life. Toney told me he was surprised that I showed no fear, and he later told a reporter, "That Shapiro, he came in here with a big mouth. We went at it for two rounds. He was tough."

Chapter Five

I didn't want to prohibit any of the lawyers on the defense team from answering casual questions posed by reporters, especially when we walked out of court each day, but I insisted that we had to be perceived as a united, cohesive team—to speak, in effect, in one voice. Although Bailey and Dershowitz had always appeared on television during their own cases and often offered commentary on cases they were not involved in, I had decided that I would not give any interviews during the trial. I even turned down the December *Playboy* interview, which would have given me an opportunity to discuss some of the complexities of the case. I did, however, make comments on each day's proceedings to courthouse reporters.

Bailey and Dershowitz continued appearing on television, making sometimes contradictory comments about the case. One day I was denying reports of a plea bargain; the next day I was reading that the ice cream that Nicole had purchased at Ben and Jerry's before her death was somehow going to give O.J. a rock-solid alibi. Mickey Rudin, Frank Sinatra's longtime lawyer, sent me a gift—adhesive tape—engraved "For Lee and Alan." Finally, I had to lay down the law that there had to be no television interviews by anyone on the team unless pre-

viously cleared. Dershowitz graciously agreed; Bailey, however, remained a loose cannon.

∞

Dean Gerald Uelmen arguing for evidence exclusion, citing
California's Supreme Court in *People v. Smith:* "The belief
upon which an officer acts must be the product of facts known
to or observed by him, and not a fanciful attempt to rationalize
silence into a justification for a warrantless entry."

He then continued, explaining, "If we were to carve out an
exception to the Fourth Amendment for detectives who don't
know what they have, in effect we would turn the Fourth
Amendment on its head and say, 'The less you know, the more
you can search.'"

∞

Much to my disappointment, Judge Kennedy-Powell ruled that
the evidence gathered at Rockingham was legally obtained and
thus admissible. Her decision (which went against Gerry Uelmen, her former law school professor) wasn't unexpected, given
the unwritten rule (remember the example of the marijuana versus the murder weapon) that the more important the evidence
to the prosecution, the lower the constitutional standard.

Most clients don't understand why, if we are correct on the
law, rulings go against us. They learn quickly that where the
credibility of police witnesses is at issue, it's a rare judge with
guts enough to rule that the police can't always be believed.
The public misconception about weak or lenient judges who let
criminals off on a technicality is pure fiction; for instance, even
when Judge Ito criticized Vannatter's "reckless disregard for the
truth," he ruled the search warrant valid and let the evidence
stand.

Early in the preliminary hearing we discovered that at least
one witness who had appeared during the grand jury hearings
would not be called by the prosecution. Jill Shively, who alleged that she had seen O.J.'s Bronco leaving Bundy, sold her

story—on the same day she testified—to TV's *Hard Copy* for $5000 and to the *Star* tabloid for $2600—which in my opinion consigned her testimony to the cash-for-trash bin. Perhaps Clark and Hodgman concurred, since she was never called to testify.

The early witnesses, all Nicole's neighbors, were used to establish a time of death, roughly between 10:00 and 11:00 P.M. Pablo Fenjves talked about hearing the "plaintive wail" of a dog—which we were clearly meant to believe was Nicole's Akita—between 10:00 and 10:30. At 11:00, Steven Schwab, out walking his own dog, saw the Akita with blood on his paws. Sukru Boztepe and Bettinna Rasmussen then testified to finding the bodies of Nicole and Ron on the sidewalk at Bundy at midnight.

On July 5 and 6, Gerry Uelmen carefully cross-examined Mark Fuhrman, pushing for inconsistencies in his version of events. I had seen Fuhrman earlier, out in the hall. "This is your lucky day," I told him.

"Oh, really?" he said. "And just why is that?"

"Because I'm not doing the cross, Uelmen is." Fuhrman was the prosecution's central seizure-of-evidence witness, and Uelmen was the defense point man for search-and-seizure issues. I would get my chance to cross-examine Fuhrman at the trial itself, and I didn't want him to be prepared for me. For now, I just wanted to watch and listen.

Fuhrman first became concerned about what was going on behind the security fence at Rockingham, he told Uelmen, because of O.J.'s Ford Bronco "carelessly, haphazardly parked . . . its rear end jutting out into the street, maybe a foot farther than the front." When he examined the car, Fuhrman saw a plastic bag and shovel in the rear, a blood dot above the outside handle on the driver's door, and also something that looked like blood brush marks or swipes on the bottom of the door. That's when he decided to go over the fence—which led, ultimately, to discovery of the glove.

The "plastic bag" was standard to the Bronco; it was part

of the cargo-carrying equipment. The shovel was used to clean up after the dogs at both Bundy and Rockingham. Neither item, in any context, was particularly sinister.

I then cross-examined Detective Philip Vannatter, the senior member of the investigative team. I knew I needed to be as aggressive and forceful as possible, not just to unravel the facts in his testimony, which would eventually impeach his credibility, but also to keep him slightly off balance. Almost immediately I challenged him on the maintenance of the L.A.P.D.'s murder book for the Simpson case. The book is provided to the prosecution, which in turn shares it with the defense as part of the discovery process. In this case, Bill Pavelic had convinced me that the record-keeping had been particularly sloppy. On the subject of the blood on the Bronco, Vannatter testified that indeed, he needed glasses to see the speck of blood near the door handle and did not see—and did not record—the blood "swipes" near the bottom of the driver's door that Fuhrman had seen.

There was also a brief and revelatory exchange regarding Fuhrman's reason for leaving Bundy in order to lead the others to Rockingham. Vannatter testified that he was familiar with the neighborhood and would have been perfectly capable of getting to Rockingham on his own.

Vannatter agreed with me that the police didn't go personally to notify Mr. Goldman's family of his death, as they did with O.J., nor did they take pictures of Kato's car as they did O.J.'s, even though it was also at Rockingham. Obviously, their focus was only O.J. from the very beginning. "If Mr. Goldman had been the sole victim of this case under the same circumstances," I asked him, "would the same investigation be taking place?" Clark objected; the judge sustained her objection. But I felt that I'd made my point.

Gerry Uelmen on direct examination, to Arnelle Simpson: "Did you tell the officers they had your permission to search the premises or to seize any property on the premises?"

"No," she answered, "I did not."

"Did any officer ask you if he could take any item from the premises?"

"No," she said.

Dennis Fung, the L.A.P.D. criminalist, questioned by Uelmen, testified that he'd first received a call at 5:30 A.M.—to go to Rockingham, not Bundy. He arrived at 7:10 and tested the Bronco for only one blood spot.

On July 7, the testimony of Detective Tom Lange primarily established the late coroner call to Bundy and contamination of evidence because of "loose" securing of premises. Lange stated that they found a total of five dime-size droplets of blood not belonging to Nicole or Ron Goldman at Bundy, but there was no way to ascertain when they were left there.

Marcia Clark, as she finished up with Thano Peratis, the nurse who took O.J.'s blood at the lab and put the bandage on his finger: "One more question, Your Honor?"

Judge Kennedy-Powell: "You always have one."

Clark: "I know. It might be a prosecutor's last-word thing."

On July 8, L.A.P.D. criminalist Gregory Matheson testified that after performing standard blood-typing, or basic serology, tests on Nicole's blood (type AB), Ron Goldman's (type O), and O.J.'s (type A), he then analyzed a dime-size blood drop, one of five discovered at the Bundy crime scene. The serology testing ruled out that drop as belonging to either Nicole or Ron and indicated a likelihood that, according to the crime-lab data, the crime-scene blood drop had the same characteristics as the blood from one out of every two hundred people. O.J., he said, was in that blood group.

Watching Dean Uelmen's careful cross-examination was like observing a quietly determined chess master. He elicited the information that because the police lab primarily runs tests on people arrested or suspected of criminal activity, the data base resulting from those tests is not representative of the population as a whole; in fact, ethnic and racial minorities are substantially overrepresented. For example, the African-American population in California is about 7 percent of the total population but accounts for approximately a third of the arrests.

"The tests . . . are exclusionary tests, is that correct?" asked the Dean. "None of these tests can tell you specifically that a particular bloodstain was left by a particular person?"

"That's correct," answered Matheson. "There's nothing here that would individualize a stain to any one particular person."

"So any attempt to analogize this to fingerprints or precise identification of a person would be inaccurate?"

"That's correct," Matheson said.

During his cross, Uelmen was able to successfully raise questions about contamination in the lab and point out problems with the collection and storage of blood samples. When asked whether the blood at the scene could have been a mixture of blood of both victims and assailant, Matheson said he didn't have a test that could either ascertain that or rule it out. In addition, we were able to get on the record that anywhere from 40,000 to 80,000 people in the Los Angeles area carried the same genetic markers contained in the blood drops found at Bundy but ruled out as being Nicole's or Ron Goldman's. All in all, I felt that Uelmen had laid some fine tactical groundwork for the trial.

Additional groundwork was laid with my cross-examination of Dr. Irwin Golden, the Los Angeles deputy coroner who had performed the autopsies. In addition to helping establish the time and cause of death, the main contribution a coroner can make is to determine the type and size of the murder weapon. I had gone over Dr. Golden's report with Michael Baden and knew that his testimony would be both grim and graphic. I also knew his report was full of errors; ultimately, the coroner's office would own up to making at least sixteen mistakes.

In the absence of an eyewitness, pinpointing a time of death is difficult. The sooner a coroner begins an examination (using such criteria as body temperature, stomach contents, and degree of rigor mortis), the more likely it is that an accurate time can be estimated. In this instance, the L.A.P.D. delayed calling the coroner for ten hours. In addition to mislabeling forensic evidence (fluid samples from Nicole's body), the coroner discarded Nicole's stomach contents, although he saved Ron Goldman's. On direct examination, Golden stated that he could only put time of death somewhere between 9:00 P.M. and midnight. On cross-examination, however, he stated that three out of four forensic criteria for setting the time would put death *after* 11:00 P.M.—which was, of course, critical to O.J.'s alibi.

No one in the courtroom was immune to the horror and sadness that Golden's descriptions of the two bodies evoked, and as I cross-examined him, I was acutely aware of Nicole's father and Ron Goldman's young sister sitting somewhere behind me. The senior Goldmans had gone out to the hall when they just couldn't listen anymore. My wife was also in the courtroom. She'd come every day during the preliminary hearing, and we took these images home with us each night. But there was no way to tiptoe through cross-examining someone I believed had been incompetent, especially since it was Golden who had assured Lange and Vannatter that the knife O.J. had purchased could have been the murder weapon. It was consistent with "*some* of the wounds," he said, "with *many* of the wounds."

"There are two morphologically different types of stab wounds on the victims," he said. "Some . . . are indicative of a single-edge blade, some of the wounds have a characteristically double-pointed or forked end." This indicated, he said, that the wounds could have been made by two different weapons, a single-edge blade and a double-edge blade, thus raising the distinct possibility of a second assailant. I moved in on him a little, asking why he hadn't yet done more detailed, definitive testing to try to exclude the weapon similar to the one O.J. had purchased. Such a test existed; he just hadn't done it yet. Why was that? His response was that he figured that testing could be "done at some other time."

"You understand a man is sitting in jail, facing charges of double homicide, do you not?" I asked. "When could those tests be done, to protect his rights? When would you suggest doing these tests?"

"Now?" he responded stiffly, with a somewhat puzzled look on his face.

Months later, when I heard Michael Baden say on television that "the coroner's office is not just a body removal service," I remembered that moment in court with Golden. Baden's tremendous respect for human life contains within it an equal respect for death and the mysteries that surround it. Baden has always maintained, as does Dr. Henry Lee, that the job of forensic specialists is not to answer the whodunit question but rather to find out *what happened*—to reconstruct the way that someone's life ended and not take sides or make assumptions in the process. The difference between these two men and Golden, I've decided, is that Golden is the kind of man who can eat lunch and examine bodies at the same time.

∞

On July 8, I made my closing arguments to the preliminary hearing, which included the following:

> If in fact the killer lived at the Simpson residence [Rockingham], the court would have to believe the following: that in a window period of less than an hour, the killer was able to leave the crime scene that has been described with a victim with two arteries in the neck cut, two jugular veins cut, and massive blood from both victims. A clear inference would be that the murderer was indeed covered with blood. The murderer would then have to do the following: abandon the bloody clothing, because they have not been found or presented; abandon the murder weapon, because that has not been found or discovered; abandon bloody shoes, because they have not been found or discovered, and then go back to his house and leave a bloody glove in his backyard. That just doesn't stand up to logic. . . . This is a case that the police admit is still under investigation, where other suspects are being sought, where the

medical examiner admits that two weapons could have been used—a clear inference that there may be more than one killer.

I don't want to go through each and every area of impeachment with the witnesses, but I think it is very, very clear that everybody who has participated in this investigation has not done so in a professional manner. From the time the Los Angeles Police Department arrived on the crime scene, it was nearly ten hours later until they started the scientific investigation and even took the temperature of the body. There was testimony that the fire department obviously was there and left and didn't do anything, yet the coroner's records clearly indicate that the fire department chief was the person who pronounced the bodies dead. I doubt if he did that from a distance.

This is a case that everybody has jumped to an immediate and unrealistic conclusion as to the state of this evidence. This is a case that is not ready yet to come to court.

At the end of that day's hearing, Judge Kennedy-Powell returned her ruling that O.J. Simpson be bound over for trial, for two counts of first-degree murder. The formal arraignment was scheduled for July 22. Just as he'd spent Father's Day in jail, he would spend his forty-seventh birthday there as well.

The sudden prominence of Mark Fuhrman in the preliminary hearing rang all of Bill Pavelic's alarm bells. Prior to that, we'd barely been aware of Fuhrman's involvement in the case, let alone that he was a key—if not *the* key—police detective in the investigation, at least in the all-important first hours. In the early reports provided to us by the prosecution, Mark Fuhrman's name never appeared at all: He wasn't in the arrest reports filed on O.J. and A.C.; the property reports didn't mention him; the coroner's report didn't mention him; the June 15 follow-up report didn't mention him; the murder reports didn't mention him; the June 13 and June 28 search warrants and affidavits didn't mention him. Furthermore, nowhere was it stated, in *any* L.A.P.D. report, that Fuhrman was the one who discovered the glove at each scene.

"Why are they shielding him?" Bill wondered. He had a nodding acquaintance with Fuhrman; they'd both once moonlighted for Johnny Carson. In addition, we had reports that Fuhrman was involved in a lawsuit, in something called an "officer-involved shooting" case.

Months before jury selection had begun and soon after Mark Fuhrman had testified in the televised preliminary hearing, Bill Pavelic reported that he was in communication with an attorney named Robert Deutsch, whose client Joseph J. Britton was suing the City of Los Angeles for excessive use of force. In the fall of 1993, Britton was apprehended while fleeing from a robbery which he'd committed. Mark Fuhrman had been one of the police officers involved, and he had reportedly fired ten rounds at Britton, both as he was falling and after he was down on the ground. Britton took five bullets, and his injuries were quite serious. Fuhrman's personnel records were included in the records Deutsch had compiled in the suit, which was eventually settled by the city for $100,000.

As a consultant to Deutsch, Bill had done what he calls a "biopsy" of the case, reconstructing the time line in conjunction with the police logs and Britton's testimony. He came to a strong conclusion that the knife Britton had dropped while running from the police had later been planted near his body in order to justify the shooting.

After Fuhrman's televised session at the preliminary, we started receiving phone calls on both the 800-number line and the office lines, from attorneys who'd had dealings with Fuhrman, from anonymous police personnel, and from anonymous people who had known him. Everybody had a Mark Fuhrman story.

Bonnie passed these messages on to Bill; Bill checked out the ones that he could. In the meantime, Gerry Uelmen and I immediately prepared a motion to obtain Fuhrman's police-department personnel records, certain of which were already part of the lawsuit against him.

The information we received on Fuhrman was deeply troubling. In the early eighties, in an attempt to get a disability-related early retirement with full benefits from the police department, he underwent a battery of physical and psychological tests in order to establish his self-described inability to do the job anymore because of his hatred for the people he had to deal with, in particular Mexicans and blacks. In a process that went on for more than two years, and included a lawsuit that Fuhrman filed because he wasn't granted the retirement, various medical specialists described him as "narcissistic, self-indulgent, emotionally unstable" with a "history of depression, tension, and stomach aches" and a great rage "with the public and the city."

By his own words, Fuhrman acknowledged his anger, as well as his propensity for violence. In his years in gang-ridden East Los Angeles, he said, he routinely put suspects in the hospital with "broken hands, faces, arms, and knees." After he was transferred to the downtown Central division, he had to deal with "more slimes and assholes." If anyone resisted arrest, he said, "they went back unconscious." His three rules when dealing with a crime situation were quoted as being, "You don't see, you don't remember, it didn't happen." The L.A.P.D. was fully aware of his negative behavior toward minorities and women and had "counseled" him on its inappropriateness. Months later, we heard that one police officer had even kept a personal log of "Fuhrman incidents" but had destroyed it when our investigation became known.

The physicians who examined him were not unanimous, however, on what Fuhrman's fate should be. "There is some suggestion here that the patient is trying to feign the presence of severe psychopathology," said one. Another wrote, "This suggests a person who expects immediate attention and pity." Yet another said, "This man is no longer suited for police work."

With specialists in both physical and mental health unable to agree, Mark Fuhrman didn't get his early retirement. What he got instead was a promotion. In my opinion Mark Fuhrman was either mentally unstable, even dangerous, or a skilled liar. Either way, his credibility as a witness had simply disappeared.

∞

Just before the preliminary, the editors at *People* magazine informed me that they were preparing a piece on me and wanted to send a reporter for an interview. Initially I was quite reluctant. My rule has always been that if it doesn't do anything on behalf of the client, don't do it. But they let me know that they were prepared to put the story together without my cooperation, and it would be a better—and fairer—story if I would agree to be part of it. When they said they wanted photographs, I contacted Peter Borsari, a West Coast freelance photographer that Linell and I had used previously for our charity events and family pictures. The magazine wanted informal shots, so Peter took pictures of me hitting the punching bag in my garage, bungee jumping at Lake Tahoe, relaxing in the pool with Linell. There was one particularly nice family shot of us with the two boys.

Throughout I remained somewhat apprehensive; I think of myself as a serious professional, and here, I thought, would be all these images that might contradict that. On the other hand, I play as hard as I work, believing that mental health doesn't come from sitting at a desk, and the pictures were an accurate reflection of that belief. The time I spend with my wife and sons, the discipline I learn from trading punches with a sparring partner, the joy I get from skiing or boating—all these things enrich and strengthen my life and, I believe, make me a better, more focused lawyer. And as hard as it was for O.J. to sit in that small cell, he never seemed to begrudge these activities. As an athlete and competitor, he understood and respected my need for them.

When the article was published, my professional credentials and integrity were given equal time with the bungee jumping and the boxing, and I decided that all in all it was fairly harmless. However, my family was now in the celebrity spotlight in a way they hadn't been before.

For eight years, Linell had been involved with a charity organization called Quest, for children afflicted with Prader-Wille syndrome. Prader-Wille, somewhat similar to Down syndrome, results in mental and physical retardation, immune-system deficiency, and a sometimes fatal eating disorder. When the Simpson trial began, Linell was president of Quest, leading a fund drive for a home for the children. She asked friends to lend their support; in return, they asked her to support their causes, and of course she did.

Attending charity-related black-tie events had always been a normal part of our lives. Now, however, my appearance at them, and the resulting media attention, would divert attention from the cause and focus it on me instead. When someone was quoted in the *Los Angeles Times* as saying, "Bob Shapiro goes everywhere now, you can see him at a supermarket opening," Linell was stung. We started second-guessing not just black-tie events but ordinary evenings out at our favorite restaurants. They were keeping track of what she wore, where we went, what we ate and drank. "This is starting to feel like an out-of-body experience," said my wife.

∞

My second experience with a national magazine was a more complex one. I had been contacted by Susan Mercandetti on behalf of the *New Yorker*. They were preparing what they called a photo essay of all the people involved with the Simpson case, and the black-and-white portraits were to be taken by famed photographer Richard Avedon. There would be no text, no need for an interview, but if I was willing, we needed to set up a mutually convenient time for the photo shoot.

Shortly after the pictures were taken, I received a call (as Susan Mercandetti said I might) from Jeffrey Toobin, a reporter for the *New Yorker* and himself a former litigator and former law student of Alan Dershowitz. Toobin was one of a number of writers who had already become regular fixtures around the courtroom. Dominick Dunne, Joe Bosco, Joe McGinniss, the AP's Linda Deutsch, Bill Boyarsky, Jim Newton, and Andrea Ford of the *Los Angeles Times,* David Margolick of the *New York Times,* and Shirley Perlman of *Newsday* were among the others.

As a courtesy to Toobin—and by extension to my friend and his former teacher Dershowitz, and Mercandetti and the *New Yorker*—I told him that although I could not give an interview, he was welcome to drop by the office and talk for a while. When he came in, I made it clear that the discussion was off the record. He asked if he could tape it or take notes, and I said no, that it was not an interview, it was an off-the-record discussion.

We talked about the case in general terms, as any two lawyers might have done under similar circumstances, and he asked what direction I thought the defense might be going, in light of any information we'd been able to gather during our investigation. I told him that we were taking a closer look at Detective Fuhrman, that there were some L.A.P.D. records on him that indicated he'd had an antagonistic history with minorities and had in fact attempted to use his hostility toward them to get a disability-related early retirement. The city attorney had taken the position that Fuhrman had lied in this instance. So I said it appeared that Fuhrman was either an admitted racist or a skilled liar. Either way, he had a significant credibility problem. In addition, one of our investigators had heard a hypothesis floating around that the person who found the glove at Rockingham—and thus became a hero—was the person who had been replaced on the case initially, and that was something that a skeptical observer might view as curious.

When the *New Yorker* with the Avedon photographs was published, I was appalled to see that directly opposite a full-page picture of me was a long article by Jeffrey Toobin titled "An Incendiary Defense," in which he cited "leading members of Simpson's defense team" as "floating" the theory that Fuhrman had planted the second glove at Rockingham. The defense team, Toobin reported, was characterizing the detective as a rogue cop, a racist, and an integral part of a police conspiracy to frame O.J. Simpson for the murder of his ex-wife.

I felt like I'd been sucker-punched. This was exactly why I hadn't wanted to talk to Toobin, or to anyone else in the press, until this case was over. I was told that the photos were to run without text. I believed that my conversation with Toobin was exactly that—a conversation, off the record, between two professional people talking about potential strategies.

In the months that followed, Jeff Toobin would write many articulate articles about this case. I came to respect his work. It was a supreme irony to both of us when we and the *New Yorker* were jointly sued by Fuhrman for libel, a suit that was quickly dismissed. But just as Linell and the children had their lives exposed in a new way because of the *People* article, things radically changed for me because of the *New Yorker*. Although I thought I was a media veteran, what I'd believed to be an off-the-record conversation found its way into print, with my name—and face—attached to it. Thereafter, I answered most queries with a firm but definite no.

Chapter Six

After the preliminary hearing, it seemed a good idea to take stock of where we were, where we were going, and how we were to get there. O.J. had a number of friends and business associates who had advised him on different business ventures. Many of them were treating this, a criminal trial, as if it were the same type of situation. One of these men, Wayne Hughes, wanted to take over the entire financial aspect of the case—and also dictate how the case itself should proceed.

He asked me to come to his ranch house in Malibu. When I arrived, Hughes came out on the verandah to meet me. He introduced me to the man who was standing there with him— who turned out to be his lawyer. This is strange, I thought.

Hughes, I discovered, wanted to be the CEO of the defense team. With little knowledge of criminal law, he had a lot of questions, many of which it would have been unethical for me to address. I tried to explain the conflict, but he persisted. He wanted to meet with Dr. Lee and Dr. Baden; he wanted to know what the investigators had discovered. Hughes had theories of how the case should be handled and who should do it, and he wasn't prepared to hear no for an answer. We were supposed to be on the same side; why did it suddenly feel so adversarial? I prefer negotiations to confrontations, but it was clear to me that we weren't going to be able to work this one out.

I told him that if he wanted to be a good, supportive friend, we would welcome that; if he wanted to lend financial aid to O.J., that would be appreciated also. But I could not go beyond that. And I would not be able to answer any more of his questions.

I had never directly discussed with O.J. the fee for my services or any additional costs that we might incur, such as those for expert witnesses. Another attorney and colleague of mine, Larry Feldman, had negotiated my fee with Skip Taft. This was somewhat extraordinary, but I didn't want to be haggling at the same time I was already representing O.J. My friend Feldman negotiated the fee. The case would go on for seventeen months, and my fee would end up being significantly less than I usually earned for a comparable time. The other lawyers on the case, and the expert witnesses we had contacted, sent in estimated projections of their fees and costs. Skip watched the budget and let me know when we were close to the bottom line. All O.J. ever said was, "I don't care what it takes, I want the best." But he was hearing from many other voices, and he had to listen to them while he was sitting in a small cell.

He was adamant that I was to stay on as team leader, lead counsel, or quarterback. My title might've changed from day to day, but his decision stayed the same. So we began to focus our efforts on what we needed to do for the trial ahead. From the beginning, it was clear to me that this would be a team defense, which would require another trial attorney to work with me in court. It was time to decide who that person was going to be.

In civil litigations, the team approach—usually a combination of senior trial lawyers, partners, and associates within the same firm—is used all the time. In the criminal arena, it's not often done, unless there are multiple defendants, in which case each defendant might have his own attorney, but they all pursue the defense together. California law states that a defendant in a capital case is entitled to two lawyers; if he can't afford them, the court appoints two lawyers on his behalf.

Economics is one obvious reason why the team approach isn't often used for criminal defense. A second reason, probably the most compelling one, is ego. Defending a criminal case is an art, not a science, no matter what the pundits preach about trial techniques. Defense attorneys, like artists, have sizable egos. Few are interested in sharing the limelight or the decision-making process, no matter how doing so might benefit the client's interest.

My own ego is in pretty good shape; after practicing law for twenty-five years, I believed that I was the best trial lawyer for this case, and from the very beginning I knew the strategic challenges it might present. We would be attacking the credibility of some members of the L.A.P.D., we would be attacking the competency and ethics of the coroner's office and numerous crime labs, and all the while we would be under the most intense press scrutiny of any trial since (we later discovered) the Lindbergh baby kidnapping. Given all of that, I knew that it was necessary to expand the group of experts I'd already assembled by adding a second trial lawyer. If what I do is an art, then what evolves from it is creative, and two of us would double the creative output. I believed that any disagreements—banging heads together, raising the level of emotion, showing great passion—would result in a synthesis ultimately benefiting our client.

The press had been speculating about who would fill the "second-chair" position, but I didn't like the hierarchy that term conveyed, preferring "co-counsel" instead. I thought of the team as a mosaic, with plenty of work and responsibility to go around, and everyone employing individual strengths and talents.

As I've indicated, my ideal candidate would have been a female African-American lawyer, and I found many outstanding candidates. But they were primarily academics. I was unable to find anyone with a national reputation and the kind of trial

experience in high-profile cases that I thought this case warranted. And I didn't want to put anyone at the table for the
sake of tokenism.

For me, this decision was a difficult, gut-wrenching experience. I have so many talented colleagues around the country
who may well have done justice to this case; I neither wanted
to insult nor hurt anyone I respected. I also didn't want to
sacrifice this particular client's good, with these particular allegations, in front of a jury that would be selected in downtown
Los Angeles. With that in mind, with the information I'd gotten
in my summit meeting with my lawyer friends, and with the
persuasiveness of those closest to O.J., we finally narrowed the
field to half a dozen lawyers, both men and women, and ultimately came down to a choice between Gerry Spence and Johnnie Cochran. "It's your call, Bob," O.J. said. "You decide."

O.J. had been leaning toward Johnnie Cochran for some
time, primarily because of his good reputation and political ties
in the black community. Not only was he a good lawyer, he
also got high marks for his fine commentary on NBC during
the preliminary hearing. Cochran, like me an alumnus of Loyola Law School, had been a prosecutor in the city attorney's
office and later an assistant district attorney early in his career.
Ironically, it was Cochran who brought Bill Hodgman into the
D.A.'s office in the late seventies. Well-liked by judges and
prosecutors (he, too, had campaigned for Gil Garcetti), he'd
had tremendous success with downtown juries. He had also
been effective in influencing changes in police procedure. In
1982, the result of one Cochran lawsuit outlawed the carotid
"choke hold" that the L.A.P.D. had often used on suspects. My
longtime friend Richard Hirsch, who'd served as defense co-
counsel with Cochran on behalf of a judge who'd been accused
of fixing parking tickets, felt that Johnnie and I shared a similar
courtroom style. We'd both rather speak extemporaneously
than use notes, and we're both high-energy and positive think-
ers, preferring to pay no attention when negative things are said

about us. Both Uelmen and Kardashian also believed Cochran would be a good choice.

On the other hand, some of O.J.'s friends had been arguing for Wyoming attorney Gerry Spence, impressed by the case analysis he had done on television. Dershowitz, who didn't know Cochran, admired Spence, whose Wild West personality was outsize and whose case record was not only admirable but nearly perfect. Alan had monitored the Imelda Marcos racketeering case as the appellate expert (Marcos stood accused of stealing millions from the Philippines) and felt that Spence had done a masterful job in getting an acquittal. For myself, I thought his early TV commentary on the Simpson case had been extraordinary. I was particularly gratified one night to hear Gerry say, "If they had a wonderful case, they would stay home just like good, ethical prosecutors are supposed to do, keep their mouths shut, and not try this case in the press."

Bailey, however, was dead set against Spence. He had never liked him and disparagingly referred to him as John Wayne. In fact, Bailey had been pitching himself for co-counsel, unsubtly lobbying Taft and O.J. for the position by saying things like "Bob Shapiro is the only lawyer in the country that I'd sit second chair for." O.J.'s coterie felt that Bailey had lost his fastball. In addition, his reputation for hard drinking was still alive and well. They didn't want him in the courtroom, they told me, but agreed that I could use him behind the scenes, strategically coordinating the investigators and the complex computer work that would be a major factor in our strategy.

On the evening of Thursday, July 14, I met with Cochran at his suggestion at the Beverly Hills Tennis Club, where he was a member. We had known each other for twenty-five years and had worked on a case together many years before. It was abundantly clear that he wanted to be a defense attorney on this case. He was friendly and charming as always; his reputation for getting along with people was one of his strongest suits. Neither of us were in-your-face lawyers; we each had strong ties to the judiciary and the prosecution, and we believed that both of us being "good guys" would serve us, and the defense, very well.

Because he had joined with Howard Weitzman to represent pop singer Michael Jackson on charges of child molestation, which the district attorney's office was investigating, his primary obligation at this point was to Jackson. Cochran's plan was to go to New York over the weekend to discuss whether or not Jackson would okay his joining this case as well. It wasn't a question of whether or not he wanted to be a member of the team; it was a question of whether or not we wanted to ask him to join us.

The following afternoon, Gerry Spence flew into Los Angeles. Fifteen years before, my friend Richard Sherman, a noted criminal lawyer, had gone to Spence's Trial Lawyers College in Wyoming and brought back a tape of his voir dire of a jury. What I heard was revolutionary: a lawyer not only ingratiating himself with a jury but asking risky, open-ended questions that brought back amazing and telling responses. He addressed the negative aspects of his case with these potential jurors, extracting a pledge from them that these negatives wouldn't be held against his client when the time came to deliberate. It was sheer brilliance.

An expert in psychology, with a strong belief that everyone is worth rehabilitating, Spence advocates forming an emotional relationship with a client, contrary to what students are often taught in law school. Critics may carp at his Western attire (no suit for him—he wears cowboy boots and a soft buckskin jacket in court), his down-home approach, and the likelihood that outside of Wyoming his style might not play. But in New York City, where more attention was paid to his wardrobe than to his presentation, he won an acquittal for Marcos. His record of civil victories is unprecedented, besting corporate giants like McDonald's, Aetna, and, in the Karen Silkwood case, Kerr-McGee.

As a legal junkie, I have always followed the careers of great trial lawyers, and I had always wanted to try a case with Spence.

We finally met at a criminal law seminar in Aspen some years ago. We had both brought our wives, and Linell and I were amazed to find that Spence's wife (whom he calls Imaging) is really named LaNelle. When he came to Los Angeles to meet with me, I arranged for him to stay at the home of my dear friend Michael Klein (who was out of town), where we could have total privacy for what I knew would be a long conversation.

From the minute he arrived, he made no secret about his desire to be involved in O.J.'s defense. "I'm an old trial lawyer, Bob," he said, "and this is the case of the century. I want to be part of it." We talked about his philosophy of trial law and the role of the team approach in a defense. "It's just like a jazz band," Gerry said. "Everyone has to play together. But every once in a while someone gets a solo."

I had some concerns about Spence's limited knowledge of DNA, but he assured me he could easily get up to speed. "Bob, you have to keep in mind that the jury has to understand this stuff, too," he said. "We have to keep it simple. Maybe we attack the science, maybe we accept the science. It's gotta be done in a way that's understandable to a jury."

The real drawback to Spence was his schedule: The months of August and September were out for him, because he was running his trial school at his ranch in Wyoming, with fifty lawyers who had been handpicked from around the country already committed to attend. He suggested that he would have some of the lawyers from his own firm come to L.A. to work with me and that we in turn could go to the ranch and brief him, but I knew that it just wouldn't work in this case. I needed someone here hands-on, every day. As much as I regretted it, I realized I couldn't hire him.

Later on, when Spence was interviewed and asked about the team approach to a criminal case, he said that for him, trying a case is like Picasso making a painting: Only one person can control the brush. When Alan Dershowitz and I were in the car on the way to court a few weeks later, I repeated the jazz band versus Picasso analogy, and he laughed. "Spence must've been talking about Picasso's jazz band," he said.

Johnnie Cochran got back into town the following week. Michael Jackson had given him the go-ahead to join the Simpson defense. On July 19 we met at my office. I told him that I was authorized to bring him on board. He accepted enthusiastically.

We never talked in terms of lead counsel and second chair; it was, to me, a joint effort. Initially I was referred to in the press as the lead trial lawyer; within a couple of days I was being referred to as co-lead counsel. I had no problem with our relationship, since it fit my concept of how we would work together. Fittingly, we used an analogy to football. There would be a team owner and part-time coach: O.J. Then there would be the quarterback: me. I would be O.J.'s Joe Ferguson, who had been his quarterback on the Buffalo Bills. And then the quarterback would hand off to somebody as good as O.J. Simpson, and that would be Johnnie Cochran.

In that first meeting, Cochran and I discussed the issue of race, and our hope that a black lawyer and a white lawyer working together on behalf of another black man would be a good message to send. He then told me that because his law practice was primarily civil, and because he had a great deal of legal and clerical support in his offices, he would continue to maintain his civil calendar, which produced substantial income, during the Simpson trial. We shook on our new relationship, agreeing to keep our collaboration confidential (not even telling O.J. and the other members of the team that the decision was definite) until we got to court on Friday, July 22, for O.J.'s arraignment. However, NBC reported the night before that Cochran was definitely joining the defense. I supposed it was because he'd told them he wouldn't be commentating for them anymore.

Friday morning, Cochran and I met at my office and we went together to the courthouse, where two or three hundred people, not to mention satellite dishes and sound trucks, were waiting for us. Eight uniformed officers tried to cordon the people off, but the cameras and microphones came at us as we walked into Judge Cecil Mills's courtroom.

Judge Mills took the bench promptly at 9:00 A.M., announcing that his selection to hear the case was Superior Court Judge Lance A. Ito. This came as a surprise to me. Judge Paul Flynn, a law professor and former assistant U.S. attorney, had been the original choice, and we were comfortable with him. However, I was told that at the last minute, Ito had lobbied for the position. Speculation was that since Judge Flynn belonged to a country club that had previously been restrictive, his presiding over the case would've been either objected to by us or a potential cause of embarrassment to the superior court. In my opinion, neither would've been the case.

Judge Ito had been the presiding judge on the Charles Keating securities fraud trial (which Bill Hodgman had successfully prosecuted) and afterward had been named Trial Judge of the Year by the Los Angeles Bar Association. I'd had previous experience with him, the most recent, of course, when I presented our motion to recuse the grand jury; and I thought that not only was he very smart, he was also the most desirable on the list of predominantly pro-prosecution judges.

Almost every judge appointed in the state since Ronald Reagan was California's governor has been a former prosecutor, either from the district attorney's office or the U.S. attorney's office, and for that reason it's not unusual to run head-on into a pro-prosecution agenda on the bench. Governors reap political capital when they appoint "tough" judges who impose maximum sentences and aren't swayed by the "legal loopholes" that the rest of us call the Constitution. Judge Ito, I believed, could be counted on to be balanced.

Judge Mills made sure that we all knew that Ito was married to an L.A.P.D. captain, Margaret York (the highest ranking woman officer at the time). If any of us felt that fact would be prejudicial to our case, we could request another judge. However, I said that Judge Ito was acceptable to us. I was later to learn that Captain York and her former police partner, Helen Kidder, had been the original inspirations for the television show *Cagney and Lacey*.

Judge Ito proved to be a man of great contrasts. A graduate of UCLA and UC Berkeley's Boalt Hall Law School, he certainly had the academic credentials for excellence on the bench. His physical appearance and demeanor sometimes suggested harshness, but his heart was filled with compassion, learned from his family's experiences in the Japanese internment camps in California during World War II. In fact, the judge wears his heart on his sleeve, treating people with patience and respect, expecting that common courtesy to be returned. He dislikes controversy, and throughout the Simpson trial, whenever he had to sanction a lawyer for unprofessional conduct in the courtroom, he later either apologized or said, "I don't want this to be personal." On occasion he would retire to his chambers for his soon-to-be-famous "ten deep breaths," and then return as if nothing had happened. He strove for balance and pragmatism. I would come in each day and say, "Good morning, Your Honor." His response was always, "So far."

That Friday, July 22, I finally saw the change in O.J.'s demeanor that I had been looking and hoping for. No longer on suicide watch, no longer on medication, he seemed to have passed through the initial period of depression and shock. His eyes were clear and his back was ramrod straight when the judge asked him how he answered the charges against him. "Absolutely, 100 percent not guilty," he said in a strong voice. It had been forty days since his arrest, and my client seemed at last the strong and confident O.J., the one we needed at the defense table. The next few weeks, which to our dismay would turn into months, would be taken up with legal procedures, including hearings, motions and countermotions, debates on blood typing, evidence inclusion and exclusion, and, eventually, the selection of the jury. Each step is part of creating a trial's road map, what one publication called the "pre-trial jockeying for position"—not the first time we would hear a sports anal-

ogy, as news anchors and commentators began to refer to the
trial as if it were a game, with the score being posted daily.

After O.J. was returned to lockup, Johnnie and I left the
courthouse through a throng of cheering well-wishers, an army
of photographers, and some new and somewhat bizarre addi-
tions: noisy hawkers of customized O.J. T-shirts and baseball
hats, someone from the Jewish Defense League yelling slogans,
and people from the Women's Action Coalition who were walking around in masks made to look like Nicole.

On Saturday, Linell and I slept late, then spent the rest of
the day—the first in a long time—just resting, reading around
the pool, and throwing the ball to the dog. The kids weren't
home; Brent was at a friend's house for the night, and Grant
was due in the next day from ice-hockey camp. We ordered out
turkey from Koo Koo Roo's, a restaurant that kept us all in
protein throughout the entire trial, and we rented a video. It
was, I knew, a small calm between storms.

Sunday morning, July 24, Johnnie Cochran and I met at the
county jail, he in a suit, I in jeans and a Connecticut State
Police baseball cap I'd gotten from Henry Lee. We visited O.J.
together on the third floor. He was behind glass, and the three
of us had to converse on phones, O.J. holding one to each ear
so he could hear us both.

In an effort to fill Johnnie in, we retraced what was now
familiar ground, with O.J. repeating over and over that more
than anything he wanted to be with Sydney and Justin. Although I could see that he was pleased to hear of polls reporting
that 60 percent of the black population and 30 percent of the
white population believed he wasn't guilty, I knew he wanted
100% of both populations to believe it.

After I drove Cochran home, Linell and I went to the airport
to pick up Grant from hockey camp; it would be a quick turn-
around for a ten-year-old, since he was scheduled to check into
Magic Johnson's basketball camp that very night, but this was
a schedule he had dreamed of for months. As we drove, I received a call on the car phone from Peter Neufeld in New York,

stressing how important it was that we get access to the blood samples and duplicate the tests. Neufeld and Scheck wanted to examine further the possibility that there had been tampering. I thought our argument to the jury should be that the prosecution's evidence had been improperly collected and preserved, was quite possibly contaminated, and therefore shouldn't be admissible. Neufeld told me that Scheck was in San Diego and would meet me at the office the next day so we could hash this out further.

When we arrived at the basketball camp in Thousand Oaks, I went with Grant for his late check-in. As we walked, the kids already assembled for drills suddenly started a "Go O.J.!" cheer. In minutes, some of the coaches had walked over to shake my hand and wish me good luck. Grant just looked down at his feet. I hoped it was only because he was self-conscious at checking in late, but I suspected that part of his discomfort was the growing hoopla.

Chapter Seven

∾

Everyone who came into the courtroom (especially after seeing it on television) was shocked by its intimate size. The spectator section (capacity: fifty-eight) is directly behind the lawyers' counsel tables, which in turn are less than a dozen feet from the judge. On their side of the room, the prosecuting attorneys can literally reach out and touch the jury. We presented a motion to switch sides midpoint during the case, so that we could take our turn being close to the jury. To no one's surprise, this unprecedented motion was summarily denied.

Across the room from the jury sits the bailiff at a desk, right next to the defense attorneys. Just behind the bailiff is a door that leads to the prisoner lockup area.

The lockup, where defendants in custody wait as their case is being called, is a small holding cell that serves two courtrooms. A dank and somewhat foul-smelling room, it has a toilet with no seat, a sink with no soap, and benches carved with the most profane graffiti imaginable. Since O.J. was in a special keep-away status for his own safety, no other defendant ever shared the holding cell with him. If the lawyers needed to speak with him, he would be taken to the adjacent attorney room, which was about five feet square, furnished with two chairs and a small table.

There's a steel sliding door that allows entrance into the cell, and just beyond it is a small foyerlike room for four people, with another steel door behind that for added security. Once inside the holding-cell area, attorneys must then pound on the wall to be allowed back into the courtroom.

From the first day, courtesy of Judge Ito and the sheriff's department, we arranged that O.J. would be able to change from prison garb into civilian clothes. He would be brought to court in his jail blues and tennis shoes and go into the second five-by-five room to change. Bob Kardashian brought O.J.'s clothes in each morning—two suits and four or five ties to choose from. O.J. was always concerned about looking sharp, and just before we'd go into the courtroom, we'd check that his tie was straight and his collar down. Guy Magnara, the sheriff's deputy in charge of Ito's courtroom, who was unfailingly kind and pleasant, would come back into the holding cell and tell us when the judge was ready to enter the courtroom. At that point, the attorneys would walk into the courtroom, and O.J. would come in behind us. He was handcuffed and wore a steel chain around his waist, but these restraints would all be removed before he entered the courtroom, as if to give the appearance that he was not in custody.

Our motion, requesting that the prosecution give us half of their blood and tissue samples, so that the defense could run its own DNA tests, was scheduled to be heard on July 25. Keno drove us all—Barry Scheck, Johnnie Cochran, Sara Caplan, and me—to court for the 9:00 A.M. hearing. As was now routine, O.J. joined us at the table, taking notes on his legal pad and asking the attorneys questions throughout the hearing.

The hearing, our first since Judge Ito had been assigned the case, was three hours long and contentious from the first five minutes. Marcia Clark was strongly opposed to sharing any of the blood-sample evidence at all, constantly referring to it as "the People's evidence" and suggesting that if a portion of it was given to the defense for its own testing, it would "deprive the People of their right to be fair in the prosecution."

Because prosecutors are the representatives "for the People" they often operate with a certain arrogance, speaking with the moral authority that they, and only they, carry the torch of justice into the courtroom. It is *their* courtroom, where *their* evidence is presented, and where defense attorneys (and defendants) often seem to be admitted grudgingly, like distant and somewhat disreputable cousins. I was a prosecutor for three years, so I know where the attitude comes from and how easy it is to acquire. It's my experience, however, that arrogance never serves anyone well; in this case, the prosecutor's arrogance would prove to be an important factor for the defense.

We countered Clark's objection by arguing that the forensic evidence belonged to the court, and that if these tests were to have any validity, we needed equal access. Under California law, the defense is entitled to perform its own tests—*if* the sample is large enough to be divided. Initially Ito agreed and granted our motion. Clark then came back with an impassioned plea that evidence "was going to be taken out of our hands forever . . . taking away prosecution evidence and giving it to the defense."

After some consideration, Judge Ito reversed himself and ruled that our defense expert, Dr. Edward Blake, could observe the prosecution's testing (at Cellmark Diagnostics lab in Germantown, Maryland) and could also "cut" and keep 10 percent of each sample in case more testing was necessary in the future. Our testing, if we ultimately chose to do it, would be performed at a private lab in Northern California supervised by Dr. Blake, a respected forensic scientist and close colleague of Gary Sims, the senior criminologist at the California Department of Justice.

And so the pattern began. Ito, in his attempts to remain fair, began his battle with indecisiveness. If the prosecution screamed loud enough, they would not only get a rehearing but possibly a reversal. It's certainly no disgrace when judges reverse themselves upon finding their rulings in error, but over the term of the trial, Ito's willingness to reverse looked like indecision. On the other hand, with the television cameras in the courtroom,

Ito was charged with making instantaneous decisions in front of the watching world. And because of the rules of judicial conduct, he didn't have the luxury that the rest of us did of later explaining and defending decisions that were often criticized and always second-guessed.

I was glad that Barry Scheck was with us during this session, although his style was a little more in-your-face than I might've wished. Ito took great stock in intellect and legal ability, and he immediately recognized Scheck's expertise in this complicated field. Marcia Clark appeared to be paying careful attention to Scheck's comments as well. He would prove to be even more formidable in court.

After the trial had ended, Scheck recalled two things about this, his first encounter with Judge Ito. One was Ito's comment that while he knew this was going to be a hard-fought battle, he also knew that we would all be very professional and responsible. He hoped, the judge said, that we would all be able to go out to dinner together once the trial was over; in fact, a restaurant in Pasadena had already volunteered to host us.

The second thing Barry remarked upon was hearing Ito say, "I'm glad I have this case."

"Most judges might have viewed this particular trial as an awesome responsibility and been a little apprehensive," Scheck recalled. "He seemed so confident, so energetic about it."

While in the courthouse presenting that first DNA motion, we heard a story that after my cross of Dr. Golden the previous week, the medical examiner allegedly brandished something that seemed to be a gun in the coroner's office, yelling, "This is all you need to take out six or seven lawyers!" I didn't know whether to be amused or appalled.

∞

Over the past few years, jury consultants have been used consistently in major civil cases without much knowledge or fanfare; it's only recently that their talents have become utilized in criminal cases as well. First, most clients can't afford the luxury of paying for consultants, and second, criminal lawyers fancy themselves experts in being able to read people and pick their own juries. This is especially true on the prosecution side. I've heard many prosecutors, when offered the service of experts, say, "I don't need anybody to tell *me* how to pick a jury." In fact, my guess is that's what went on with the district attorney's office in the Simpson case. Although they had the help of DecisionQuest's Don Vinson, one of the leading experts available, they didn't seem to pay much attention to what he had to say. During jury selection, Vinson was in the courtroom for only a couple of hours; after that, we didn't see him again. We heard reports that he'd advised the prosecution against building their case on domestic abuse, cautioning them that black women jurors often have conflicting, defensive, and even occasionally protective reactions when a black man is being accused of that behavior.

When we began interviewing for our own jury-selection experts, I became most impressed with Jo-Ellan Dimitrius, who came in the door with computerized exhibits and a thorough knowledge of current jury-pool demographics. We had asked for written proposals and cost estimates from everyone we spoke with, and I knew that cost would be a factor in who we ultimately chose. But I was going to hold out for Dimitrius.

Tuesday morning, July 26, we held our first major roundtable meeting for the entire defense team: Cochran, Uelmen, Pavelic, McNally and McKenna, Sara Caplan, Shawn Chapman (an associate in Cochran's office) and Carl Douglas (a junior partner), and Barry Scheck. Dr. Lee came in later, and we spoke with Baden and Dershowitz by speakerphone. The meeting lasted two and a half hours, and its purpose was to draw up a detailed battle plan. From the investigators, we needed minute-by-minute timetables, starting with Nicole's dinner at Mezzaluna and going right up to when O.J.'s letter was read by Kardashian, including O.J.'s phone calls, Kato's phone calls, the Browns' phone calls to Nicole, and calls to anyone else that any of the key figures might've talked to during that time. We needed background information on essential witnesses, including everyone who had testified in both the grand jury and preliminary hearing, with a special emphasis on Detective Fuhrman. We needed interviews from all known and potential witnesses on Bundy and Rockingham, in Los Angeles and Chicago, as well as those on the flights to and from Chicago. Of major concern was O.J.'s purchase of a stiletto knife just weeks before the murders. And I was additionally concerned about the story we'd heard that the witness to the dog "plaintively wailing" on the night of the murders reportedly worked at one time as a *National Enquirer* reporter.

After the investigators had left the office, the lawyers discussed the DNA evidence and what, if any, benefits would be gained from observing the prosecution's tests at Cellmark. Henry Lee was adamant that just observing would be of no benefit at all; on the other hand, not doing it might reflect negatively on us in front of the jury. The choices came down to these two: We could get a blood split so that we could have our own samples and test them if we decided that it was warranted; or we could forego testing completely, and instead challenge the collection and preservation procedures that the L.A.P.D. lab had performed, and the subsequent contamination of these samples.

At noon on Wednesday, July 27, I received word that Judge Ito was holding an emergency hearing that day regarding the prosecution's request to set aside his order of Monday which would allow our experts to cut a sample. It seemed that Cellmark labs had written a letter objecting to that ruling. "Our laboratory policies and procedures preclude anyone other than the appropriate Cellmark staff from doing any analysis in our laboratory," the letter stated. "We strongly prefer that Dr. Blake and/or Dr. Lee observe the cutting. . . . This avoids the necessity of a transfer of evidence custody and control."

I notified the court that even though we were given the opportunity to observe, we declined. "The guidelines are totally unmanageable," I said. "We won't be participating." It wouldn't benefit us or the jury, we decided, and would be a waste of everyone's time.

Once again, I was aware of Clark's growing impatience with me. My unwillingness to flirt with her or be less than business-like made her angry. The invective was getting sharper, the expression on her face was frequently disdainful or disgusted. Her remarks were running to things like "Shapiro's being outrageous, unethical, unprofessional. I have never seen such conduct from a lawyer." We weren't, I suspected, going to walk hand in hand out of the courtroom when this was all over.

Later that afternoon, I had a conversation with Don Ohl-meyer, the West Coast president of NBC and close friend of O.J.'s who had visited him often at the county jail. After one recent visit, during which they'd had a long and impassioned discussion that had convinced him that O.J. was innocent, Ohl-meyer was worried that their conversation had been overheard.

It wasn't the first problem we'd had with the way the visiting area was set up. The deputies stood barely five feet away, on O.J.'s side of the glass. I was never sure whether conversations were "accidentally" overheard or not, but I was almost certain that real confidentiality was nearly impossible in that space. A few months later, we would grapple with this issue again, when Roosevelt Grier, the former football great who had become a Christian evangelist, visited O.J. on a Sunday afternoon in November. At that point, they'd been meeting regularly, reading the Bible and discussing private matters; and on this particular day, O.J. spoke quite emotionally to the large and gentle man who had become, in his opinion, his spiritual advisor. The conversation was overheard by a sheriff's deputy, who then reported it to the prosecution—who then alleged that by virtue of raising his voice, O.J. had waived his right to confidentiality. They then went so far as to subpoena Rosie Grier in an attempt to get him to testify as to the content of his conversations with O.J., which he appropriately declined to do.

∞

On Wednesday, July 27, I spent two hours with O.J. at the county jail. It was becoming more and more obvious to me that his frustration with the press coverage was growing each day. He couldn't understand why the media kept hammering at him, especially on the issue of domestic violence. For most of his life, O.J. Simpson had easy access to the press, as well as a good relationship with reporters; now, he simply didn't understand why he just couldn't talk to the reporters himself.

I didn't want to get into a situation where we opened the door to or participated in a public debate on the issue of domestic violence. It wasn't an argument that we could "win," because there aren't two sides to it. It's intolerable behavior that takes place too often, and in this case, it would be presented by the prosecution in a complex way, going beyond physical abuse and moving into areas of psychological and financial control as well. Some of these resonated strongly with me because of my earlier representation of Tina Sinatra; I was well aware that they resonated with the public as well.

O.J. had pleaded no contest to spousal abuse in 1989 and had gone through the legal system as he'd been directed to do, getting counseling and performing the required public service. Talking to the press or challenging their interpretation of events now that he'd been accused of Nicole's murder would give them a reason to replay the 911 tapes, setting up what would in effect be a parallel public trial. Only this one would be outside the rules and constraints of a courtroom. As his defense lawyer, defending him in a capital murder case, I couldn't allow that door to be opened. I'd learned that each time the issue came up, O.J. was going to react with understandable frustration. "I'm just venting," he'd say to us. "You have to let me vent." He had to blow off steam; we had to let him.

∽

Also on July 27, we were served notice that Ron Goldman's mother, Sharon Rufo, had filed a wrongful death suit against O.J., but we made no response. Ultimately the Browns and

Fred Goldman would also file suits. The filing of a civil lawsuit during a criminal proceeding is not unusual—and in this case, I had expected it. For many families, civil suits are one way to assuage pain and, seemingly, to take control of the system and inflict their own punishment. Civil suits generally have no effect on the outcome of a criminal case; the criminal case has priority, and so, because of Fifth Amendment privileges, depositions can't be taken for the civil suit until the criminal case ends.

We live in a civilized society, governed by laws. However, grief for a dead child is primal, governed by no law and softened only by the passage of time. I had great compassion for the Goldman family, as I did for the Browns, and never lost sight for a moment that they had buried their children, a son and a daughter that they loved as much as I love my own. My sorrow for the families was of no consequence to them, of course, nor should it have been, and I wasn't surprised to see the civil suits begin to develop.

That Wednesday night I flew up to San Francisco. I had a business appointment there the next day to meet with the U.S. attorney on a case I'd been involved with previous to Simpson's. Outside the courthouse I was stopped by two women who asked for autographs. While I was standing there, a city bus came to an abrupt halt, and the driver jumped out, ran over, and asked for an autograph. It was getting stranger and stranger.

When I returned to Los Angeles on the twenty-eighth, I met with Larry King and his producer for dinner at Eclipse, an elegant restaurant on Melrose Avenue that had quickly become one of the only places where I could count on having any privacy, whether I was eating with my wife or having a business dinner. It was the first time I'd met King, although we had mutual friends who'd grown up in New York City and were his lifelong buddies. I liked the fact that he did live interviews on his show—no editing or tailoring quotes—and I thought his Clinton and Perot interviews had made a new kind of history.

That night, King was good company, full of witty stories and observations about the law, and he was very informed about the Simpson case. He made not-so-subtle hints that someone from the defense team should come on his program to talk about the defense's version of the case.

"I don't think my making appearances outside of court are in my client's best interests," I told him, still smarting from my *New Yorker* experience.

"Bob, you've gotta come on the show. You know this case so well, you can explain it so the viewers understand it," he said, combining his natural charm with an appeal to my trial lawyer's ego. "It'll be great. Besides, the prosecution's case is already out there; you have a responsibility to counterbalance it." Now he was hitting me where I lived, in the inherent characteristic I carry around from my cultural upbringing: guilt.

It was an easy evening. After dinner we exchanged phone numbers, and I agreed to think about the invitation and meet with him the next time he came to Los Angeles.

∞

On Friday July 29, Uelmen, Caplan, and I met at the courthouse with Bill Hodgman to set the date for the trial. Cochran, who had another matter that morning concerning rapper Snoop Doggy Dogg's murder case, said he'd meet us later.

Hodgman, as always, was low-key and friendly. Ito suggested a date of September 20, but the defense wanted no delays, so I asked for the earliest possible date—the first Tuesday after Labor Day, September 2. The prosecution objected, saying that they needed more time, but I didn't want to waive another day. Cochran suggested a compromise of September 12, then Judge Ito settled on September 19.

Afterward we visited with O.J. in the lockup. Kardashian was with him, and I knew he wanted to hear something positive. All he could think of was getting out and being with his children. I don't think he had any comprehension of how complicated it was going to be to even seat a good jury, let alone see this trial through to completion.

∞

On the last weekend in July, Linell and I took Brent and Grant to Las Vegas for the James Toney fight. We'd been invited to join Bob Arum, the fight promoter, as Toney's guests after my sparring match with him three weeks before, and we certainly got the royal treatment. When we walked into the MGM Grand Hotel that night for the fight, we were immediately recognized, and someone from the VIP desk offered to escort us into the arena. I was so proud of my family: the boys looked handsome and happy, and Linell was practically glowing in an all-white Richard Tyler suit. When we entered the arena, the crowd started cheering and clapping. I looked up to see who they were applauding, and there, on the four big screens in each corner of the arena, were the four Shapiros. One of the boys said, "They're cheering you, Dad."

Once we got settled in the second row, we were immediately surrounded by people asking for autographs and pictures. "If Muhammad Ali had walked in here," said Bob Arum, "he probably wouldn't have gotten a bigger response."

Jackie Kallen, Toney's manager, came down and invited me back to the dressing room to see James before the fight. James was taped up, concentrating and focused, refusing to break his poker face as he waited for this championship fight to begin.

Looking at him, I thought about the letter I'd received that day from the California State Boxing Commission. It seems they'd heard about my two rounds with James earlier that month and were writing to inform me that I was not licensed as a sparring partner, which the law required. In addition, as an attorney I should be aware that "people over thirty-six years of age are not allowed in the ring with a professional boxer," let alone anyone with the talent of James Toney. They further stated that the law required anyone over thirty-six to have a complete neurological and physical examination before fighting.

I joked later that George Foreman and I would take that exam together.

Seeing the look in Toney's eyes as he prepared to walk into the ring, I decided that I probably *should* have had a mental competency exam before ever stepping into the ring with the man. "You're going to kick butt, James," I said, pledging that we'd be back after the fight to congratulate him.

While I was making my way back down to my seat, they kept putting the celebrities up on the big screen, people like Sugar Ray Leonard and Phil Collins, and whenever I turned, there was my picture up there, uncomfortably large, and people would cheer each time. This was a sports crowd, a crowd that was likely to root for the underdog. On the other hand, the predominantly male audience that loved boxing also loved football, and O.J. had been one of their great heroes. Were they cheering me because I was representing an underdog? And was it even me they were cheering, or was it O.J., and I was just here in his stead? My eyes met my wife's. What *is* this? she seemed to be asking.

James Toney's fight with Prince Charles Williams was twelve rounds and mostly took place in the corners, with lots of blows exchanged. The crowd booed consistently, even though a lot of punches were thrown. Toney would not take him to the middle of the ring, and it seemed to be very close right up until the end when Toney took control. Those sitting close to the ring said he had it by three or four rounds, but going into the eighth it was clearly even. He was finally able to KO Williams by the twelfth round, but it was a tough fight. Later, Toney said he'd been suffering from the flu.

At some point in the middle of the frenzy, a large man came up and introduced himself as a private security person who had worked for Marvin Hagler and Sylvester Stallone. "Do you think you'll need any help tonight, Mr. Shapiro?" he asked. Normally I would've turned him down, but as I looked around the room, I decided it was a good idea, especially since Linell and the boys were with me. It turned out to be a *great* idea. We needed five linked-arm escorts just to get back to James's dressing room, and the same number to get out the front door.

It was hard to get to sleep that night. I knew about courtrooms, and I thought I knew about human nature. This was something altogether different. Entertainers, politicians, and athletes covet the public spotlight; it's not only integral to who they are, it defines their professional worth in a measurable, palpable way. For lawyers . . . well, recognition is wonderful, applause is great, people asking for autographs can make you feel good, but I kept asking myself why. What was there about being a lawyer for a man accused of double murder that caused people to treat me like a celebrity?

Of course, it was still early in the case; things would change. Just as quarterbacks must get used to both cheers for touchdowns and boos for interceptions, I'd soon hear a different sound coming from the stands.

Chapter Eight

They're taking potshots at him already; every lawyer in the country is auditioning for his job. That's something Bob would be terribly upset by—he's always been a team player and a gentleman.

—Leslie Abramson

On Sunday, July 31, Johnnie and I visited with O.J. in the county jail, where once again we heard him tell the story of his life with Nicole. It was a mantra he repeated no matter who was visiting him, no matter how easily the sheriff's bailiffs could overhear. That he'd loved her, that they'd had their problems, that he'd accepted their marriage was over, that he'd moved on, that he only wanted to do what was best for the kids, that he had a good life, that he never would do anything to threaten it.

We had to get him to focus on the task at hand, to understand that what lay ahead of us was work. I know he wanted our support, our friendship. But being his best friend wasn't my job, it wasn't what he was paying me for. I know my bedside manner could stand some improvement, but I didn't think we had the time to indulge O.J. anymore. On the other hand, Johnnie seemed to have infinite patience with him, telling him what he wanted to hear, approving of everything he said, listening to him tell the story of his life over and over. We had work to do, and it was time for O.J. to *think* of it as work.

O.J. just couldn't stay with it; he kept veering off to Nicole, to the stories that had been printed about them, and to some of the grand jury testimony that had inexplicably been leaked to

127

the media. There was one story in particular, about Keith Zlom-sowitch, who had dated Nicole shortly after the divorce. Zlom-sowitch, who was a potential witness for the prosecution, had alleged that O.J. followed Nicole, stalking her, and had watched through her window when she and Zlomsowitch were having sex.

As he would later repeat in his post-trial video, O.J. insisted he never stalked his ex-wife. It was a small neighborhood, and they often simply ran into each other in the same bars and restaurants. The reason he'd seen them being intimate on that one occasion was that he'd gone there on what he thought was an invitation from Nicole. The curtains were open and he saw the two of them having sex in the living room. He went away then, he said, and waited until the next day to tell Nicole that he'd seen them. He told her that he didn't think their behavior appropriate, considering that his two young children might walk in the room. He didn't hit anybody, he didn't yell, he didn't break anything. He just said, "Don't do that so openly around my kids."

After hearing this story, it occurred to me that Zlomsowitch might be a good *defense* witness; after all, in similar circum-stances—an ex-wife having sex with someone on the couch, his two small children upstairs—what man wouldn't go completely ballistic? And yet, O.J. didn't.

∞

As we began preparations for the trial, a simultaneous grand jury investigation started up regarding A.C. Cowlings, who had been arrested after the Bronco chase on suspicion of aiding and abetting a fugitive. Christopher Darden was the assistant district attorney in charge of the grand jury's investigation.

I was more than a little suspicious of the prosecution's mo-tives. By investigating A.C., they could gather information, witnesses, and testimony (given under oath) that could be used in the case against O.J.

The law says that once a trial is in progress (and we were

considered "in progress" once O.J. had been arraigned), a grand jury proceeding related to witnesses in that trial is not allowed. Nevertheless, Bob Kardashian was one of the first people subpoenaed; Cathy Randa was right behind him, and so was almost everyone who had been involved in the case since the first week, including Michael Baden, Henry Lee, and even Keno Jenkins, my driver.

Normally very soft-spoken and polite, Keno became completely unnerved during the grand jury hearing when it was suggested that he—and I—had somehow been part of a plan for O.J. to evade the police with A.C. Cowlings. "They said they didn't believe me," he said. "They called me a liar!" His blood pressure immediately spiked, and he had to see his doctor the following day.

I even heard from an anguished Henry Lee in Connecticut, who was also completely unaccustomed to having his integrity questioned. "Bob," he said, "I think I might have to resign. My department is very upset with me." He was very upset about being subpoenaed, he'd been criticized by his bosses for giving me the Connecticut State Police baseball cap, and the press was making his life miserable. "They follow me, they follow my wife. Wherever we go, there they are." He would continue to consult on the case, he said, but he couldn't do so in a senior position.

When I received a subpoena demanding that I produce O.J. Simpson's datebook for 1994, I called Chris Darden myself.

"Chris, I just received a subpoena, and I'm certainly willing to cooperate in any way possible. But I don't have this datebook here. I don't think I ever had it."

"Cathy Randa told us she'd turned it over to you," Darden said.

I called Cathy, who told me she'd given the datebook to her own attorney, Melvyn Sacks. I called Sacks and asked him to seal the datebook in an envelope and bring it to my office the next day with a letter declaring the envelope's contents. I then presented it to the court, under seal, arguing that I objected to turning it over to the grand jury. It was "privileged material beyond the scope of the Cowlings investigation, but containing information pertinent to the Simpson prosecution" that they were not entitled to get by this method. As Dean Uelmen argued, "The grand jury is not empowered to conduct roving investigations."

We were assured by the district attorney's office that what is euphemistically known as a Chinese wall had been built between Chris Darden's investigation of A.C. and Bill Hodgman's prosecution of O.J., keeping the current grand jury investigation confidential. While I trusted Bill Hodgman implicitly, I never believed for a minute that there was a wall high enough or thick enough to keep these two matters from spilling over onto each other.

In November of 1994, when the grand jury concluded its investigation, it was announced that there was no sufficient cause for the D.A. to seek an indictment of A.C. The very next day, Christopher Darden became part of the Simpson prosecution team; when Bill Hodgman fell seriously ill in January, Darden became co-lead counsel. There was a great hue and cry (from Johnnie Cochran, among others) that Darden had been added to the prosecution team primarily because he was African-American. However, to my mind it had less to do with that than it did with the grand jury hearing that Darden had overseen and the confidential information he was privy to. So much for the Chinese wall, I thought.

∞

On Monday, August 1, I was surprised to read in the *Los Angeles Times* that Judge Ito had released O.J.'s grand jury transcripts to the public. He did it, he said, to "level the playing field," since significant portions of the transcript had already been leaked in previous weeks. We hadn't been notified, and it took me by surprise. Of course, it made big news all day long, with Keith Zlomsowitch and the alleged "stalking" incidents taking center stage.

Later that afternoon, we received a letter from Robert Tour-telot, an attorney representing Mark Fuhrman, notifying us that all the defense attorneys for O.J. were going to be sued for defamation, as were Jeffrey Toobin and the *New Yorker;* however, if we publicly retracted our "statements," the suit wouldn't be filed. I forwarded the material to Larry Feldman and Tony Glassman, my own attorneys.

On Wednesday, I was called to the jail to meet with Skip Taft and Captain Albert Scaduto, who ran the facility. O.J.'s security needs in the jail, with special sergeants assigned to guard him, were costing $36,000 a month. They wanted to move him to a different location, to what they called a "high-power unit," and use a twenty-four-hour-a-day video camera in place of the extra guards. I strenuously objected that a video camera trained on someone around-the-clock would be a significant invasion of privacy, especially where bodily functions were concerned. All I could think of was the thriving tabloid market and what someone might pay for a video of O.J.'s activities in his cell.

Skip and I then went to inspect the new cell location. Once again, it was the standard nine by seven. I was discouraged to see that since no one would be in any of the seven neighboring cells, O.J. would for all intents and purposes be in solitary confinement. Because he was technically a "protective custody" inmate, he wasn't allowed to eat in the community mess halls, work out in the rooftop exercise area, or attend services in the jail chapel. Thus far, he'd been a model prisoner, still presumed innocent of the crime he'd not yet been tried for, and yet he was completely isolated. A telephone within his grasp (he couldn't receive calls but could make them during limited time periods, like all other inmates) and two hours of television a day—with the channels selected by the guards—weren't going to do much to mitigate that.

My mood wasn't helped when I got a quick look at that week's *Time* magazine, in which they reported the results of a *Time*/CNN poll. Sixty-three percent of whites believed that

O.J. would get a fair trial; only 31 percent of blacks felt the same. Seventy-seven percent of whites believed the case against him was very strong; 45 percent of blacks agreed. I didn't worry so much about the numbers as I did about the distribution. They're polling readers by race, I thought.

That afternoon I met Joel Siegel for lunch at the Grill, a discreet restaurant off Rodeo Drive. While there we ran into Mort Zuckerman, owner of the *New York Daily News,* and then-superagent Michael Ovitz. Zuckerman, whose newspaper circulation had steadily climbed since the murders, joked, "Keep it going as long as possible."

Ovitz, who lives quite near Rockingham, protested. "No, no, Bob," he said. "Get it over with, so I can return to a normal life."

∞

When Johnnie Cochran came on board, so did his associate, Carl Douglas.

A former public defender who was intelligent and knowledgeable about the law, Douglas had an astonishing capacity for detail and organization. Long entrusted with running Johnnie's practice, there is nothing Carl doesn't take care of; in fact, if Cochran is a metaphorical airport, Douglas is his air-traffic controller. I did, however, have some reservations about his actual trial skills. He didn't project well in court, and I felt that his style before a jury was somewhat pedantic. He often seemed to lecture, rather than draw them in, and the net effect was boredom. In my experience, boring a jury can be more dangerous than making them angry.

Carl was made case manager, in charge of keeping track of the discovery material, which quickly became voluminous. He also kept track of the defense motions to the court and prepared the agendas for all the defense-team meetings. After I'd known Carl for a while, and understood how much Johnnie depended on him, I was asked to give a toast at his birthday party.

"You know," I said, "when Johnnie first introduced me to

Carl, I wasn't sure what his last name was. For months, I thought it was 'you-take-care-of-it.'" It brought the house down.

∞

For years, Linell and I have taken the kids to Lake Tahoe for a family vacation in the later summer. In 1994, we had gone ahead and rented the house from mid-August through Labor Day. I had warned her that with so much work on the trial, and jury selection a huge hurdle we still had to get over, I wasn't sure how much time I'd be able to spend with the family, if any.

"Bob, they really need you to be with them," she said. "They're not reacting to all of this very well."

She was right. We'd gone to a screening at producer Robert Evans's only a few days before, and the first words out of Grant's mouth this time were, "Are there any celebrities here?" Earlier, at the airport coming back from the Toney fight in Las Vegas, Brent said, "I wonder how many people are going to ask for your autograph this time, Dad. How much do you think it's worth?"

I tried to wave him off, but he wasn't buying it. "Oh, come on, Dad," he scoffed, "you're probably going to end up on a baseball card or something."

One night, Linell told me that our friends had been talking to Michael Klein and Bob Koblin, saying that I was changing, acting differently—signing autographs, stopping to shake hands, allowing perfect strangers to come up to a table in a restaurant and interrupt our private "off-duty" time and personal conversations.

I was taken aback; nobody had said anything to me about it, and now two of my best friends had gone to my wife, not wanting to confront me directly. I'm *not* changing, I wanted to tell them; the environment around me is different. The idea that my closest friends would think that I was turning away from them—or worse, that they would turn away from me—was very upsetting.

"This is a no-win situation," I told Linell. "When people come up to me and ask for autographs, if I don't sign, I'm a jerk. If I do sign, I'm still a jerk."

When I was growing up in Los Angeles, there were no pro basketball teams, no major-league baseball teams. Instead, we had the Pacific Coast League, with the Hollywood Stars and the L.A. Angels. The Hollywood Stars were on Fairfax, quite near to where I lived, so I saw them play as often as I could. When the Dodgers came out to Los Angeles from Brooklyn, I quickly got a part-time job selling Cokes and hot dogs in the stands at the Coliseum. I would ask players for autographs, and most of them were generous and kind, not just to me but to all the kids who worked there, and to the fans who came to see them play. Others weren't so kind, and I remember vividly their faces and voices when they said "Get lost, kid. I don't have time for you."

A person who aspires to be good, or even the best, at what he does wants recognition for achieving that. Anyone who denies it is denying something basic about being human. And when people came up to me, as they increasingly did, and said "You're doing a great job" or "My daughter's in law school, would you please sign this for her?" or "My father would love your autograph," what was I supposed to do? I didn't hit home runs or score touchdowns; I was a lawyer. Yet kids wanted my autograph. I simply could not look anyone in the face and say "Sorry, I don't have time for you."

I finally talked with Michael Klein about my mixed feelings, and his. "I know the publicity and everything is an intrusion, on all of our lives," I said. "Ultimately, though, it's not about me. It's about O.J." I reminded him that we still had a jury to pick. "Everybody's watching me, Michael, all the time, everywhere. I can't be a hard-ass with people; you know I'm not like that. Besides, I can't take the risk of alienating anyone at this point."

He understood, he said. He just reserved the right to complain about it once in a while. Ultimately, I decided to stop signing autographs when there were cameras around, and I stopped doing it at the courthouse entirely, because that was a place of serious business—T-shirt hawkers and trial groupies notwithstanding. I always responded, however, asking people to write or call my office, and I would send them something. In other circumstances, I tried, and still do, to be as courteous as I can be to people who are courteous to me.

And by and large, people *are* courteous. Plus, there's no denying that VIP treatment can be pleasant. Convenient parking, hard-to-get tickets, front-row seats, good tables in wonderful restaurants. I soon realized that there was another reason for the velvet-glove routine. Browsing quietly in a bookstore one day, I quickly drew a crowd, all of whom were talking at once, some of whom quickly ran out to buy disposable cameras so that they could get pictures. The management was not happy. And at a Kings hockey game one night, a group of a dozen or so people gathered around my seat for autographs—which didn't much please the hockey fans in back of me. Celebrities, I discovered, are not isolated simply because they're particularly special but because they're often security risks, crowd-control problems, and traffic-jam instigators.

Before the trial began, I went to an annual charity gathering called the Sports Spectacular, which raises money for Cedars-Sinai Hospital in Los Angeles. At the Spectacular, fifteen or twenty star athletes come together to auction off sports memorabilia, meet fans, and give autographs. In other years, O.J. would've been front and center, but not this time.

I was introduced to Joe DiMaggio by my friend Tommy Lasorda. Standing in front of the legendary DiMaggio, trying to talk to him without stumbling all over my words, I felt all the old boyhood feelings—hero worship, awe, respect. In the noise of the athletes and fans swirling around him, DiMaggio was a quiet, authoritative presence, almost majestic. As he autographed baseballs for my sons, I was struck by how large and strong his hands still were. Little wonder that in his prime he could wield a bat as easily as other men swing flyswatters.

The three of us—Lasorda, DiMaggio, and I—then went to the men's room together. In retrospect, it probably wasn't a good tactical move. Security had to close off the door to the men's room while we were in there, and I was very aware of the people on the other side of that closed door. What were they saying? DiMaggio's in the head with Lasorda and Shapiro. Lasorda's in there with Shapiro and DiMaggio. Shapiro's in there with DiMaggio and Lasorda. Or more likely, "I wish whoever's in there would get the hell out, so they'd open the damn door and let *me* in!"

∞

O.J.'s new cell and his isolation in it were very difficult for him to adjust to. As stoic as it was in his nature to be, he was completely miserable. His bunk, which was steel, had only a very thin mattress on the top of it. With his arthritis, he could barely lie down on it. He couldn't sit up in it either, because his head hit the upper bunk. And when he was full-length on the bed, his face was practically in the toilet. The television, just beyond his reach outside his cell, was often set on the news— which was more often than not about him and the case, and he was unable to shut it off. One night he'd been watching the Dodgers game, and in the bottom of the ninth, with bases loaded, the guards shut off the television set.

He was supposed to take his arthritis medicine with his breakfast, but the food arrived at 6:00 A.M. and the pills didn't arrive until 8:00. If he waited until 8:00, the food was cold, and the roaches were more interested in it than he was. The same thing happened with his evening meal. At one point, when he realized that the video camera was (in spite of assurances to the contrary) pointed right at the toilet, he draped a towel over the camera. Within minutes after the first time he did it, the deputies came down and told him to remove the towel.

In addition, when they walked him out of his cell for any

reason, they handcuffed him from behind, which aggravated his arthritis. Couldn't he be handcuffed in front? "And why do I have a pillow case that hasn't been changed in fifty days?" he asked a bailiff. "On the other hand, I guess I should be glad I have a pillow. Some people in here don't even have that."

I spoke with Captain Scaduto, and he met with O.J. to talk about the problems. Scaduto agreed to find him a thicker mattress and take the camera off the toilet area. He would do his best to coordinate the food-and-medicine situation and also agreed that from now on, O.J.'s hands would be cuffed in front, not in back. Thereafter, O.J. was generally treated well by the deputies in this, one of the most troubled, overcrowded, gang-infested jails in the entire country.

In addition to his living arrangements, O.J. was concerned about my treatment of his friend Bob Kardashian, whose constant presence in court I had questioned. In fact, Lee Bailey had told me straight out that I'd been too hard on Kardashian. While I was grateful to him for all of his cooperation, and especially for the day-to-day care and attention he was giving to O.J. in jail, I just felt it wasn't necessary for him to be at the defense table every day. He wasn't actively involved in the pretrial preparation, and in all likelihood he wouldn't play a role once the trial began. However, I certainly didn't want to alienate him; he was one of my client's best friends. I promised O.J. that I'd make a point to call Bob, get together with him, and talk it through.

That day, O.J. had a few things to say on the subject of violence and the way the media had been portraying him. Anyone who knew anything about football would tell you that he'd never been an attack player. "In eighteen years of playing football," he often said, "I only had one fight—and that's just because somebody jumped on my old friend Reggie McKenzie."

∞

On Monday, August 8, we held a meeting of all lawyers and investigators in the office. The people who were out of town were linked to the rest of us by speakerphone. We finalized the decision on jury consultants; as I'd hoped, we hired Jo-Ellan Dimitrius. Of the three groups we'd been reviewing, Jo-Ellan's was based in California, and had a great deal of experience with local juries.

Johnnie broke into the jury consultant discussion. No one knew downtown juries like he did, he said. After all, it was his jury expertise that had gotten Todd Bridges off. Bridges, a former child star charged with murdering a drug dealer, was acquitted of those charges in a very highly publicized case that had contributed to Cochran's reputation.

That night Cochran and I spoke briefly on the phone, primarily about the lawsuit that Mark Fuhrman was talking about filing against us. I had discussed the matter with Larry Feldman and Tony Glassman and decided not to respond. But Johnnie had prepared a lengthy response and had engaged his own lawyers to send it out.

"Johnnie, I don't think anybody on the team should write anything or file anything without running it past me first," I said. "We have to stay cohesive, and focused, for the good of the case."

"This isn't about O.J., Bob," Johnnie told me. "I have to protect myself. You don't have to worry about me, I know what I'm doing. I wasn't even involved in the case at the time."

The next day, Captain Scaduto called from the jail; he'd heard through the grapevine that someone in Cochran's office—Carl Douglas, maybe—was filing a motion concerning O.J.'s complaints about the poor condition of the jail. "I thought we were going to try and work this out between us," Scaduto said.

I assured him that nobody was filing anything, and we were of course willing to wait a reasonable time to see that the problems at the jail were addressed to everybody's satisfaction. After I'd spoken to Scaduto, I called Johnnie and requested in the strongest terms possible that Carl proceed no further on whatever it was he was doing. "I have thick skin, Johnnie, so you can argue with me on issues if you want, I have no trouble with that. But you and I have to speak and act with one voice on legal procedures and defense team strategy." Happily, he agreed.

That night I had trouble sleeping for the first time since I'd taken on the Simpson case. I hadn't eaten much all day, I'd canceled my boxing session with Jason, my trainer, and I tossed and turned much of the night. When I abruptly awoke the next morning at 6:15, I felt anxious and jumpy. I'd never been either a plaintiff or a defendant in a court action, and now I was being threatened with a libel suit. It was all a little unsettling.

On August 10 we conducted a hearing to bring Judge Ito up to date, to let him know that we (the defense and the prosecution) were making good progress on discovery; that is, we were each responding to the other's request for information. There had been a request from the press asking that they be allowed to see photographs introduced at the preliminary hearing, in particular the coroner's photographs of Nicole and Ron Goldman. They evidently wanted only to see and then describe the pictures, not reproduce or broadcast them. I argued that while we had a right to a fair trial, the press had no corresponding right to try the case in the media. Ultimately, ruling that even the descriptions of the pictures would be prejudicial to the case, Ito kept the photographs sealed.

Afterward, Bill Hodgman, Marcia Clark, and I met in chambers for about forty-five minutes, talking about the different effects the case was having on all our lives. The story about my work related to the shooting of her ex-husband had come out, and we agreed that it was completely bizarre—a real case of truth being stranger than fiction. We were doing the jobs we'd always done, yet our personal lives didn't seem to belong to us anymore. Complete strangers commented on Marcia's hair, Hodgman's manners, my suits, even my tan. All of our children were being affected by our constant presence on television and our absence from home. Brent was acting out even beyond what I'd expected once he hit adolescence, and Grant's nightly question was "When will this be over?"

We talked about DNA for a few minutes. To date, we were dealing with more than one hundred samples, and the last batch of discovery material had come to nearly two thousand pages. In one memo, I had categorized it as "ecologically improper material."

Marcia and Bill weren't optimistic about the results they were going to get, since RFLP testing wasn't particularly successful with leather, asphalt, or concrete. "It would be a happy day if the results exclude O.J.," Marcia said. "Then we could just dismiss the case and move on."

I was pleasantly surprised by that comment. I guess we were all a little weary. "I'm having quite a time running my bureaucracy," I told them.

"Our bureaucracy is bigger and much harder to deal with than yours is, Bob," joked Hodgman. It was the most relaxed discussion I'd had with them since the case had begun.

∞

On Wednesday, August 10, I got a call from NBC's Don Ohlmeyer, who was somewhat dismayed at his network's coverage of the case, which he felt had been pretty negative. Ohlmeyer had been to see O.J. often, and on one visit he'd even offered to help pay the $30,000-per-month overtime charges so that he could move to a more comfortable cell. O.J. refused the offer, saying that he couldn't allow Don to do that. "Isn't it nice that I have a friend like him?" he said to me.

O.J. was going to Cedars-Sinai Hospital the following day, for the long-delayed lymph node biopsy. The surgery, an outpatient procedure, was at his expense; the trip to the hospital alone, complete with three unmarked cars and five special deputies, would cost two thousand dollars. He was understandably nervous but trusted Dr. Huizenga. He'd been thinking about the results of the test, about what he'd do if they showed positive for cancer. His greatest concern was for his children, especially the two little ones. At the end of that month, he would sign over guardianship of Sydney and Justin to Louis and Juditha Brown, the term of guardianship to last only "until his release."

When I left the office that day, KCBS Channel 2 anchor Harvey Levin was waiting for me out in the parking lot. "Bob, can I get you on camera?" he asked.

"Sure you can," I said, smiling, and then gently took the microphone out of his hand. We did a quick Abbott and Costello routine, where I was the interviewer and Levin was the subject. I peppered him with questions about the negative press coverage we'd been getting.

"Hey, I think I need a lawyer for this," he said, laughing.

Handing over the microphone, I changed positions with him and stood in front of the camera. "Well, Harvey, business is slow today," I said, "so I'm available for hire."

He didn't want jokes, he wanted something solid. "Just give me ten seconds, please," he asked. "Anything you've got, on the record."

I shook my head. "I've got nothing to say about anything having to do with this case. Absolutely nothing."

The next morning, the phone rang at six-thirty. It was Dr. Huizenga. Although it would be a while before we'd know the results of the tests (which ultimately proved negative), he said the procedure itself had gone well, although the *National Enquirer* was supposedly scaling the walls of Cedars-Sinai.

O.J. called later that morning when he returned from the hospital. He was tired and irritable; he'd been awakened in the jail at three-thirty that morning, at four they handcuffed him—from behind—but then didn't take him out of the cell to leave for the hospital for another half-hour. He couldn't sit down on the bed, he couldn't go to the bathroom. And when he came back from the hospital and went to make his phone calls, somebody accidentally slammed the iron gate on his hand.

"It doesn't hurt right now," he said. "I'm probably still

loaded with anesthetic." He was upset that the early news reports of his trip to the hospital said he was suffering from hem-
orrhoids. "They can't even get that right," he said, disgusted.
"News is just entertainment to them."

Chapter Nine

In August, we gave O.J. our copy of the police murder book to examine closely. If he testified, he had to be solid on the facts. As the most important person in the case—the one who knew more about his relationship with Nicole than anyone else did—he would be able to spot inconsistencies and errors, which we could then point out to a jury.

He was unhappy with our pursuing avenues of reasonable doubt. Understandably, he wanted to be proven innocent. That would have required our producing proof of who committed the murders. That was not the defense's obligation, and it was beyond our resources.

After this meeting, I heard from Sara Caplan that she'd been called to be present during a search of O.J.'s business office by four deputies and, I was happy to hear, a Special Master. The search warrant was specific to material dating from January 1 to July 17, 1994. When the deputies discovered brochures on domestic abuse in O.J.'s files—brochures that he'd been given while on probation—Sara promptly declared that these were beyond the scope of the warrant and couldn't be seized. The Special Master agreed. That material became the "mystery document" that Cathy Randa later shredded—which of course made it into the tabloid headlines as something dire and sinister.

In late August, we met with Jo-Ellan Dimitrius about the questionnaire we would prepare, with the prosecution, to give to the prospective jury members. We had a tentative draft of the questions we wanted to use, based on responses that Jo-Ellan had gotten from focus groups. In her meetings with O.J., she was getting to know him and becoming familiar with the themes of his life—his relationship with Nicole, his feelings for his children, the unlikelihood that he would have committed these crimes.

I attended one of Jo-Ellan's focus-group sessions in Santa Monica. I sat with her behind a glass wall, watching a facilitator work with a racially mixed group of nine people, reflecting what we believed the jury pool to be. I was fascinated as I heard their responses to questions ranging from "How many people here have heard of O.J. Simpson?" (unanimous) to "What do you think the trial verdict is likely to be?" (mixed). Many of them were familiar with the Simpson preliminary-hearing proceedings and understood some of the legal terms and the issues of evidence as well.

They weren't particularly concerned with what they'd heard of the 911 tapes, although they didn't think the prosecution should've released them to the news media. The tapes did show that O.J. had a temper, but, said one woman, "What couple hasn't had a really bad fight or two?" As for Mark Fuhrman, although he might've been a racist, no one believed he was a bad cop, and jumping over the wall at Rockingham made him seem brave and daring to them. They thought the DNA evidence was the strongest part of the D.A.'s case, although they said that if O.J.'s Bronco was used after such a violent murder, there should have been blood soaked all over everything. While they had no particular criticism of the coroner's office, they were concerned about the pivotal role in the evidence-gathering part of the investigation that had been played by neophytes or trainees.

While they didn't expect O.J. to testify at the trial, they did say that they would "feel better about him if he did." Not surprisingly, they showed a fundamental confusion about the role, or mission, of the defense. In order to keep O.J. from being convicted, they said, we either had to identify the real killer or prove somehow that he had been framed. And they were familiar with the dynamic between the defense and prosecution. "Marcia Clark's going to be really disappointed if it turns out that someone else did it," said one man.

∞

Linell and I had been invited, along with the boys, to the wedding of Miko Brando, Marlon's son. The wedding and reception were going to be held at Michael Jackson's Neverland Ranch, which, although it's almost as secure as the Pentagon, is nevertheless the subject of constant press scrutiny, with helicopter flyovers the order of the day.

A few days before we were scheduled to go, I had been the subject of a somewhat negative piece on local television, commenting on the fact that since I'd taken on O.J.'s case I had also gone with my family to the World Cup soccer matches, the glittery and well-publicized opening of a Los Angeles country-and-western–themed restaurant, and the James Toney fight in Las Vegas. Linell was upset not only at the implication—that instead of taking care of business, I was celebrity-showboating—but also because these were events and activities that we would've attended in any case, long before I was associated with O.J. Simpson.

"I don't think we should even go to Miko's wedding now," said Linell angrily. "Our being there would probably wreck his special day. I think I'm going to take the kids to Lake Tahoe and stay there until it's time for them to come back to school. It's all getting really ridiculous now, Bob. Cameras everywhere we go, people pointing and yelling at you, practically hip-checking me and the boys out of the way to get to you."

I knew there wasn't much I could say that could take the edge off the way she was feeling. Our quiet dinners out often turned into social events, our social events became roundtable discussions of the Simpson case, complete with confrontations and critiques of my performance to date. At one dinner party, Tina Sinatra took me outside and read me the riot act on the terrace. "How can you represent him?" she demanded heatedly, not waiting to hear my answer. "Isn't this hypocritical, what you're doing?"

And all the while, the other party guests were trying not to listen, and Linell was trying not to notice that once again the focus was on me and the case. She was stuck in the awkward position of being my most loyal defender and protector at exactly the same time that her own life, *because* of me, was getting more and more uncomfortable.

"Well," I told my wife, "remember when I told you a long time ago that I didn't want to be famous? That I just wanted to be known for being a good lawyer? This is why."

"Back then, we didn't know about *this*," she said. "This, *nobody* could have predicted." Ultimately, she and the boys stayed at Lake Tahoe, and I went to Miko's wedding alone.

∞

As the tension surrounding jury selection and pre-trial preparation began to rise, we were plagued by a series of leaks to the press, and the leaks seemed to be coming from all directions. The TV tabloid *Hard Copy* ran a story about Marcia Clark's former mother-in-law, Gaby Horowitz's mother, who lived in Israel. She had some bitter feelings about her ex-daughter-in-law and was more than willing to make disparaging remarks about Marcia—including that she was a racist—on camera. When I found out that our investigators were privy to this information, I was appalled to think that there was a possibility it had been leaked from our office. Anyone who knew Marcia Clark, as I had for two decades, knew that any suggestion that she was a racist was so far from the truth as to be completely laughable.

Pat McKenna and John McNally were quick to assure Bill Pavelic that they didn't leak anything to *Hard Copy*, or to anyone else, and told him that they had very strong reasons to believe that our investigator Barry Hostetler had done it. Skip Taft, who had been monitoring the budget, had already suggested that we could afford only three investigators. Letting Hostetler go, it was decided, was appropriate given the circumstances. It would be six months before we learned that the leak had in fact come from inside, though not from Hostetler.

In August, there were both television and newspaper reports that lab tests on the strands of hair in the blue knit cap found them to resemble O.J.'s hair; in addition, one television reporter said that the item in the "mysterious envelope" still in the court's custody was a new knife, with its original price tag. The first piece of information could only have come from the prosecution; the second one, the reporter said, "was confirmed by a defense source."

Judge Ito told us in chambers that he was particularly angry to have learned key information in the case while he was taking a shower and listening to the radio. His response to the leaks was to draft a gag order. "A trial court not only has the authority but the affirmative duty to protect the right to a fair trial," he wrote. "Given the amount of media interest and coverage that this case has ignited, the court must use its inherent authority to control the judicial procedure." He wanted all motions sealed and not made public until they were argued in court. Prosecution and defense lawyers were not to comment on anything that might come before the jury, any evidence or information specific to guilt or innocence. Ito went on to say that violation of the order would incur sanctions, although he didn't specify what those sanctions would be. They could range from monetary fines to charges of contempt.

Although some members of the ACLU and the press corps thought Ito's order was harsh, my own response was that an information embargo was long overdue. There had been leaks since the beginning, not the least of which was the "Simpson-is-guilty" drumbeat that came regularly from the district attorney's office. However, because I had always maintained a comfortable relationship with the press, I was often the one assumed to be responsible for the leaks. It would be nice for the playing field to be not only level for a change, but regulated by the judge. Now the challenge would be to keep my own troops quiet.

∽

In addition to the information we'd gathered on Mark Fuhrman's racial attitudes, we had also been contacted by a woman named Kathleen Bell. After talking to Bill Pavelic, Bell, a white woman, ultimately filed an affidavit with the court that reported a casual conversation she'd had with Fuhrman in the mid-eighties. He'd told her that in his capacity as a policeman, he frequently pulled over cars driven by black men, for no particular legal reason, and he especially did so when he saw black men with white women. Mark Fuhrman had met Nicole in the mid-1980s, when he was the responding officer on a call Nicole had made initially to the Westec security service. In that incident, she reported that O.J. had shattered a car windshield with a baseball bat. What, then, must have gone through his head when Fuhrman arrived at Bundy and realized who the murdered woman was?

When we moved to obtain Fuhrman's records, our request had included not just his personnel records but his Marine Corps records as well. This had been Lee Bailey's idea; if there was a pattern of Fuhrman's behavior that went back further than the L.A.P.D., he said, we ought to know about it. Although Ito did give us access to the police records, he denied the military records, stating that there was nothing in them relevant to the Simpson case. Robert Tourtelot, Fuhrman's attorney, called us "desperate snooping defense attorneys" whose request for the records was "replete with factually unsupported accusations of racism."

"This is not a fishing expedition," argued Johnnie. "This officer harbors animosity against African-Americans, especially African-Americans married to Caucasians."

Once the press learned of the defense's interest in Fuhrman's records, they were all over us for making race an important issue in the trial.

"Race is not the issue here," I responded for what seemed like the millionth time. "Credibility is the issue. And the documentation of Fuhrman's attitudes toward black men—and possibly toward this black man in particular—goes directly to his credibility as a witness, and as an investigating police officer in this case."

Privately, Cochran told me I was naive in believing that race wasn't an issue.

"I never said it wasn't *an* issue," I argued. "I said it wasn't *the* issue, and at any rate it shouldn't be part of this case. A defense built on race will never help us."

"Never say never, Bob," he replied.

∞

In late August, a column published in both the *New York Times* and the *Los Angeles Times* stated the following: "Unlike clinical laboratories which perform tests for hospitals and doctors' offices, the nation's crime laboratories are exempt from regulation and external review. There are no minimum certification requirements for lab personnel." Written by Paul Giannelli, a law professor at Case Western Reserve University, the piece cited the case of one serologist who had falsified "test results in hundreds of cases since 1979. . . . Defendants who have since been exonerated were sentenced to long prison terms on his testimony. . . . For more than a decade, he worked closely with prosecutors and the police and apparently tailored his findings to conform with their theories of the cases." Proficiency testing for crime lab personnel has been voluntary since 1984, reported Giannelli, but the results of that testing haven't been made available. "Many people assume that the accused will have the opportunity to challenge expert witnesses who present faulty evidence," he wrote. "In fact, 80% of defendants can't afford to hire a lawyer, much less pay expert witnesses."

The information came as no surprise to Barry Scheck and Peter Neufeld. "Bad science puts good people away all the time," Barry said.

At the time the column was published, we had been assured by the prosecution that all the blood samples for DNA testing had been sent to the Cellmark laboratory in Maryland. However, we discovered that a small portion, two drops, had been retained by the police department, ostensibly so that the prosecution could submit it at a later date to a second laboratory for a second set of diagnostic tests—because, Peter Neufeld suggested, some of the sample material had deteriorated to such a degree that it was no longer fit for testing. The prosecution had originally told us that there wasn't enough sample material to share with the defense, yet evidently there was enough for the police to retain for "backup" testing. In a pre-trial hearing called to resolve pending DNA and discovery matters, Marcia Clark stated adamantly that she wasn't aware that material had been retained.

"It seems very bizarre to me that the lead prosecutor in the case does not communicate with the laboratory charged with handling essential evidence in the case," I said.

Dean Uelmen then accused the prosecution of playing the old shell game. "What we're dealing with is an attitude problem," he said. "The attitude is they own the evidence, and when they're through with it, we can have whatever scraps are left over."

"Hysterical proclamations and hypocritical ramblings," was Clark's response.

In late August, Uelmen, Scheck, and Neufeld laboriously argued that the collection and subsequent handling of the blood samples had been compromised, possibly even contaminated, by the inefficiency of the police crime lab personnel. To support this argument, the pre-trial information they managed to elicit—from such witnesses as criminalist Dennis Fung, Gary Sims, the DNA specialist and criminologist with the California Justice Department, and crime lab assistant director Michelle

Kestler—was so minute and technical (and, we nonspecialists later had to admit, tedious) that Judge Ito grew irritated with the pace, snapping at Neufeld three separate times in an effort to speed up the questioning. "Move on to something that has to do with the size of the samples!" he said. Later Neufeld turned to me, saying, "Only I could come out from New York and immediately put everyone on this case to sleep."

The second day of the hearings, I joked that the scalpers were losing money. Visitors were walking out of court, three reporters in the front row were dozing, and O.J. was struggling to keep his eyes open, too. "This is cruel and unusual punishment," he joked in a stage whisper. "Any more of this and I'll wish I *had* killed myself."

However, the scientific evidence was as crucial as it was boring. It allowed us to learn how bad the L.A.P.D. criminal lab personnel had been in the collection and preservation of the blood evidence—which later allowed us to challenge the evidence itself.

Nevertheless the scientific testimony threatened to put us all to sleep—until suddenly I heard an odd piece of information: that when O.J.'s blood sample was drawn at the police department a little after 2:00 P.M. on June 13, Detective Vannatter "took it back to Rockingham and at 5:20 P.M. *he gave it to Dennis Fung.*" Wait just a minute, I thought. What's this detective doing walking around for what sounded like three hours or more with a suspect's blood sample in his pocket? The blood was drawn at the police department. Why didn't it go directly to the evidence unit or the crime lab just three minutes away?

∞

On August 26, Judge Ito finally ruled that the prosecution was not obliged to share blood samples with the defense. Nor did he find significant fault in their dealings with us. Ito said that the prosecutor's handling of blood evidence was "a picture of confusion, miscommunication, and noncommunication between the prosecutors, the attorneys, and the Los Angeles Police Department. Such conduct, while less than exemplary, does not rise to the level of bad faith or misconduct."

∞

O.J. was irate about an August cover story in *Newsweek* on his alleged "dual life." There were allegations of drug use and orgies throughout. They even showed a picture of him alone, watching a white stripper, but they cropped it to give it a more negative inference. "It was my birthday party!" he stormed. "Nicole threw the party, she hired the stripper, and there were 250 other people there!"

There was also a somewhat disparaging reference to his beloved golf game, and to his membership in a predominantly white country club. "I thought it was supposed to be about progress," O.J. said. "It's like I'm not even supposed to be playing golf, like golf is a 'whites only' sport. I thought being one of the first blacks to get in someplace meant progress, meant equality. I thought breaking color barriers was a good thing. I remember when Sidney Poitier was the first black member at Hillcrest, and Gene Washington got into the L.A. Country Club. It was a big, big deal. Like Jackie Robinson in baseball."

He was essentially taken to task for not contributing to black causes, yet I knew for a fact that he was a longtime major contributor to two charities. His habit of keeping this information private was now working against him. And what really made him angry was the not-so-veiled criticism of the way he spoke—the inference that by working to improve himself, he'd ended up "talking white."

"Do people get on Julian Bond or Bryant Gumbel for the way they speak? Bob, did you know that Sir Laurence Olivier kept going to a speech coach way into his eighties, just to keep improving his diction? It's like I'm too black for half these people, too white for the other half."

Chapter Ten

As the September 19 date for the trial approached, the competition among the prime-time TV newsmagazine anchors to book Simpson case guests began to resemble the NFL draft. "So-and-so's got the Brown parents!" "So-and-so's got the Brown sisters!" "So-and-so's got Arnelle and Jason!" Every day we were receiving phone calls from various network producers who were updating the O.J. sweepstakes, trying to "get" me.

I was heeding Ito's order, as well as my own vow, not to give any interviews until the trial was over, but that didn't mean that I couldn't interview *them* while they were trying to interview *me*. As a result, I had some fascinating conversations with a number of respected television reporters, men and women whose work I had long admired or recently come to know through our ever-expanding video archive collection.

Television can be a seductive medium, and the people in it are skilled persuaders. When someone you've seen on TV calls and asks you for an interview, you think it's a pretty important day. When ten nationally recognized journalists personally call you at home, you're now completely convinced that not only is it an important day, but that you are the very center of that importance. They never state outright that *they want to know something;* rather, they charmingly suggest that it's vitally important that "your views should be told."

The topper came the night I met with Connie Chung and her producer for drinks at her hotel. Clearly, what she wanted was an interview with O.J. or me. Connie is a charming, elegant, and quite funny woman, and it was a thoroughly enjoyable evening. There was some talk about the law in general and some observations about the Simpson case—the issues that would be addressed at trial, the way it was being covered in the news. I was as curious about how these people did their business as they were about how I did mine. I was fascinated by the powerful effect they had on our culture, and even more fascinated by the way they continued to work the O.J. story.

At the end of the evening, the three of us said our goodnights, with hugs all around. A few minutes after I had left the hotel I realized I had left my cell phone behind. I went back inside and called Connie from the lobby to ask if she'd picked it up. "I'm so glad you called, Bob," she said cheerfully, and then delivered the best line I'd heard since the case began: "I just spoke to my husband. He gave me permission to sleep with you—in exchange for an exclusive with either you or O.J."

Laughing at the joke, I declined what I called her "very kind offer." As I drove home, I thought to myself, if this had been the real thing, a good negotiator would have asked which would've come first, the interview or the sexual favors.

∞

Because it had been our decision not to waive any time, we knew that the trial would begin before the prosecution had even commenced testing the majority of the DNA evidence—which was unprecedented. When we received word in late summer that the prosecution's preliminary DNA testing on two of the blood spots at Bundy had come up positive for O.J.'s blood group, I knew that the experts on our team would have to do as I had suspected early on: challenge the methodology and competency of the L.A.P.D. lab technicians.

When attorneys wish to present scientific or forensic information as evidence, often a hearing must be held before the judge and outside the presence of the jury. In this procedure, called a Kelly-Frye hearing, lawyers on both sides argue for and against the acceptability of particular evidence—that is, the degree to which it is accepted within the scientific community and the legal precedents that may exist for its use in trial. The judge weighs the arguments, rules on the admissibility of the evidence, and then sets the parameters within which the evidence can be presented to a jury. In the Simpson case, we anticipated that the Kelly-Frye hearing on DNA evidence might be held in early September. However, on the last day of August, Marcia Clark announced that the prosecution wouldn't be ready for the hearing until some time after jury selection was completed, which at that point we figured would take at least a month.

When he heard this, O.J. realized that the trial itself probably wouldn't begin much before the holiday season, and he broke down and cried at having to once again adjust his dream of being home with his kids. Almost everyone on the defense team had at one time or another represented clients who had waited a year or more before their trials were held. Long delays, due to factors such as crowded court schedules, pretrial hearings, and frequent continuances, were common. We knew it wouldn't help matters to tell our war stories to O.J. We could only comfort him, and counsel him to try to be patient with the unwieldy process. (Ultimately, the defense team would decide to waive the Kelly-Frye, and agreed not to challenge the admissibility of the prosecution's DNA evidence.)

We had also been waiting on the prosecution's decision on whether or not to seek the death penalty. I believed that they would not. The defense had prepared a letter to go on record in the D.A.'s office, basically to the effect that since our client was innocent, we would take no position nor make any recommendation regarding his sentencing.

This was a major strategic decision. A death penalty trial

would require a special voir dire on what's called a "death qualified jury," that is, a jury who could vote to impose a death sentence. This type of jury is obviously pro-prosecution; anti–death penalty jurors are excluded. However, in the guilt phase of a trial, a death penalty jury generally requires a higher standard of proof—which would favor the defense.

On September 9, the district attorney's office announced that the People were not going to seek the death penalty but would instead ask for life without parole. I wasn't surprised. No matter how solid the prosecution believed their case to be, I couldn't envision a scenario in which either Bill Hodgman or Marcia Clark would stand in front of a jury and ask them to return a verdict that would send O.J. Simpson to death row.

In September, we heard that the prosecutors had conducted a weekend-long mock trial in Phoenix, Arizona. Using their jury consultants and presenting the evidence they had to date, they selected seventeen local citizens as the jury. The mock jurors liked Bill Hodgman; they were less enthusiastic about Marcia Clark, claiming that her courtroom style was too aggressive. For my part, I felt that her style and obvious personal antagonism toward me would be favorable to us and off-putting to the jury, and I did what I could to elicit those responses from her at every opportunity. While she openly flirted with Johnnie during much of the trial, my presence almost always kicked off a hostile reaction.

The Arizona mock jurors were, however, quite clear about their verdict. As one "juror" told a local reporter, "The prosecution asked if there was just circumstantial evidence, DNA and this and that, could you find him guilty?" Evidently the jury's answer was no: They found O.J. not guilty.

We also heard that the prosecution wasn't going to put Dr. Irwin Golden back on the stand again for the trial. Reportedly, they had been looking for a medical examiner to testify as an expert witness in order to counter Golden's performance under my cross-examination in the preliminary. One candidate, Dr. Boyd Stephens, the president-elect of the National Association of Medical Examiners, turned them down, as did others. Ultimately the prosecution would use Dr. Lakshmanan.

There was a lot of discussion about why the district attorney was going to try this case in downtown Los Angeles rather than in Santa Monica, which would have been the natural venue. The explanations were many and varied. One possibility was the need for both a high-security courtroom and extensive news facility.

A second possibility was that in the wake of the racial tension that was created by the Rodney King verdict and escalated during preparations for this trial, it might have been a political move on Gil Garcetti's part to try O.J. in an area where the jury pool would include more African-Americans than did Santa Monica.

My own thought was that Garcetti wanted close personal control over the case, and instant access to the press—which was permanently located right next door to his office.

Technically, the trial could have taken place anywhere in Los Angeles County, and we were prepared to present the defense's case in any courtroom Garcetti wanted, but we were pleased that it would be a downtown courtroom and a downtown jury. I heard from an old friend in the district attorney's office that there was great resentment there at the tremendous personnel and resources being devoted to this one case. "D.A.s are complaining that they can't get simple investigations done on other cases," she said. "Everything but Simpson comes in very low on the priority list."

∞

Right after the Labor Day weekend, the prosecution filed a motion requesting that once the jury was selected, Judge Ito should sequester it. Initially, the defense didn't think that sequestration was a good idea, primarily because it presents significant hardship, especially to people who need the income from working at least part of every day, and thereby narrows the jury pool. Jo-Ellan Dimitrius also advised that sequestration can make some jurors become bonded with the bailiffs who care for their every need. Understandably, bonding with law enforcement creates a pro-prosecution jury. We also didn't think sequestration was necessary because we believed the jurors would follow the judge's instructions to not be swayed by outside influences. Put simply, we trusted them. Just before the trial began, however, events would persuade us to agree with the prosecution, and the jury was ultimately sequestered.

As we prepared for the trial, we knew we had to confront the existence of the 911 tapes and the issue of spousal abuse, and be prepared to argue that such abuse does not automatically lead to murder. Our own surveys showed that 92 percent of the people polled had heard the tapes; of those, a majority believed that they were an accurate reflection of Nicole and O.J.'s relationship. Trying to get the tapes excluded would be a pretty futile move at this point.

There was no point in hiding it—after all, O.J. had pleaded no contest to the charges. They'd fought after coming home from a party, where they'd each had a great deal to drink. Nicole admitted later that she went after O.J. first, throwing things at him, accusing him of being with other women. He overreacted, he blew up, and he wrestled her, which was wrong, and he admitted it. And he went to counseling because of it. He also readily admitted to yelling at Nicole and kicking at the door in 1993. He wasn't proud of any of it. They had fights, they had battles. They broke up, they got back together, they broke up. After the 1994 reconciliation—initiated by Nicole—didn't work out, O.J. was resigned to their marriage being over, and he resumed his relationship with Paula. If he were truly a man out of control, he would've gone over the top with Keith Zlomsowitch, or the rumors about Marcus Allen. And he didn't.

∞

In mid-September, we observed Yom Kippur, the Day of Atonement, the most solemn of Jewish high holy days. Accompanied by my parents, Linell and I attended services at Stephen Weiss Temple, a magnificent sanctuary high atop Mulholland, overlooking the San Fernando Valley.

A reform temple, where the prayers are translated from Hebrew into English, Stephen Weiss has one of the largest Jewish congregations in the United States. Because of this, simultaneous services are held at six different venues on the temple grounds.

We first had occasion to meet with the chief rabbi, Rabbi Isaiah Zeldin, when Brent applied to Stephen Weiss–Michael Milken Community High School, which is affiliated with the temple. I had found Rabbi Zeldin to be a warm, compassionate man, equally adept and wise discussing temporal matters as well as spiritual ones. Quite often, when helping children apply for admission to a private school, parents find themselves answering a variation of the question of what the child can do for the school. Here, we had experienced the reverse: The people at Stephen Weiss were always concerned about what they could do for Brent, and for us as a family. I was surprised to find myself feeling quite emotional about being part of such a place, and great pride at being a Jew.

However, I hadn't been attending temple regularly, and on this particular night I expected to feel only the usual dutiful responses. I was tired, achy, anxious. Was I getting the flu? I'd been restless at night, waking up and thinking of things to talk to Johnnie about, questions I had for the investigators, procedural questions for Uelmen, science questions for Scheck and Neufeld. We'd started out ahead of the prosecution; had they gone past us?

As the Yom Kippur services went on, I found that the rich voices of the rabbis and cantors singing the ancient prayers were deeply moving to me. When services were over, I came away grateful for the opportunity to have a brief time of spiritual contemplation in the midst of what was distinctly unspiritual turmoil.

∞

Johnnie Cochran had established himself as a leading criminal defense lawyer when he was asked by then–District Attorney John Van de Camp to be an assistant district attorney in the late seventies. It was the first time in the history of the office that a criminal defense lawyer had been appointed to that position.

Cochran was a visible presence as a prosecutor and took a lead role in investigations of police shootings. Upon leaving the D.A.'s office, he reestablished his private practice, concentrating primarily on civil cases in which he represented civilians against the police department and, in more recent years, entertainment figures involved in criminal cases. Cochran's entire practice is staffed by African-Americans, and he is justifiably proud of the reputation the firm has established over the years. Most of his career has been in the downtown Los Angeles courthouse, and he viewed himself, quite correctly, as an expert with downtown juries. He carries himself well, with both dignity and energy, and has a unique ability to vigorously represent his clients and at the same time maintain good relations with prosecutors, police, and government officials alike. This is a quality and attitude I pride myself on, and I welcomed it in Johnnie.

From the beginning, I liked his intuitive understanding of people. A consummate politician, he prided himself on being able to get along with everyone. He is especially good at speaking on his feet; he's completely extemporaneous, even in trial, and eloquent on the issues he's most passionate about. In private, I rarely saw him show anger, and when negative things were said about him, he shrugged the comments off as unimportant. When the *Los Angeles Times* published a particularly unflattering article, Johnnie simply ignored the story. I respected his ability to know when to be tough and when to tone things down, both in and out of court. We made frequent jokes at each other's expense—I chided him about his unduly loud neckties, he kidded me about my diminishing hairline.

I had expected there would be competition between us, and I wasn't surprised or unduly alarmed when I started seeing the signs. Competition is, as I've said, as intrinsic to the nature of defense attorneys as their muscular egos.

In September, I was contacted by the editors of *Vanity Fair* magazine and asked if I would assent to an all-defense-team photograph, including lawyers, support staff, and investigators. The portrait, to be taken by Annie Leibovitz, would be for the December "Hall of Fame" issue. I agreed, and on the appointed day, as everyone began to gather at the office, and Leibovitz and her crew of eight or nine people spent the better part of the morning setting up to shoot in the firm's law library, I got a call from Johnnie.

"Bob, I can't be in this picture," he said. "Michael Jackson hates *Vanity Fair*, and he's said he doesn't want me to have any part of this."

I was taken completely by surprise. But I knew that Jackson was a valued, longtime client, and Johnnie had to honor his wishes. I realized that was why Carl Douglas and Shawn Chapman hadn't shown up yet, either.

When I apologetically repeated what Johnnie had told me to Annie Leibovitz, she said, "That can't be true about Michael Jackson hating *Vanity Fair*—I've just been contracted to do a cover story on him!"

Whatever the reasons, it seemed that no one on Johnnie's staff would be participating.

With the other lawyers, the office staff, and the investigators, there was enough of the Simpson defense team to make a decent showing. But there wouldn't be a single black professional face in the picture. This wouldn't represent either the composition or the spirit of the defense team. In fact, it would signal dissent among us. I saw that I had no choice. Over Lee Bailey's strenuous objections, and with great apologies to Annie Leibovitz and her hardworking crew, I canceled the picture.

Everyone who had assembled for the photo session was very disappointed. The lead lawyers had been in the spotlight for months, and this would have been a chance for those who had received little or no public acknowledgment to be recognized for their long days and weeks of hard work, and maybe even have some fun.

The following day was miserable for everyone, with tension and a new uncertainty permeating the office. In addition, there were news reports that Johnnie had given interviews announcing that O.J. would testify on his own behalf. I was upset to hear this. We hadn't even finished picking a jury yet, the evidence wasn't all in. It was only September. We were nowhere near making that decision, or helping O.J. to make it.

That night I scheduled a staff party at a friend's home for a private screening of a new Tom Hanks film, *Forrest Gump,* and to celebrate investigator Pat McKenna's birthday. It was a long-overdue social break for all of us. Everyone but Cochran attended.

I was so distracted the whole evening that at one point Jo-Ellan Dimitrius came up to me and said, "What's going on with you, Bob? You're in awful shape." Right then I knew I'd picked the right jury consultant.

After Jo-Ellan and I had talked for a while, I realized that what was happening between Johnnie and me had to be confronted and resolved. I headed for the phone and quickly arranged a meeting for the following morning.

Later that night, I ran into Michael Viner of Dove Books. Viner told me that he'd be publishing a book soon by Nicole's friend Faye Resnick.

"I just wanted you to know there's nothing negative in the book about you," he said.

"Resnick can say whatever she likes about me," I told Viner. "I'm not on trial for murder. But my client is. At this point, anything published having to do with this case raises the serious possibility of compromising his right to a fair trial."

The next morning I began the meeting with Johnnie and our crew on a firm and somber note. Although Bailey had headed back to Boston, Gerry Uelmen was on the speakerphone, and Jo-Ellan and her assistants were in the room, as were all the other lawyers and investigators. I simply restated the facts of my being hired as lead counsel to conduct the defense. All decisions relative to the case and to our client—and all public statements or interviews about those decisions—had to first go through me. As to our client's testifying, the press didn't need to know each step of our decision making. Staking out a position in public, before all the evidence was in, was unwise. Furthermore, and Johnnie agreed with this, the defense team not only needed to show an image of solidarity, we actually had to *be* in solidarity with each other. The battle we were waging was daunting enough without faction fighting.

As we talked, the meeting relaxed into something more closely resembling a bull session, with everybody saying what was on their minds. None of us could've done this alone, we agreed. "It's almost impossible just to keep up on the reading," Johnnie said.

When we adjourned, I was glad we'd all had the chance to air our differences, no matter the initial reason. The tension seemed to have dissolved, and we all appeared to be on the same team again.

Later, I called Annie Leibovitz and once again apologized for wasting her time. She said I could make amends to her and her editors if she could take my picture, alone, for the magazine's Hall of Fame issue. Mindful of O.J.'s concerns about lawyers wasting time and money, I checked with him first, and then agreed on the condition that it could be done easily and quickly. She assured me that it could.

I met with her at the office, late on a Friday afternoon. I had boxed that week and was sporting a black eye. Because it looked more like dirt on my face than anything heroic, I assumed Leibovitz would want to make it disappear with some kind of makeup. After taking a look, she decided instead that it was a good metaphor, and we got down to the no-time-wasted business of a fast photo session. No hair stylist, no makeup, no jacket, and the office around me looking like a tornado had blown through it. In retrospect, maybe *that* was the metaphor. (We used the picture on the jacket of this book as well—but somebody cleaned up the eye.)

∞

In late September, Tracie Savage, a reporter with Channel 4—KNBC, the local NBC affiliate—reported that DNA tests performed on O.J.'s socks found at Rockingham identified the blood as Nicole's.

When I heard Savage's report, I almost smacked the side of my head with my hand, the way you do when you come out of a swimming pool with water in your ears and a ringing in your head. If this information was true, I thought angrily, it had gone directly from the police to a television reporter, completely bypassing the lawyers, the judge, and the discovery process. If it wasn't true, it was misinformation from an inside source and manipulation of a reporter.

The next morning there was a heated chambers conference with Judge Ito, who acknowledged, "If I was in your shoes, Bob, they'd have to peel me off the ceiling."

Marcia Clark assured us that the socks had not yet been sent to Cellmark for DNA testing. Only standard serology tests had been done at the L.A.P.D. lab, and only she and assistant district attorney Lisa Kahn knew the results, which thus far excluded O.J. and possibly included Nicole.

I told Judge Ito that I strongly suspected that Tracie Savage's information came from the Scientific Investigations Division (SID) of the police department. He agreed to schedule an immediate hearing and brought in Michelle Kestler from the L.A.P.D. crime lab (whose husband was a police detective) and Donna Jones, the deputy city attorney (who is married to a police captain). Kestler, who adamantly denied being the source of the leaks, said that the socks would be sent out for DNA testing on Monday, September 26, which coincidentally was the first scheduled date of jury selection.

Although I wanted the attorney general's office to investigate, Ito felt that response was too harsh. Instead, he instructed Donna Jones to begin an internal affairs investigation. The following night, KNBC's Tracie Savage not only stuck by her story on the air but embellished it: Both types of DNA testing had been performed on the blood on the socks, she reported, and the blood was unquestionably Nicole's.

Judge Ito was livid. Publicly chastising Savage for inaccurate and false reporting, he threatened to keep the news media out of the courtroom entirely. Again, this wasn't the remedy I sought. I wanted to know where the false information was coming from and stop it, arguing that it was maliciously interfering with O.J.'s right to a fair trial. The leaks always seemed to come after we'd had a good day in court with favorable rulings.

When Ito continued to take off on the media's irresponsible behavior, I said, "You know, this may not be a media problem at all. In fact, the media may be relying on what they believe to be good sources." I made it clear on the record that I didn't believe the leaks were coming from the district attorney's office, and I knew they weren't coming from us. I didn't say outright that the L.A.P.D. was conducting a deliberate misinformation campaign to taint the jury pool, but I did continue to insist that there be an official investigation. Ito said that he'd take it under advisement. And he let us know that he was still reconsidering the whole idea of the media in the courtroom—television cameras in general and Channel 4 in particular. One ultimate result of the furor over the news leaks was that Judge Ito issued an order that all test results go directly and only to him.

A few days later, I spoke with an old friend who had met with the news director at KNBC. The employees of the station absolutely stood by their story, which they insisted came from a source inside the police department.

"I guess they'd rather stick with their story—and call the judge and the district attorney liars while they're at it," I said.

"Evidently so," said my friend. "They're acting like their job is to make the news, not report it."

I could see that this kind of thing frustrated O.J. to no end. The degree to which wrong information was repeated, or confidential information was leaked, simply confounded him. As the jury selection and pretrial hearings progressed, he became more knowledgeable about the legal issues and more active in decision making. Watching him, I understood how it was that he had come so far from his difficult beginnings. He would be the first to argue that he wasn't a scholar, but he had an acute and curious mind, and an obvious vital interest in how his case was being conducted.

Yet O.J. was also keenly aware of what was happening in the "outside world," especially with his friends. He grew quite agitated and sad when Bobby Chandler, an old Buffalo teammate and one of O.J.'s dearest friends, was diagnosed with inoperable lung cancer at the end of September.

Throughout the early days of going in and out of O.J.'s office at Kardashian's, I would often run into Bobby Chandler. He was a spectacular man, a gifted All-American with great style and humor who had become a lawyer, practiced for a short time, and then pursued a broadcasting career. He understood the law; but more important to all of us, because he visited the jail almost religiously, he understood O.J.

Not yet fifty—and looking much younger—Chandler seemed the least likely candidate to be diagnosed with a terminal illness. He never smoked or drank, he worked out regularly, and he seemed a source of boundless positive energy. O.J. told me that four of their Buffalo teammates had died of cancer, and there had been some speculation about toxic material adjacent to a practice field. In spite of his diagnosis, Chandler was about to undergo an arduous chemotherapy regimen in hopes of arresting the progress of the disease, if not its ultimate outcome. O.J. was distraught with worry for his friend, who had been so stalwart.

"He's been so great to me," he said. "Now he needs me, and there's nothing I can do for him from in here."

∞

As we continued to argue the pretrial evidentiary motions, we focused on a second Rockingham search warrant that had been issued three weeks after the murders. The warrant had turned up two home video cassettes with notes on each, written by Nicole. "O.J., it's probably too late, but I thought you'd want to have these," she had written. The videos were taken during O.J. and Nicole's wedding, and the births of Sydney and Justin.

Although the district attorney's office and the police said that these pointed to a motive for O.J.'s rage and the subsequent murders, to anyone else they indicated a desire on Nicole's part for another reconciliation. If Nicole hadn't desired to remind her husband of the good times they'd shared, and the children that had come from their marriage, why would she have sent these videos to him, in a gesture that seemed almost loving? This didn't seem like the action of a woman who was hunted or stalked by someone she wanted nothing further to do with.

I did, however, object to the fact that we weren't informed of the existence of this material until very late in the game. "Oh, yes, you were," Marcia Clark argued in court, gesturing at me with a document. "It was in the property report."

Glaring, I took the document out of her hand and read it. "In this report it makes no mention of the notes from Nicole," I said adamantly. The newspapers later reported what O.J. whispered at the table. "Clark's busted, busted."

There seemed to be a new Marcia Clark in court that day. Her clothes were different, her hairstyle was different. Overall, her demeanor had been quieter, calmer, almost as if she'd been taking tranquilizers intravenously. Obviously, she'd taken to heart what some of the participants had said at the mock-trial weekend in Arizona. However, our exchange over the videos and the notes brought out the Marcia that had been my sparring partner over the past months. My continuing suggestion that procedure wasn't being followed by the prosecution, that the defense was somehow being short-changed, made her notice-ably angry. She seemed so intent on finding flaws in defense strategy that I wondered how much attention she was paying to her own.

Bill Pavelic, our investigator, kept reminding me that the district attorney's office hadn't turned over to us the police logs and tapes for June 13. Some months before, he'd heard from a source inside the L.A.P.D. that Fuhrman and his partner, De-tective Phillips, were using a department-issued cellular phone in the early morning hours of June 13. This source contended that Fuhrman and Phillips called from outside O.J.'s house to the West L.A. police station, where Sydney and Justin had been taken, and asked the watch commander to find out from the children where O.J. was. Pavelic's source reported that the kids had said something to the effect of "out of town for business." Therefore, contrary to what they'd testified in the preliminary, the police knew quite early that O.J. was not at Rockingham. This meant the police had no reason to scale the wall in order to notify him or protect him from danger. Pavelic was adamant that we obtain the watch commander's log and the cellular phone records to document this call, because his informant was suggesting that it was made before the robbery/homicide detec-tives, Lange and Vannatter, were in the picture—which gave Fuhrman time to manipulate evidence.

"Hodgman knows how important this stuff is," Pavelic fumed, "and he and Clark are deliberately withholding it."

I told him there was a more likely explanation. "It's the L.A.P.D. that doesn't want us to have it," I said, "not the D.A. That's why they're stalling. I'll bring it up before Ito again, he's already told them at least once to turn it over. Don't worry, Bill, our chance will come."

∞

In September, to celebrate Brent's fourteenth birthday, Linell and I took him and thirty of his friends to play paintball at a concession out in the hills of Newhall, about thirty-five miles from our home. Paintball is where you get all dressed up in camouflage combat gear, form teams, and run through the fields and hills playing guerrilla warfare—with mock guns filled with bright, splattering paint.

Linell and I and the kids all rode out to Newhall on a chartered bus, and once we got there we had a twenty-minute hike up a dirt road. As we got closer to our destination, I was astonished to see that TV satellite trucks had arrived there before us. A reporter called out a question, but I shook my head and turned away, heading instead into the building with the kids to get fitted out with our gear and fatigues and instructions. Linell, ever the diplomat, walked over to the reporters and said, "Please. This is a private party, for the kids. Nobody's going to say anything to you today about the case, Bob's not going to give you anything. There's nothing going on here about O.J. So won't you please be kind, and respect our privacy?"

As we left that afternoon, the reporters tried again to talk to the kids, asking their names, asking what their parents thought of the case. "Does your dad think O.J. is guilty?" one guy shouted. That night, Linell's civilized request for respect and privacy for the kids showed up on the local news.

Chapter Eleven

At one point, Judge Ito considered doing something very un-usual: asking jurors to sign a contract, stipulating that they would not sell their stories nor profit in any way from their participation in this jury for six months after the verdict. I could certainly understand his motivations; we still were weeks from actually beginning the trial, and every day there were two, three, four stories about the inner workings of both the defense and prosecution teams, on television and the newspapers. I felt that giving jurors a contract to sign would have a chilling effect and compromise their autonomy at the very beginning of what would no doubt be a difficult task for them. Some might even want to consult with lawyers before signing—or, worse, during the case itself, if they were surreptitiously approached by re-porters or publishers. Ito wisely decided not to ask for con-tracts.

I was learning that behind the scenes Lance Ito was a very complex, intense man. He arrived at court at six-thirty in the morning, the first one there and always the last to leave. His chambers looked like the archives of a pawn shop, with memo-rabilia in every nook and cranny. We had in common a passion for pens, and Ito proudly displayed his collection to me, telling me where I could find collectible pens at good prices. Anything that came in relative to the case—cups, pennants, buttons, posters, even the most devastating editorial cartoons—found a niche in Ito's small office, and he gave away as much as he kept. In one instance he passed along to me a baseball card with my picture and stats on it; in another, he showed us a button that read, "O.J. Defense: No Comment."

The judge prepared diligently for the case, putting in three months preparation for the DNA alone, and his books—on law, science, and any number of other subjects—were strewn everywhere. In the center of all this chaos were two computers on which he typed his daily rulings, a printer, and a complete set of all the evidence in the Simpson case. His desk was piled high, but he could always immediately find whatever he needed.

Initially, Judge Ito took pride in reading five newspapers a day, but midway through the trial, he stopped. "I wouldn't read a word of what they're printing about all of this," he said disgustedly. His finest moments were when both the defense and the prosecution were displeased by one of his rulings. "I must be doing my job," he'd say.

Ito is a great storyteller, and he loves a good joke. We told a lot of them in chambers, often about the case, frequently at our own expense, and he gave as good as he got. He was a good sport about Jay Leno's Dancing Itos. Marcia Clark, who had studied dance, wasn't nearly as sanguine about the dancing Marcia.

Near the end of the trial, Ito gave me one of his pogs, the cardboard disks that kids trade and play with that resemble old milk-bottle caps. One side of the pog read "guilty," the other "not guilty."

∞

The following is a conversation I had in my car with Johnnie Cochran, on the way to the courthouse September 26, the first day of actual jury selection:

> RLS: Good morning, Mr. Cochran! How are you today?
> JLC: Good morning, Mr. Shapiro, I'm just fine, thanks.

RLS: I'm taping this, if you don't mind, Mr. Cochran.

JLC: [laughing] Don't mind at all. Got enough newspapers in here, Bobby?

RLS: [laughing] Oh, shut up. Hey, did you get a good night's sleep last night, Mr. Cochran?

JLC: I did, I certainly did. I worked hard yesterday, got enough sleep last night, and I'm ready to go. How about you?

RLS: I'm ready to go, I feel great.

JLC: Then we're both ready. A couple of clever minds. The prosecution better be ready, too.

∞

What greeted us at the courthouse was simply incredible. Although we had been mobbed by reporters before, now the chaos was somewhat more organized, with red cones out in front and two L.A.P.D. officers standing guard. These were the early days of what came to be known as Camp O.J. By the time the trial actually began, the staging for lights and cameras would be nearly five stories high, and the parking lot would be filled with large vans for the reporters, anchors, and television crews.

We walked in greeted mainly by cheers and a few shouts—no boos yet. There were cameras behind roped-off areas stretching one hundred feet on either side of the sidewalk. There was a sea of still photographers, video crews, radio and television announcers, lookie-loos, shouters, and souvenir vendors creating a noisy, somewhat gala carnival-like atmosphere. Like a medieval mob about to witness a beheading, they had all come to see if a man would be convicted of two brutal murders and sentenced to life imprisonment without the possibility of parole.

Inside the courtroom it was eerily silent. Court cameras were covered in dark fabric, and the public was not admitted. Only three press representatives were present. The judge had made an unprecedented decision of allowing us to walk in with O.J., rather than having him come in through a separate door from the holding cell. Even though everyone in the courtroom knew he was in police custody, he was allowed to have the appearance of someone who was not. He walked in first, followed by me, Cochran, and Jo-Ellan Dimitrius.

The room seated 250 potential members of the jury. In that group were some who would ultimately be on the jury, and the awesome nature of their task—and ours—was palpable. The security was subtle but obvious; there were six or seven armed sheriff's deputies in uniform. I recognized another six undercover deputies, and there were probably more.

At first, O.J. was in an upbeat mood, positive and energetic, ready to go forward. While all eyes were on him, however, his were on Ito, as the judge stood at the podium and made his opening remarks, explaining that he needed the help of everyone in the room to find a jury. When he announced that the trial would go through at least to February 1995, everyone heard O.J. moan, "Oh, God, no. My kids, my kids."

Judge Ito explained to the potential jurors that he had good news and bad news. The bad news was that the jury questionnaire that the defense and prosecution had ultimately agreed upon was 79 pages long. There were 294 questions, 12 alone having to do with potential jury members' comprehension of the science of DNA. The good news was that the original proposal had been 125 pages long. The selection process, he warned them, would be painstaking, and it might take some time. Ultimately, it would take five weeks.

During the voir dire process, we were seated at a small conference table. I was eye-to-eye with Marcia, which wasn't particularly enjoyable for either of us. O.J. was at one end of the table, and Ito was at the other. Cochran was next to me and Jo-Ellan next to the judge. Each prospective juror would come in and sit down, directly across and six feet away from an accused murderer. Both sides continued to say, of course, that they wanted a fair and impartial jury. In actuality, one side wanted a convicting jury, the other an acquitting jury.

When jury selection finally began, Judge Ito had ruled that if jury consultants were going to be used, they had to sit in front of the bar, not in the audience of observers. So Jo-Ellan

Dimitrius and her colleagues sat at the table with us, and we introduced them to the potential jurors.

The prosecution, however, seemed to take a different tack; only Marcia Clark and Bill Hodgman sat at the prosecution table, as though to convey to the jury pool, "We're just the poor underdogs sitting here representing the People, up against the army of the big-bucks defense."

But I knew very well that their jury consultant, Don Vinson, was sitting in the back of the courtroom. As I began to question the prospective jurors, I pointed Vinson out to Judge Ito. "Your Honor, can you have that person identify himself, please?" I asked. "I don't believe he's a juror." The main focus of my objection to where he was sitting was that it was next to potential jurors. An abashed Vinson identified himself. After that day's recess, he was gone. Clark and Hodgman evidently preferred their instincts over his expertise, in spite of his advice to downplay the importance of domestic abuse as a precursor to murder.

Frustrated and often angered at the ongoing publicity about the case, which neither he nor anyone else could censor or control, Judge Ito had basically excluded from the jury any candidates who regularly read newspapers, magazines, or watched television news. "Both sides lost some good people in the process," Jo-Ellan said.

"I'm not looking for hermits," Judge Ito told the prospective jurors. "The issue is, can you set aside whatever you heard? Can you put aside your impressions and opinions and judge this case solely on the evidence presented in court?" Although those questions are posed to every jury, we were all aware that this jury would face a number of challenges unique to this case and this defendant.

Although there was a sense of drama and ritual surrounding this first day, the day itself was fairly uneventful. The first round of eliminations from the panel was for "hardship," which described jurors who, on the one-page questionnaire from the court, said that under no condition could they be available for a trial that would run at least through February. One man in particular put on quite a show. "I'm just too stressed to do this," he claimed, although he looked to be in as good a shape as most of the panel, if not better. His brother had suffered a heart attack, he said, and his mother had died of one. If we made him serve on the jury, what would we do if he had a heart attack and died during deliberations? The speech was creative, and effective. We excused him.

One of the challenges of picking a jury is finding people who are not only honest but honest with themselves as well—that is, honest about their feelings. In a voir dire setting, with the solemn rituals of trials and courts all around, it's awkward for a prospective juror to say he cannot be fair, cannot be impartial. In many ways, it's almost a trick question. I phrase it somewhat differently by putting jurors in the defendant's position, by trying to get them to understand how they would feel in that same position. What qualities of deliberation would they hope to find in a jury judging *them?*

Bill Hodgman and Marcia Clark had filed a motion requesting a continuous hearing, asking that once the hardship cases in the prospective jurors were identified, the trial be continued—that is, delayed—until their DNA testing was complete. They had ten more items to be sent to Cellmark. I thought it was ironic that the evidence they were seeking to test had been discovered months ago. They wanted to complete the hardship portion, then go to the DNA hearings, then return to final jury selection. The defense argued against the motion. Now that selection had finally begun, we didn't want any further interruptions, and neither did the judge. "I want to get this jury selected," said Ito.

That first day, Johnnie and I left together, walking out through the same chaos. Every reporter had a question, shouting out comments, introducing themselves, throwing their microphones out in front of them so that if we made any remarks, they could later edit tape to make it look like they had interviews with us. We said nothing.

I dropped Johnnie off at his office and went back to my own, where I had an appointment with Skip Taft to talk about the money situation. The preliminary figures for the trial alone were overwhelming. The clock had now been running for five months, and we still didn't know for sure when the trial would begin, let alone end.

The tab for the three investigators, who were paid a specified weekly rate plus living expenses, was one concern. Their fees had been negotiated by Skip, and there was no question that the crew had been working diligently seven days a week, around the clock, but we had to do something to cut costs. John McNally indicated that he would be willing to leave the case and would go back east within a month. Pat McKenna said he would take a cut in pay but wanted to stay on. In the meantime, we agreed to find a two-bedroom apartment and get them out of more expensive hotel rooms.

I then called Alan Dershowitz, whose hourly rate was accumulating steadily. I wanted him and his brother Nathan to stay with the case. Alan had been key to strategy since the beginning, and in terms of motions he was a creative master. He pledged to reduce his fee in the event of having to prepare an appeal. "I don't even want to talk about appeals now, Alan," I said. "We're not going to see a conviction in this case." He agreed to stay on, with a flat fee that was agreeable to Skip.

Scheck and Neufeld were another problem entirely. For the preliminary hearing and pretrial motions, they'd been working for a flat fee. We needed them for the trial, but they were anticipating a three-week Kelly-Frye hearing plus three weeks preparation for it, which would've been a tremendous added expense. Skip was frustrated, saying that he sometimes felt like he was watching O.J.'s money drain through a sieve. "We just can't do this," he told me. "We've got to find ways to cut the money or cut the time."

I told him we'd do what we could, but Scheck and Neufeld were essential. We hadn't even begun the trial; it was no time to cut down on lawyers or experts. We did, however, begin to reconsider the Kelly-Frye.

The second day of jury selection, O.J.'s mood was down again. He had had a very sad conversation with Bobby Chandler. They had talked about their children: Bobby had three of his own, and O.J.'s daughter, Sydney, would be celebrating her birthday in a few days. Chandler had tried to impress upon O.J. the power of prayer. Although he himself was not afraid to die, O.J. was grieving for the pain his friend was going through. In one hushed, surreal moment in court, he unexpectedly sang a few chords of "Memory" from *Cats,* and the reporters, of course, took down every note.

Rather than returning to the holding cell over the lunch break, O.J. was allowed to stay at the table with us. During the breaks, he and I learned to play solitaire on the computer, although we both had some initial trouble moving the mouse around. When he'd win, his mood would brighten up a little, and then he'd remember where he was.

⚭

In the wake of the KNBC report about blood tests on the socks, the court's concern about news leaks became increasingly apparent. Ito showed us an article from *Newsday* that reported that blood on the floorboard of the Bronco had been DNA tested and identified as Nicole's. Neither Scheck nor Neufeld knew anything about this. Ito reacted angrily to *The Daily Journal* (a law newspaper) for publishing the jury questionnaire before he had released it, and temporarily took away the paper's seat in the courtroom. I was convinced that reporters weren't pulling their information out of thin air. Someone was feeding it to them.

Ito told the attorneys he was seriously considering keeping television cameras out of the courtroom. At any rate, he wasn't going to decide one way or the other until the last possible moment, hoping that it would put some kind of pressure on the media to moderate themselves and to take his threats seriously.

We filed a motion for the judge to take some kind of action to find the source of the news leaks, since their cumulative effects seriously threatened the defendant's right to a fair trial. Johnnie argued very passionately that these problems in the press began on day one, with the leak of the 911 tapes and Gil Garcetti talking about a Menendez defense.

The morning we were to file the motion on the news leaks, Clark was late to court. In chambers, I kidded Judge Ito: "I've got bad news. Marcia won't be here today, she's sick." He looked at me with some surprise. I said, "She's recovering from her personality transplant."

In addition to following up on the news leaks, I queried Ito and Hodgman about the discovery order we'd filed weeks before for the logs and communications tapes from the L.A.P.D. The judge had signed that order, but the material still wasn't forthcoming, and Bill Pavelic kept reminding me how important it was to see the detectives' reconstruction of their actions on that first critical day.

"I don't want anything more or less than what we asked for and what you signed," I told the judge.

Hodgman interrupted, saying that producing all that material would be difficult. I stopped him. "Your Honor," I said to Ito, "haven't you already ruled on this?"

He nodded. "Yes, I have, and we'll put this back into the record."

I mentioned that we kept going back and forth on these issues of discovery. "I thought the procedure was that the proponent argues, the respondent argues, and the proponent gets the last argument," I said. "But on this case, we have surrebuttal, sur-surrebuttal, sur-sur-surrebuttal, and super-surrebuttal. Then the judge rules. Then, if the ruling goes against the prosecution, they present a motion for a new ruling."

∽

For Grant's birthday in September, we took fifteen kids to Raging Waters theme park. I was dressed in a hat, sunglasses, and loose jogging clothes. Linell bought the tickets, I stayed off to the side, but one of the ticket takers recognized me and insisted that security be called. I spent the rest of the day sitting in a secluded back corner of the park, reading one of Gerry Spence's books, while Linell ran shuttle between me and the kids.

At the end of the day, as we were gathering up everybody to leave, a security guard came running up, all wide-eyed and out of breath. ABC had a news crew waiting just outside the front gate. So we all turned around and made a quick, discreet getaway out through the back way.

A few days later I was invited by Art Harris, the CNN correspondent who had been reporting on the case, to have dinner with Tom Johnson, a former editor of the *Los Angeles Times* and current president of CNN. We talked about tabloid journalism and whether or not the First Amendment could be passed today. Johnson and Harris both said they didn't believe it could.

"If I were a journalist watching this case," I said, "I'd want to know if the money that the people of California were paying was being well spent. Whether the district attorney's office was doing a good job, whether they were understaffed, the way they keep claiming whenever they can't provide us something, or if they have adequate resources. I'd want to know how many other murder cases they're trying while they're putting on this one, and how the resources available are comparable."

We discussed the increased role of DNA evidence in criminal trials. Tom Johnson was concerned that scientific evidence seemed to be used solely for the purpose of convicting someone. I told them a bit about Scheck and Neufeld's work with the Innocence Project.

And, of course, they wanted to know if television cameras were going to be allowed in Judge Ito's courtroom. "Three weeks ago it was a sure thing," I told them. "Now, I don't know which way he's going to decide."

"Why doesn't he let the cameras go in," suggested Art Harris, "and have them turned on and off at the attorneys' discretion. At the end of the trial, the tapes could be edited and then used solely for educational purposes, not for commercial ones."

I rolled my eyes at that one. The prosecution and the defense attorneys would argue over when the cameras should be on or off. They'd argue over who would edit the tapes and how. And then there would be arguments about whose educational benefit the tapes were for. And, of course, the tapes would be leaked. And then everybody would have to be subpoenaed. And they'd all bring *their* lawyers with them. No, I told them. As anxious as Ito was to do the right thing, I knew he'd either have the cameras all the way on or, if he changed his mind, all the way off. My belief was that we'd have cameras.

"Bob, if you were president of CNN," queried Johnson, "how many countries would you air this trial in?" At the time he was thinking about airing it in around forty countries. Later the count went close to two hundred.

Faye Resnick's book, *Nicole Brown Simpson: The Private Diary of a Life Interrupted,* landed on the jury selection like a bomb.

The day of October 18 started off badly. Johnnie and I arrived at court to find that Ito had denied all of our motions for exclusion of DNA evidence, in spite of "telegraphing" Marcia Clark the week before that some of the prosecution's evidence was going to get thrown out. This was because we had documented that the prosecution had failed to complete its testing in a timely manner. They'd had this material for three months and hadn't sent it out for analysis, but no one could explain why this was. Ito had even indicated that he was considering sanctions against the prosecution. "You had your chance before," Ito told them. "I'm not going to consider this." While I'd expected to lose part of the fight, it was a significant setback to have lost all of it.

The first order of business was a discussion in Judge Ito's chambers about the imminent release of Resnick's book and what effect, if any, it might have on our jury candidates. Co-written with Mike Walker, a *National Enquirer* editor, it was a sleazy "reconstruction" of the last months of Nicole's life and a sad commentary on what Resnick alleged was the loving friendship she shared with Nicole. I thought it was the height of irony that the pundits had been mistakenly assuming for months that we would impugn Nicole's character as part of the defense strategy, and here her "best friend" was doing it instead. There she stood, safely behind the shield of the First Amendment, during what she and her publisher knew was still an ongoing and unsequestered jury selection. As Greta Van Susteren was later to observe on CNN, "A book that's this tawdry, this sort of mean-spirited, suggests something far more than news. It suggests that someone is greedy and wants to make money."

No one knew for sure when the publication date was, so Judge Ito's clerk called Dove Books directly. We were dismayed to hear that the book had hit the newsstands that very morning. I suggested that we excuse the jury for a long lunch break so that everyone else could examine the book.

When Ito excused the jury panel for the lunch break, he made a poor judgment call by suggesting that they go to the nearby mall to get an early start on their Christmas shopping. At the mall there's a big chain bookstore. Resnick's book was one of their "picks of the week." That afternoon, I was unnerved to see that a couple of jurors had returned with bags from that very bookstore.

After Judge Ito and the defense and prosecution attorneys read the book during the break, I requested a recess until the next day, so that we could all consult and try to formulate a plan for damage control. The book itself was one thing; the press furor that was even now heating up to accompany its release would only raise the stakes.

Ito then ordered a temporary halt to jury selection, instructing the jury to return in two days. As they left, he said to them, "Oh, I neglected to tell you, you are to stay out of bookstores." It reminded me of that old psychologist's joke where you tell someone not to think of elephants—at which point all they're able to think of is elephants.

For the first time since the case began, Johnnie and I gave a joint statement to the press. I said, "I've had a great fear that O.J. Simpson could not get a fair trial; after the events of today I'm *convinced* that he cannot get one."

Johnnie criticized the judge for his ruling on the late DNA evidence. "We thought we'd be able to get twelve people who would judge this case solely on the evidence they'd hear in court," he said. "Now I don't think that's possible."

That afternoon Johnnie and I, with Sara Caplan, had a conference call with Bailey in Florida, Uelmen in Santa Clara, and Dershowitz in New York. Bailey started things off, and he was as angry as I'd ever seen him. "Gentlemen, this is war and we have to start treating it as such! We must be very, very aggressive and immediately move to have the case taken away from Judge Ito; file a writ of mandamus in the California Supreme Court; ask that it be transferred to federal court. Severe sanctions and remedies must take place!"

Dershowitz agreed that we should take a more aggressive position, but Cochran and I argued that we didn't want to file a motion that we were sure to lose, and delay the case even longer. "Gentlemen, it's time to get tough!" Bailey insisted.

"We don't want any more delays," I said, "and at this point we're doing better with the jury selections than the prosecution is. We have to find a way to protest this strongly, and make a legal record of it, without crashing the whole thing. The appellate court is just waiting out there to get their hands on this. I don't want that to happen." We began to formulate a plan of attack.

On October 19, I presented a motion before the judge, in a closed courtroom. Gerry Uelmen had worked late into the night on the motion we had all met early that morning to review. In it, we asked for two things: one, to continue the trial for one year and to grant bail to O.J., releasing him under stringent conditions of house arrest, "allowing the frenzy that has taken place to die down, and allow an opportunity for a fair trial to be presented"; and two, to investigate a conspiracy among Faye

Resnick, her attorney, the *National Enquirer*, and Dove Books to deprive O.J. Simpson of his constitutionally guaranteed right to a fair trial, to plant false and misleading information in the minds of the jurors, and to seek financial gain. Dershowitz had added that we did not want a sequestered jury, and we did not want a change of venue.

Emotions, mine and everyone else's, ran high throughout the arguments of this hearing. The judge, of course, ruled against my motion, and I objected strenuously. O.J. couldn't stop talking at the counsel table, and at one point I admonished him that if he didn't be quiet, I'd quit as his lawyer. The "threat" made it onto that night's news.

During the discussion, Marcia made a flip remark about prospective jurors lying to get on this jury, that she wished they all had to take polygraphs. I later said that was "one of the most idiotic statements made in a courtroom anywhere," and I meant it. I don't think I've ever had an angrier day in a courtroom.

That night I was awakened by some radio talk show host calling on my direct line at home. The first time, I hung up on him. He called back. "This is a private residence," I snapped. "I view this as a serious invasion of my privacy and ask you please not to call back here again."

To his credit, the man said, "I understand, I apologize," and he hung up. I had the feeling the brief exchange had been broadcast on the radio, live.

The following day, Judge Ito asked both prosecution and defense to join in a motion to close the proceedings to the public and press. He anticipated arguments from the media, but he believed that if we presented a united front on this issue, it would strengthen his argument. In addition, we would now voir dire the jurors individually, away from the rest of the panel.

I had always been in favor of open courtrooms and televised court proceedings. Now I found myself in the ironic, uncomfortable position of agreeing with the prosecution and a very conservative judge that the press and public should be banned.

I suspected, however, that without an "audience," we might get more honest answers from the jurors.

Although the press covered Ito's closure of the courtroom very negatively, the jurors did seem to be more comfortable when there was just one of them at a time in the room. They were certainly more forthcoming. Three admitted that they had watched television in the two days that Ito excused them: one saw the news, one watched a program on clairvoyants on PBS, one watched The Movie Channel. We also discovered that several jurors knew of Resnick's book and had heard some of the furor surrounding it. Some had become aware of it only because of Ito's instruction to stay out of bookstores. Quite naturally, when they went home or to work, someone told them why bookstores were off-limits. Then there was the one woman who said, "I come home, I go in my room, I do my ironing, I play Nintendo." There were others who resolutely assured us that nothing, absolutely nothing, could affect their fairness. Certainly such overeager people might have agendas of their own, and they were clearly jurors we did not want.

Throughout the upheaval surrounding the first few days after Resnick's book was published, O.J. appeared less upset than his defense counsel. She had accused us, and me in particular, of trying to stop the book in advance of its publication and claimed that tapes she'd recorded had been stolen. But O.J. did his best not to let it bother him. He knew it was full of mistakes; in fact, a couple of the errors were so ludicrous he actually laughed out loud. Faye's former boyfriend appeared on Barbara Walters's show and was quite critical; Cora Fischman spoke to one reporter and referred to Resnick as "Faye the Flake"; Nicole's father, Lou Brown, had publicly called the book "trash." I suspected that nothing would slow down sales, but I hoped that it could be seen for what it was.

Ito had asked a professor at Harvard Law School to have students prepare memorandums on whether or not media should be allowed in the courtroom. Six memorandums arrived, making articulate cases for both sides of the issue. After studying them carefully, Johnnie and I found ourselves reconsidering the question of excluding the media from the trial. Finally we went to the judge and told him that we'd changed our minds. As uncomfortable and cumbersome as the whole thing sometimes was, the American public had a right—possibly even a need—to see and understand what goes on in its courtrooms. It was clear that no one was going to understand those five amendments in the Bill of Rights unless they saw them implemented in a concrete situation.

∞

Having taken Brent and Grant to the Coliseum two years before for a Rolling Stones concert—and having enjoyed it—I'd long since purchased tickets to the Stones' October concert in Pasadena. Linell and I sat in the third row with the boys and were surprised during the opening when the lead singer for the Red Hot Chili Peppers (the group my kids *really* wanted to hear) not only announced that Robert Shapiro was in the audience but that later on, "Judge Lance Ito is going to be doing a guest set on the drums!"

Later, when Mick Jagger tore into "Honky Tonk Woman," we were completely astonished when my picture flashed up on the huge Rose Bowl video screen, right next to Jagger's, and there was a thunderous cheer from seventy-five thousand people.

It was a great night—noisy, energetic. It had been too long since the four of us had done something fun together. I was becoming increasingly concerned for my boys. With their school and ice-hockey plus my schedule, I was only seeing them on weekends. The case, and my total absorption in it, was weighing very heavily, especially on Linell. "I'm proud of you," she said, "but for me, there's no upside to this."

She had lived in Los Angeles all her life; there were restaurants and charity events and department stores she had gone to since she was a teenager. Dinners at Drai's and parties at Spago were part of her routine. Now, she never knew quite what would be waiting for her in these places, especially if I was with her. One anonymous source was quoted in the paper as saying "Robert Shapiro will come to the opening of a fucking door."

I didn't care what people said about me, about my politics or my style or my choice of clients. As former district attorney Ira Reiner said to me, "You get high-profile, and you simply have to learn to eat shit." But my family and my private life should've been strictly off-limits to anyone with integrity.

A day or so after the Stones concert, I received a care package from Joel Siegel in New York, with lots of newspaper articles and magazine clippings, including one magazine from Europe with the cover line "Robert Shapiro—The Most Famous and Smartest Lawyer in America."

The note from Joel read, "Don't let this go to your head. They also think Jerry Lewis is the funniest man in America."

Chapter Twelve

The last week of October, the prosecution claimed that their data-base research turned up O.J.'s name in 15,310 articles. On October 25, Marcia Clark asked Ito to dismiss the entire jury panel, claiming that they had been infected by all the recent publicity, including the furor over the Resnick book. Johnnie countered with, "You'll never get a better pool than this one. This pool has been more admonished than any other; they've been ordered not to see or read *anything*." I fervently hoped they'd missed that weekend's egregiously tasteless *Saturday Night Live* "Week in Review," touting the Pope's new book, *O.J. Did It, God Told Me.*

Bill Hodgman came up with the idea of planting our jury on a college campus somewhere, where people could go to the movies, the theater, listen to lectures, and so on, yet not be contaminated by outside information. I responded that it was too little too late. The only reason Clark wanted a new panel now, I said, was her jurors-needing-polygraphs remark, which seemed to suggest that they were all liars.

At which point the first juror in the box, a sixty-year-old woman, said, "Everybody talks about this case, everybody wants to get on the jury, and they all lie."

"See, Your Honor, I told you!" said Clark.

On the way to court, Dean Uelmen told me that he'd been informed by the prosecution that a blood sample in the Bronco tested positive for Nicole and that a mixture of O.J.'s and Ron Goldman's blood was on the console. This evidence would be the most challenging to overcome. I discussed it with Cochran, and he said, "Well, we'll just have to deal with it."

The question in my mind was not whose blood was where, but when and how it got in each location. I had begun thinking of our tactic as a formula: CPA and DNA. CPA stood for collection, preservation, and analysis. The third had no meaning whatsoever unless the first two were done properly. Contamination, cross-contamination, degree of degradation—these were the issues that Scheck, Neufeld, and Henry Lee would be working with.

Gerry Spence had made a comment on television to the effect that if O.J. did do it, he didn't know he did it. In the lock up, O.J. was furious. "I know what I do and what I don't do," he said angrily, "and I didn't do this."

He was depressed and frustrated, worried that perhaps now even his own lawyer might not believe him. There was no way to make things easy or comfortable for him. Being his lawyer didn't mean being soft on him. It meant putting hard questions to him, challenging him on evidence. "Best friend" wasn't in my job description.

It's unfortunate that something as vital as finding a jury should be so tedious and time-consuming, and yet it is a by-the-numbers process. With Ito's restrictions, one juror was eliminated for watching a cartoon with her children, one for turning on a Spanish soap opera, one for waking up to a clock radio, and one for walking into a bar that had a television on.

I began to see a pattern of black jurors being treated differently than white jurors by both the judge and the prosecution. In all fairness, I'm not sure they were aware of it. I didn't believe it was intentional, and I'm sure that both Clark and

Hodgman would say that they absolutely didn't do it. And Ito would agree with them. And indeed, the behavior was subtle. For example, one thing that gave reason to excuse for cause was if the panelist had violated the judge's order simply by turning on a television or radio. Ito would ask white jurors, "Have you watched television or listened to a radio?" For black jurors, he'd say, "Have you listened to music?" Invariably they'd say yes, and his next question would be, "Was that done on a radio?"

I saw Marcia Clark go after a forty-two-year-old black female postal worker whose job was to track lost and stolen mail. She appeared to be of above-average intelligence, bright, nice, but not particularly adept with her communication skills. When I questioned her, she had, like almost everyone, formed some opinions of the case. She had always viewed O.J. as a hero, had liked him, and didn't want to believe he was guilty. She thought the officers, in jumping over the fence "to save lives," weren't quite credible. But, she said, this was twenty-twenty hindsight; she wasn't on the scene at the time, and the officers might've believed their reasons were good ones. She believed she could set her feelings aside and listen to the judge and the evidence. Marcia cross-examined her in a very sweet, low-key, methodical way, leading her down the primrose path before demolishing her. Ito excused the juror for cause, because she had "preconceived conceptions of the case."

I argued that *all* jurors had preconceived conceptions, and this woman was no different, she just expressed them from a different point of view. Clearly this was a juror the People didn't want, and I could understand that, but I did not believe the reason for her excusal rose to the level of cause.

One seventy-one-year-old black man was questioned by Bill Hodgman, whose voice and articulation became very slow and level, different somehow than when he was questioning white panelists, almost as though he expected the man not to understand him. "Do you know what a polygraph is?" Hodgman asked. The juror shot back at him, as though insulted, "Yes, it's a lie detector!"

One black woman undergoing a voir dire by Hodgman finally blurted out, "You make me feel like I'm on trial!" Another began to cry when Hodgman probed deeper and deeper into why she didn't have faith in blood tests. It turned out that her sister was misdiagnosed after a series of blood tests, and died a month later of leukemia. "At least I've never made a juror cry," said Cochran later.

"There's something happening that I don't like," I said, when he and Carl Douglas were reviewing the sessions with me. "Race shouldn't be an issue here."

"It's always an issue, Bob," Johnnie said. "It's an issue in everything in life."

I just looked at him. "But I hoped it wouldn't be. I *believed* it wouldn't be."

He smiled. "That's because you're not black."

Often after these voir dire sessions I left the courthouse with my blood boiling. We haven't gotten anywhere in fifty years, I thought. We have the appearance of equality, and blacks serve on juries right beside whites, but in looking at the polls, it was clear that the tide in October had gone against us, splitting right down the racial line.

According to one CNN poll, 70 percent of those polled believed O.J. guilty; 20 percent believed he wasn't. The majority of those who believed him guilty were white; those who believed him innocent were black. The majority of black jurors had black heroes, and O.J. Simpson had been among them, for many good reasons. Should these citizens be penalized, or be assumed to be incapable of making thoughtful, considered decisions because of this fact? In our voir dire process, if blacks were excused for cause because their initial opinion was that O.J. was innocent, then all the whites should've been excused for cause if they believed him guilty.

∞

On Halloween, I arrived at court to see a half-dozen TV camera operators wearing "Shapiro masks." It gave us all a good laugh. Later I thought that it was pretty ironic. If I wore one of those masks, I could probably move through my life with some of my old autonomy.

For five weeks we'd been working with our jury panel, narrowing it down bit by bit, and we were now down to the last twenty-seven jurors. Jo-Ellan Dimitrius had coordinated all the massive material and data on each of them, the answers on their questionnaires, their responses to voir dire, and we'd ranked our possibilities on the computer. The final round was a war of nerves, like an ultimate chess game. It would result in what I believe to be the most important aspect of any case: who will judge the evidence.

This panel of possible jurors had received the most thorough indoctrination and explanation of its mission of any jury I had seen in twenty-five years. Day after day, Judge Ito had emphasized to them that "Mr. Simpson can sleep through this if he wants. In our justice system, the burden of proof is solely on the prosecution." And yet, when I asked jurors what they expected Mr. Simpson to do in this case, one prospective juror looked me straight in the eye and said, "Prove his innocence."

We had planned our strategies for peremptory challenges very carefully. Several times early on we accepted the jury knowing full well that the People would exercise their challenges. Thus we were able to hang on to our own challenges to use later. We had no intention of being easy on the prosecution if they continued to exclude blacks. Each time a black juror was excluded by the prosecution, Cochran asked to approach the bench, to build a record of a systematic challenge based on race.

On November 3 we at last had our jury. Twelve citizens sworn in; fifteen alternates to be chosen the following week. The final composition was better than we could have expected. Eight African-Americans, two Hispanics, one male Caucasian who was part Native American, one young female Caucasian. None had prior jury experience, none seemed preconditioned toward accepting DNA evidence. All seemed to have open minds. They, and we, had made it through a challenging five weeks. Picking a jury is always the hardest part of a case, and at last, it was over. Johnnie and I joined hands and together we announced, "The defense accepts the jury."

∞

November 7 was the date set for the courtroom hearing on cameras in the courtroom. The media had a field day, as lawyer after lawyer got up and delivered eloquent lectures on the freedom of the press on behalf of newspapers and networks. When Ito took the bench, he showed us his own demonstrative evidence: boxes stacked twelve feet high, full of the approximately fifteen thousand letters the court had received asking that the cameras not be in the courtroom.

Overall, I felt that cameras should be allowed. I believed they would help O.J. On the plus side, I believed that the defense team was more comfortable in front of a camera than the prosecutors. We thought that O.J. would do well with cameras, whether on the stand or simply at the defense table. On balance, we believed that all our witnesses would stand up better to camera scrutiny. The prosecution's key witnesses hadn't done particularly well with the cameras during the preliminary hearing, especially Detective Vannatter and Dr. Golden. The cameras might also serve to keep Judge Ito operating down what I thought of as the middle of the road, rather than leaning to the prosecutorial line, as most judges in my experience have tended to do.

The downside, of course, is that cameras affect everyone in a courtroom, and people get self-conscious and then act differently—and more unpredictably—than they otherwise might.

Floyd Abrams, the noted constitutional law expert who was commenting for Court TV, gave in my estimation the best reason for cameras in the courtroom. Drawing the analogy to O.J.'s plea, he said, "I represent the cameras, and to that I plead one hundred percent not guilty. The cameras haven't caused the problems." The public should see what the jury sees, he argued. We, too, wanted cameras only for the evidence that the jury would see. Any pretrial motions, evidentiary rulings, or arguments made at sidebars would not be filmed.

As was his policy, Ito courteously allowed everyone an opportunity to speak as long as they wanted. At the end of the day, he announced his decision: The trial could be televised.

Soon after our jury was impaneled, I was astonished to see, in the *Los Angeles Times*, a full-page ad announcing that Judge Ito, "the most famous judge in America, is going to be welcomed into the homes of the American people." During the November network sweeps, Ito was going to be featured in a five-part interview with reporter Tritia Toyota on KCBS, the local CBS channel. And KCBS was promoting it like it was the first moon landing.

Tritia Toyota's husband, Michael Yamaki, was a respected attorney and a man held in high regard in the Asian community, and that's evidently how the first contact came about between Ito and Toyota. We later learned that there had only been one on-camera interview, not five. Ito had no way of knowing that it would be divided into a series and shown every night for a week, let alone be hyped by the television station in a manner that suggested that he was going to give inside information on the Simpson trial and its participants. This, of course, was not the case. To Ito's credit, and to the reporter's, the only things that they discussed were personal matters—his childhood and his family internment in the Japanese camps, and his interest in the law.

Nevertheless, the whole matter put him in an unfortunate light. His detractors accused him of being on an ego trip, that it was arrogance on his part, or self-aggrandizement; his supporters said that the interview not only gave the public a behind-the-scenes look at a judge and his role in the judicial system but also an introduction to a respected Japanese-American in a position of great responsibility.

Regardless of how harmless it may ultimately have been to the case, I thought Ito's interview highly inappropriate not to mention that the timing, coming right on top of the Resnick book, contributed to the media circus. However, I knew it would be impolitic for me to begin a trial of this magnitude by criticizing the sitting judge.

As we began to head into the holiday season, it was clear that O.J. was more and more irritated at issues that appeared peripheral to his trial, that seemed to draw attention away from the trial itself. He told anyone who would listen about his exasperation when Ito did the television interview, worried that it would create more bad publicity for the case. At the counsel table, he was easily overheard joining in on the gallows-humor jokes and sotto voce wisecracks that the attorneys exchanged among themselves. He grew visibly restless and impatient when he thought the prosecution was dawdling over a voir dire of a prospective alternate juror. When Ito told potential jurors that they would be sequestered for up to six months, and that opening statements might not even take place until the end of January, O.J. audibly groaned in court.

One issue that needed to be resolved was the recurring question of Judge Ito's wife, Captain Margaret York. We had information that she had at one time been Mark Fuhrman's supervisor when he was a patrolman in West Los Angeles, and had clashed with him over his treatment of women police officers, and we raised the possibility of York being called as a witness—which in turn raised a conflict-of-interest question for Ito.

Both the defense and prosecution thought it would be fairly easy to resolve this potentially embarrassing situation. We first spoke informally with Captain York outside Judge Ito's chambers, and then in a conference with him inside his chambers we suggested that his deciding the matter might give the appearance of impropriety. We needed an open hearing, with an objective judge to hear our argument.

We went to Judge Mills and asked him to appoint someone. When he suggested Judge Steve Czuleger we reminded him that Czuleger had participated in the grand jury, and we'd prefer someone who hadn't worked on any of the Simpson matters. He said, "Fine, Robert Perry, then." Perry was a former U.S. attorney and was satisfactory to us.

"Your Honor, we don't know him," argued Marcia Clark. "We don't want to deal with anyone we don't know."

"Well, let's discuss this for a minute," said Mills. "Who would you like?"

"Judge Curtis Rappe," Clark answered promptly.

"Wait just a minute, Your Honor," said Johnnie. "If she's going to suggest somebody, then I want to suggest somebody." And he mentioned a judge that he knew and was close to.

This is going nowhere, I thought. "Judge Mills, this is ridiculous. If we all pick and choose and then argue our favorites, this will never get done. You're the presiding judge, you have lots of good judges to choose from. Why don't you just pick one?"

Mills nodded. "That's exactly what I'm going to do," he said. "I'm not going to be influenced by anyone. The matter goes to Curtis Rappe." The prosecution's choice.

After Mills appointed Judge Rappe, I spoke with York's attorney, who assured us that his client had only a dim recollection of Fuhrman and hadn't experienced any difficulties with him. That clashed with what we were hearing from Robert Tourtelot, Fuhrman's attorney, who alleged that they'd had many disagreements, including at least one that led to a formal reprimand in his file.

Rappe subpoenaed all the records and reviewed them. He announced that there was nothing beneficial to the defense in calling Captain York in the case, and the matter was resolved.

∞

Over the long Thanksgiving weekend, I visited O.J. twice, once on Thanksgiving Day itself, which, since he was away from his family, was a very hard day for him. On the following Monday, Bill Pavelic and I spent four hours at the jail, going over and over the now-familiar details with O.J. I suspected that if he took the stand he would be a typical witness—that is, not as good as he thought he would be. I often tell clients that they must *learn* to be witnesses. They must take their time, listen to questions, and answer them simply. Testimony is definitely not social discourse.

Over the course of the trial, Bill spent endless hours with O.J., keeping him informed and getting his input. During their conversations he subtly encouraged O.J. to control his constant storytelling impulses. In the time they spent together, the two men formed a bond of trust and true friendship. But that didn't mean O.J. didn't get as impatient with Bill as he did with the rest of us.

One day, in complete exasperation, O.J. said, "Bill, I hope this doesn't perjure me, and I haven't really told anyone until now, but I just remembered . . . somewhere, sometime that day, I spent some quality time in the head!"

∞

Between Thanksgiving and Christmas, Nicole's sister Denise hired famed feminist attorney Gloria Allred as her representative, and within days of doing so, it seemed that Denise was everywhere—on television, in the tabloids. To anyone who would listen, she stated over and over again, quite emphatically, "O.J. Simpson murdered my sister." Denise in the *Orange County Register:* "O.J. did it." Denise on TV, on *Geraldo:* "He did it." Denise on *Primetime Live* with Diane Sawyer: "He did it." In effect, she launched a war of words, which the Brown and Goldman families very quickly joined.

I believed that it was the defense's role to speak on behalf of O.J., and I knew that the prosecution was prepared to speak passionately and eloquently on behalf of Ron Goldman and

Nicole. For this reason, I'd hoped that their families wouldn't get caught in the judicial or media crossfire.

For months, I had admired the courage and dignity evidenced by the Browns and the Goldmans, and I respected it. I don't know that I could have behaved with anything approaching such grace if it had been one of my children who had been murdered. These people had all lost so much already. I had hoped, not just for my client's sake but also for theirs, that at the very least their privacy and dignity could be protected.

There was, of course, no way on this earth for me to express those feelings without sounding patronizing and condescending to the families. Yet I made the mistake of doing so, in response to a reporter's question about the potential prejudicial nature of Denise's remarks, and those of Lou Brown and Fred Goldman. I then compounded my mistake by saying that we understood and forgave them for the things they were saying, because of their heartbreak. My words were poorly chosen, and Fred Goldman in particular was understandably outraged.

I later gave a statement to the press at the courthouse, emphasizing that I'd had no intention of patronizing the families or their pain. For our side, from now on we were going to limit our comments to legal procedure or to clear up any questions after each day's session. There would be no interviews.

A few days later, three prospective jurors were excused from the panel after stating that they'd heard or read the Denise Brown interviews, in which she said "O.J. did it."

∞

At the end of November, Peter Neufeld called in a panic. He was scheduled to participate in a murder trial—admittedly one to which he'd made a commitment some months before—in New York City. The trial was to begin at around the time our Kelly-Frye hearings on the admissibility of DNA evidence were scheduled. The New York judge, Harold Rothwax, had ordered Neufeld to appear at the trial.

Judge Rothwax told Judge Ito that Neufeld would be needed

for only two weeks even though the lawyers had agreed the trial would take six. Ultimately it would take eight.

Even though we hadn't yet started calling witnesses, our jury had been seated: technically, our trial was under way. We couldn't afford to lose Neufeld, so I requested Judge Ito to issue a court order directing Neufeld to appear for O.J., hoping the tactic would convince Rothwax to allow Neufeld to stay in Los Angeles. Ito issued the order, but Rothwax was not persuaded. He ordered Neufeld back to New York under penalty of contempt of court, at which point Barry Scheck said, "Bob, there's too much work to do alone, I'm going to need some help."

For a time I thought that this might be a place for Lee Bailey to actively participate in the trial. Ever since the day of O.J.'s Bronco ride, Lee had been on the team essentially as a consultant, overseeing McKenna and McNally and working with his computer expert, Howard Harris, to get the case material into a system that we all could use.

Bailey continued working on his own cases, frequently heading back East. But he had stayed involved with the Simpson case, visiting O.J. and attending defense team meetings at my office. He raised Bonnie's hackles on a regular basis, telling off-color jokes that invariably had a prurient punch line, or issuing sweeping orders about computer equipment or filing systems. His mood sometimes swung from grandiose to silly, and he often went off on tangents. But he was, above all, two things: He was the legendary F. Lee Bailey, and he was my old friend and mentor. "Someone has to do Kelly-Frye with Scheck," I said. "Maybe it could be Lee."

The response to my suggestion wasn't particularly enthusiastic. After all, if we were losing a DNA expert, shouldn't we replace him with another DNA expert?

Barry Scheck had put together a thirty-five-page memo detailing what he believed our strategy should be with regard to the scientific evidence, and he readily agreed to meet with Lee to see if he could be brought up to speed. Scheck wasn't optimistic. He didn't doubt Bailey's abilities, but he felt there was a certain depth of expertise that could only be obtained by having fought in the trenches of the DNA wars for years, as he and Peter Neufeld had done. Not only that, but whoever countered the prosecution's DNA experts had to do it carefully, with finesse, not shred them on the stand, as was Bailey's style. As an alternative, Barry mentioned Robert Blasier, a lawyer colleague in Sacramento.

I remembered reading a profile of Blasier in the *Daily Journal*. He had received an undergraduate degree in engineering from Carnegie Institute of Technology and his law degree was from Harvard Law School. He had extensive experience in medical and scientific issues, especially DNA, and he'd served as an expert witness for both the defense and prosecution when admissibility of DNA evidence was in question. He had also been a legal analyst on both local and national television.

Blasier, a scholar and scientist with a great wit, was ideally suited to the Simpson case. Competitive and seemingly tireless, he had a calm, logical approach to the law and its intersection with science. The bonus came when we found out he was a computer whiz as well. He had a laptop with twice the memory of the one that Bailey had shipped from Florida. Even better, Blasier was able to immediately access all the material in the court reporter's transcription software.

Once Blasier's laptop was in gear, we had immediate access to each day's proceedings, as well as all discovery material, the evidence inventory, all motions and responses, and the full set of California legal codes. It was as though the man had an entire law library on his lap. His system was so good that when questions came up in court on past testimony, Judge Ito would often query Blasier, who could instantly locate the sought-after information. In addition, until Blasier's arrival we had been working with several talented graphics companies to prepare exhibits and demonstration boards. Blasier was able to create similar graphics as he sat in the courtroom, providing them overnight for use in court the next day. What looked like a crisis turned into a blessing. As Sara Caplan said happily, "We literally weren't all working on the same page until Bob Blasier and his computer got here."

∞

In early December, in an effort to adjust the composition of the jury and challenge alternate jury members not to their liking, the prosecution had begun an unofficial investigation of certain members of the remaining jury panel. One of them was a man who had worked for Hertz some years before. In a conference in Ito's chambers, Chris Darden quipped that this juror was about to become very famous. He then gave us a draft of an article for *Star* magazine. It was about the juror being a former Hertz employee, his presumed sympathy for O.J., and the degree to which that compromised his being on this jury. Glancing quickly through the article, I saw a reference to the reporter being scheduled to "meet with an investigator from the district attorney's office for further comments on Monday."

When I pointed this out to Judge Ito, he became quite angry. Questions or problems involving jury members were to be reported directly to him, and any investigating was to be performed only by the sheriff's deputies, on Ito's orders. Nothing was to go to the press, and no investigations were to be conducted by the D.A.'s office.

"We've had no choice, Your Honor," Marcia Clark argued. "When these matters come to our attention, we have a duty to investigate them."

"No, you don't, Miss Clark," cautioned the judge. When she tried to continue, he stopped her. "There are to be no independent investigations by the prosecution of these jurors," he said. "If you have problems, those problems are to come to me."

We had originally opposed the prosecution's motion for jury sequestration, feeling that it would work against us. But now I began to reconsider the wisdom of *not* having the jury sequestered. Maybe it would be better all around if they were not only out of the media mainstream but out of the prosecution's line of fire as well. Our subsequent motion for sequestration read, "One need only look to the Faye Resnick book as well as the media blitz currently underway by Nicole Brown Simpson's family members and representatives to provide additional justification to sequester the jury now rather than later."

∞

A few days later, someone faxed a copy of a piece by newspaper gossip columnist Liz Smith, in which I was said to have had dinner with Tony Frost, a reporter from the *Star*. Smith wrote that Frost and I met at La Veranda restaurant, and at the end of the evening Frost gave me a bottle of champagne. The following day, she said, the transcript of O.J.'s initial statement to the police, which to date hadn't been revealed, was published in the *Star*.

The transcript, and the original tapes of that interview, had been in a safe in my office for months, under double signature. Just after Thanksgiving, O.J. had requested to hear the tapes. Pat McKenna signed them out, took them to O.J. in the jail, and then returned them to the office safe.

I couldn't waste my time or anyone else's tracking down the source every time my name showed up in a bad light in a gossip column, but this leak was more disturbing than gossip. Where, I wondered, did the *Star* get that transcript?

Chapter Thirteen

After weeks of discussion with our DNA experts, the defense team decided to waive the Kelly-Frye hearing on the admissibility of DNA evidence. Fighting item by item could've taken anywhere from two to three months. We had neither the time nor the money to expend on additional expert witnesses.

Besides, I had always believed that no matter what we did, Judge Ito would ultimately admit all the results of the DNA testing. As a former prosecutor, he'd hardly been shy in revealing pro-prosecution leanings in some of his early rulings. Furthermore, we knew he had consulted with his colleague, Judge Dino Fulgoni, who was an open proponent of DNA evidence and one of the district attorney's top DNA experts before he went to the bench. We were just going to have to deal with the evidence and argue not its admissibility but its reliability and credibility.

Over the weekend of December 10 and 11, CNN's Art Harris reported the defense's decision to file a motion to waive the Kelly-Frye hearing. Confirmation of this information had come, he reported, from two members of the defense team. I was completely surprised when I heard this; we hadn't filed the motion to waive yet, nor had we told anyone about it.

"*Damn* it, this place is like a sieve!" I said. "I just gave my big speech about not talking to the media, and here we are, meeting ourselves coming and going on TV before we've even filed the damn motion!"

Gerry Uelmen, who had prepared the motion, was angry at the news leak, as was everyone else. Strategically, it didn't harm anything; psychologically, it had us all once again looking over our shoulders. And at each other.

On Monday, December 12, the jury was assembled and given cautionary instructions by Judge Ito as to what they were to do between that date and January 4, when they were told to report back and be prepared for sequestration. There were a few more pretrial matters to resolve—the admissibility of the prosecution's domestic abuse evidence and the material on Mark Fuhrman we wanted to introduce—but once we'd foregone the Kelly-Frye hearings, we knew that the trial would probably begin within a couple of weeks after the Christmas break.

∞

In mid-December, we did battle with the prosecution over Roosevelt Grier's visit to O.J. the month before.

The problems around our visiting arrangements and the visiting room had begun almost as soon as O.J. went to jail. Defendants on bail can prepare their cases seven days a week, but of course that had not been an option for us. Because we were often in court on pretrial matters during the week, it was difficult for us to meet with O.J. anytime except the weekends. But the attorney room at the jail was closed from mid-Saturday until Monday morning.

Judge Ito made another area available to us, with the required sheriff's deputies, some soundproofing, and a phone system so that O.J. could speak with a semblance of privacy, in spite of the glass wall between him and his visitor. During his visit with Grier their conversation, and specifically O.J.'s words, were overheard by a deputy. Even though neither side knew what had been overheard, Grier assured us that it wasn't anything damaging. Still, we contended that because of Rosie's status as a minister, the jail conversation was privileged; Marcia Clark argued that by raising his voice in the glass-walled visiting room, O.J. forfeited his right to privacy, and whatever he'd said would be admissible.

"If the parties choose to shout at each other, that's their problem," said Ito, leading me to believe that he was going to go along with Clark.

I exploded. "I think it's disingenuous for Your Honor to even make that suggestion. You assured us privacy with those phones!" I said. The existence of telephones and the volume of an overwrought defendant's voice hardly qualified as reason to check his constitutional rights at the jail door. Ito had approved the design of that room so that it would be private. O.J. had every right to believe that whatever he said there was said in confidence.

Ito's eyes got very steely. "Take a deep breath, Mr. Shapiro," he cautioned. "When you argue that the court is being disingenuous in that question, I'm a little concerned. I would ask you to sit back and think about that for a moment."

Cochran and Uelmen took me aside and told me that Ito wanted an apology. "No," I said angrily. "Ito personally assured us that the room was designed to protect confidentiality. He can't rule against us just because Clark wants him to. The conversation was privileged, I don't care how loud it got."

My colleagues weren't any happier than I was, but it was clear that the next step was mine, and it had better be made diplomatically. After the lunch recess, I came back and apologized to the judge. "It was something said in the heat of advocacy," I said.

Later that week, Judge Ito ruled that, indeed, O.J.'s conversation with Grier was privileged. "Counsel for Simpson were assured that the proposed modifications would make a portion of the module secure," he said.

∞

The court would be dark for the two-week Christmas break. I had long planned to take Linell and the boys to Hawaii. Johnnie was heading for New York and then on to South Africa for a long-planned trip. The New Yorkers were heading out, and Bailey was going to Florida. Baden and Lee had been back East for months, getting ready for their trial testimony.

O.J. knew that some of us were going to be out of town until after New Year's; in fact, he had encouraged everybody to take time off. We had been working almost nonstop for six months. With the trial coming up, it would be the last break we'd get for a while. He was trying to be fair; I knew he wasn't looking forward to his own "break" in jail. Even with his family visiting, it would be a very, very quiet two weeks, and we were all painfully aware of that.

As the time to leave grew closer, I became uneasy. I wasn't sure if it was discomfort at the idea of O.J. in jail over Christmas or guilt at time with my family that I suspected might be cut short. Maybe it was knowing that when we came back, we'd finally go to trial. Whatever, I fully intended to work in Hawaii. I was taking a stack of files, along with DNA reading material, and I'd made arrangements for two private telephone lines and a fax line to be installed in our suite. Anyone who wanted or needed to reach me would be able to do so.

On Sunday and Monday, before I left, I spent as much time as I could at the jail with O.J. We went over the same ground again and again, and I reassured him that the case had been fully researched and prepared, that we were ready. O.J. was working to stay optimistic, to stay focused and energetic. Much of the material in my office—witness statements, the murder book, crime-scene photos, much of what we'd received in discovery—was being packed up to be shipped to Florida so that McKenna and McNally could go over everything again on the break. When we all returned, we would be rested and prepared for the trial to begin.

A few weeks before, I'd called Mike Ovitz to get some personal advice, telling him how difficult it had been to hang on to my private life. "I'm really getting battered in the press. Any suggestions as to what I can do?"

"You're really out on a limb," he said. "I really don't know what to tell you in this situation. I know how awful it is, what's happening to Linell and the kids. You've got to pay close attention to them. When you travel, travel under an assumed name."

So that's what I did, using the name Tony DiMilo, a singer who'd been in my father's band. United Airlines and the Grand Wailea Resort on Maui were both in on it and saw to it that our real names never went into any computer. Once on the plane, Linell and I were in first class and the boys were in coach directly behind us. I worked all the way to Maui, feeling only slightly foolish when the flight crew, who obviously knew who we were, asked Linell if "Mr. DiMilo" wanted any more club soda.

Once settled in at the hotel, I left it on two occasions to go out to dinner. Otherwise, we ate all our meals in the hotel restaurants, and I spent much of each day in our suite, reading DNA texts and drafting a twenty-six-page outline of what would become the foundation for Johnnie Cochran's opening statement. Linell and the boys hit the beach or the pools, and I'd join them around three in the afternoon, bringing my homework with me. After reading in the sun for about an hour, I'd head back to the room and deal with the phones and faxes, then to the health club for a workout. In the evenings, we all had dinner together. Then I'd exchange faxes with Barry Scheck, who was in Mexico, on DNA strategy.

On the twenty-third, I received a memo from Lee Bailey regarding tactics for the trial opening. When we talked about it on the phone, he was somewhat rambling and repetitious. It was six hours later where he was; clearly he'd enjoyed a few cocktails. When he mentioned that he was planning on being at the trial for the duration—around four months, he guessed—I said, "Lee, what are you talking about? There are only three seats at the counsel table. I haven't received any clearance whatsoever for you to be there."

"Oh, yeah?" he said. "Well, have you talked to your client lately?"

"Not specifically about this," I answered. "Besides, Skip

Taft is really watching the money, there's no way he'd pick up
the tab for you to be at the table."

"Well, you're wrong," he said. "I've rented a condo on Wil-
shire Blvd. I'll be there for the trial. And I'll be at the table.
Why the hell do you think I've been coming to all these meetings?"

This was getting murkier by the minute. "Because you're a
consultant on the case, because you wanted to be involved with
what's going on. Harris is your computer guy, McKenna and
McNally your investigators. But Lee, you're a consultant to the
team, you're not one of the trial lawyers."

The conversation went downhill from there. Bailey wanted
to know why he wasn't included in my fee agreement with O.J.
and why, if he wasn't one of the trial lawyers, his name was on
some of the pleadings. (Because I thought it would help out
your career, I wanted to say.) The phone conversation ended
badly.

When I told Linell about it afterward, she said, "This is
getting sad. You guys have known each other too long for this
to happen, you have to clear it up." So I called him the next
morning. "Look, Lee, I feel awful about this," I said. "If O.J.
wants you at the table, then of course I do, too."

Later that afternoon there was a conference call, with Lee,
Johnnie Cochran, Barry Scheck, Dershowitz in Boston, and
Gerry Uelmen. F. Lee Bailey was now officially at the table.
"Welcome, Lee," boomed Johnnie. "Thanks, Johnnie," an-
swered Lee.

At the end of the conversation, Johnnie closed by saying,
"Oh, by the way, Bob, we're having a meeting in my office on
the twenty-seventh."

"What? You said you were going to South Africa!" I said.

"Nope, not going to South Africa," he answered. "I'm staying here. There's too much work to do. Plus we're having this
meeting."

"Why didn't somebody tell me about it?" I asked. "You
knew I'd be here until after New Year's."

"Well, we've just gotta move on, Bob," he said. "We've
gotta do what we've gotta do."

"Fine," I said evenly. "I'll be back in time for the meeting."

"No, no," he said quickly, "don't cut your trip short. You don't have to be here. It's really just my staff."

I then received a fax from Carl Douglas stating that Skip Taft was very concerned that costs had gotten out of hand. All future meetings would be held in Johnnie Cochran's office and all future travel arrangements would be made through Cochran's secretary. From now on, our out-of-town experts would be moved to a hotel that was fifteen dollars cheaper a night than what we'd been paying, and in-town travel would be done by taxicab.

The faxes really started flying. I said I'd pay the extra money to keep Baden and Lee in the Marriott near my office, which had always given me terrific discounts. I'd pay out of my own pocket, and I'd also pay for the Lincoln Town Cars to get them back and forth. I wasn't about to have either man flagging down a cab with an armload of papers and files, trying to get downtown to the courthouse to give costly expert testimony. *That* would have been a waste of time and money.

Then Bill Pavelic called me to report a phone call he'd received from John McNally on Christmas Day. "Hey, Bill," McNally had asked him, "what're you going to do once Shapiro's bumped from the case?"

Pavelic was alarmed. "Bob, you know the files that left your office? They didn't go to Florida," he said. "Everything went to Cochran's office."

Linell had been monitoring the goings-on with a growing concern. "Bob, something weird is going on here. What are they doing to you?"

⚮

On the flight back to Los Angeles, Linell and I speculated on what I would find waiting for me at home. "You've put your life, our lives, on hold for this trial, and now look what's happening," my wife said. "People are working against you behind your back, and you're just too nice to see it."

I tried to take a more balanced approach. "Whatever's going

on," I said, "it's important not to make it bigger than it really is. With the trial about to begin, we're all under enough pressure, this is no time to start looking in the bushes for enemies. I don't want to start worrying about who I can trust and who I can't."

But Linell was adamant. "Something's wrong, Bob, and it goes deeper than Lee Bailey fighting to get a seat at the counsel table or equal time on television. Hold your ground with O.J. He knows that you've put this all together. Do things your way, because that will be the right way. And if they decide they want Bailey and Cochran to run the show, well, fine, you can just get out of it, and we can have our lives back."

"I can't 'get out of it' unless the client shows me the door, Linell," I said. "And you know that as well as I do, I made a commitment to him, and I have to honor that."

∞

On January 2, I had to wade through a press phalanx to get into the jail. "So what's the deal on your demotion?" shouted one reporter. "Are you getting booted off the team?" yelled another. "Is Bailey taking over?"

"It's been two weeks of no O.J.," I answered. "So somebody's cranking up the wheels. If I had to spend any of my time worrying about the innuendoes, the speculation, the rumors, I wouldn't have any time for preparation."

When I got inside, Johnnie was already there. There was a tension between us that had not been there before. "What's going on?" I asked. "Am I out?"

When I'd hired Cochran, it was with the full understanding that he would have a more active role once the trial started, because he was good with downtown juries, he was good with blacks, and he had a good track record for trials. I wasn't exactly surprised that he had stepped forward, but where I had anticipated a power shift, there now appeared to be a power struggle—or a coup. Things had changed.

"O.J.'s not too happy that you're charging a thousand dollars a day for your conference room," Johnnie said abruptly.

"What?" I said. "Where the hell did that information come from?"

"We've got the records," said Johnnie. "Go talk to Skip Taft, it's all in there."

It was true, we had been paying rent to the firm for the conference room. To the *firm*, in which I was not yet a partner and from which I didn't profit one cent. "Nine hundred and seventy dollars *a month*," I told Johnnie.

Since the case had begun, we'd occupied the biggest conference room in the firm for seven days a week, almost around the clock. It was where the investigators had worked the phones, written their reports, stored their files. The paralegals and the temporary office help camped out there, sorting the stacks of mail, collating the fourteen copies of every memo and motion. It was where the take-out food was delivered and eaten on the lunch hours and evenings when no one left the office until late.

"Well, there's more to it than that," Johnnie said. "There's evidence that you leaked the story to the *Star*."

After the transcripts had shown up in the *Star*, Pat McKenna knew that he'd be suspected of being the culprit, since he'd signed the tapes out of the office to take them to O.J. in the jail. So he went to the magazine immediately, and they assured him that they'd give him a letter stating that he wasn't the one who'd given *Star* the material. That person, according to the *Star*, was me—and in fact had been paid five thousand dollars for it. McKenna reported this to Kardashian, who said, "I don't believe that. Go back and get a copy of the five-thousand-dollar check."

McKenna brought back a copy of the check, made out not to me but to a third party, because, he was told, "Shapiro is so sneaky, he doesn't want his name appearing on anything."

The transcripts were somewhat favorable to O.J., so of course it only made sense that I'd made sure they showed up in print. The source of the leaks on our decision not to hold Kelly-Frye hearings—also me. In fact, Jo-Ellan Dimitrius had it on good authority: She'd heard it from two of Larry King's staffers at a Washington dinner! The conduit to CNN, the print press, the networks—all me.

I was totally dumbfounded. "You know this is absolute and total bullshit, Johnnie!" I said. "How can you even think I'd do anything like this? I haven't busted my butt and pushed these people so hard the last six months just to see everything we've worked for go south now!" As my voice grew louder, I knew I could be heard all the way down the hall. But I didn't care. I had found myself in the role of defendant, surrounded by circumstantial evidence that bore no relationship to the truth.

Throughout our heated discussion, Johnnie never raised his voice. He seemed to take a quiet pleasure watching me grow angrier by the minute. It was all I could do not to say, "Let's just step outside and settle this."

The next morning we all met at Johnnie's office, with O.J. on the speakerphone. All the rumors and stories were on the table now, and everyone seemed to accept my absolute statement that I hadn't leaked to the *Star* or to anyone else. There were apologies all around, albeit some of them subdued, and an acknowledgment that we had to find a way to close ranks.

"We're being driven apart by the rumors and the leaks, and it's hurting the case," I said. "I think we should all take lie-detector tests."

"That kind of thing wouldn't work in this instance," said Bailey.

"What about a confidentiality agreement?" Skip Taft asked. "It doesn't guarantee anything, of course, but it would formalize where we go from here."

"No, no, we don't need formal agreements," Bailey said. "We're all professionals here."

It was agreed that Johnnie would be the lead lawyer at the trial, Carl Douglas would be the case manager in charge of all discovery, and I was once again the quarterback in charge of the overall defense team and strategy. We would make the decisions as to who was in court and who would examine witnesses on a day-by-day basis.

After the meeting, I went down to the jail with Alan Dershowitz to talk quietly with my client. I was prepared to resign if that's what was required, and I wanted Alan with me for what might have become a difficult session. However, when we left the jail and were met by the reporters, I was able to report that no one was leaving the defense team and we were prepared to go to trial.

The very next day, in Cochran's office, Bailey was ready for another fight. "You went down to the jail behind our backs," he snapped at me. "You went down there to undermine us, to convince O.J. to see it your way."

Dershowitz got mad at this. "Lee, you weren't even there. I was. Bob wasn't undermining anybody. He even offered to resign, if that's what O.J. wanted."

At that point, it wasn't clear to me what O.J. wanted. He was on the inside, we were on the outside, and he needed us. Maybe, because of this, he wanted to be everything to everybody, so that we'd all stay with him and keep up the fight.

That day, someone faxed me a *New York Daily News* column, written by Mike McAlary. It gave all the details about the trip to Maui—Linell and me in first class, the kids in coach, the name of the hotel, the Tony DiMilo alias. I was a "Hollywood character tan-deep in makeup and significance" who had been demoted by Cochran and Bailey, both "appropriate, decent men." Johnnie was quoted as saying, "I think Shapiro's gone off the deep end."

However, McAlary reported, Bailey was now "on the case. Even Cochran defers to his judgment now." Hmm, I thought, wonder what Johnnie's response was when he saw *that* line.

Directly beneath McAlary's column was another piece, this one equally detailed, on my demotion to a "lesser role" on the defense team. "O.J. told him in no uncertain terms that Cochran and Bailey will be taking control of the trial," it stated.

For Skip Taft, this was the last straw. The jury members were still out there in a post-holiday haze, not yet sequestered, and no doubt picking up reports about the squabbling defense team. Inside information was being sold, and our confidence in each other—and O.J.'s confidence in us—was eroding. Skip asked Bill Pavelic to begin an official investigation of the leaks. Where, Skip wanted to know, was our weak link?

In the meantime, we had to go back to court for motions, specifically on domestic abuse and Fuhrman. One night I got a call from Bailey. "Robert, do I have the privilege of riding with you to court tomorrow?"

"You do not," I said.

I picked up Johnnie as usual the next morning, and when we got to court, we were both surprised to see Bailey there. "You're not needed today, Lee," Johnnie told him. After court, we went back to Cochran's office for a closed-door strategy meeting. There came an insistent knock. "Johnnie, Bob, I've got to talk to you," said Bailey.

I looked at Johnnie. "It's up to you," I said. "I'm not talking to him."

Johnnie went to the door, stepped outside for a few moments, and then came back into the room. "The source of the leaks and stories," he said, "is John McNally."

Bailey had evidently decided to make retired N.Y.P.D. cop McNally his fall guy. After all, he was already off the case and safely out of Los Angeles. But I knew that McNally hadn't been present for my "demotion" meeting. The information from that meeting, no matter who had passed it on to the *Daily News*, could only have come from someone in the room with us at the time.

A lot of things made sense now. How and why Barry Hostetler ("Spence's guy," Bailey kept calling him) had been eliminated from the investigative staff. How reporters always knew where my kids' parties or hockey games were going to be. How Mike McAlary knew about Tony DiMilo. And why so much of the negative stuff was coming from the New York papers and columnists.

"There's one thing to be learned from this," I said. "Don't

ever judge anyone on circumstantial evidence. It's impossible to defend yourself."

∞

A few weeks later Bill Boyarsky, who wrote "the spin" column in the *Los Angeles Times,* called *Star* magazine directly.

"What about the release of O.J.'s police interview transcripts?" Boyarsky asked Kaplan. "Was it Bailey or Shapiro?" The answer, which the *Times* printed: "We can tell you this—it wasn't Shapiro."

While Bailey's betrayal was deeply painful for me and my family, other people paid a price, too. For nearly six months, McKenna, McNally, and Howard Harris had been trusted members not just of the defense team but also of my office family. They had all been together constantly, under the same pressure, eating the same take-out food and rolling their eyes at the same bad gallows humor, going to Bonnie's home to play pool and unwind over Mexican food and a few beers. Out of necessity, everyone's world had narrowed, and it was like being in the trenches or, as someone else said, like working in an emergency room. These had become close, trusting friendships.

For me, loyalty is the key to everything worthwhile in my life. The friendships that mean the most to me are the long-term, going-back-a-long-way ones. Long-term marriage isn't the norm in my neighborhood, and I deeply cherish my own. The loyalty of O.J.'s friends kept me believing in and committed to his case. And loyalty was what led me to bring Lee Bailey in on the Simpson case to begin with. Now that was over.

In his carefully detailed report to Skip Taft a few weeks later, Bill Pavelic wrote that his investigation had revealed a "systematic and elaborate campaign of disclosures to the press, principally to columnists for Eastern papers, CNN, and supermarket tabloids. The object . . . to denigrate Shapiro's skills and his ability to keep client confidences, and to enhance Bailey's own modest role in the case so far."

∞

Soon after the Bailey fallout, I was at home, on a conference call with Johnnie and Bill Pavelic. Bill was outlining the point-by-point chronology of everything Bailey had done, in the weeks before I was in Hawaii, and in the days since, including the leaks to the press about conversations only the lawyers could've been privy to. I was adamant that Bailey be removed from this case, from anything having to do with O.J. and the upcoming trial.

"Don't you understand, Johnnie?" I said angrily. "This isn't a disagreement over tactics, or style. This isn't some kind of personality conflict Bailey and I are having about how to conduct a defense. The man betrayed me—and the entire defense team, and O.J., too—on every conceivable level. And he undercut the public perception of the defense of this case in the process. The jury's not sequestered; they're hearing this garbage. This isn't me being wounded by a couple of nasty press clippings! This man lied, he cannot be trusted!"

"I didn't know you felt so strongly about this, Bob," Johnnie said on the other end of the line. "I thought this was something you'd get over, for the good of the client."

"Good of the client?" I said. "It's the client that I'm talking about here, don't you get it? Bailey took confidential information, and it sure looks like he or his people went to the press with it. Bad enough that I've been insulted and betrayed by someone I've trusted with my own son, for God's sake. O.J.'s been betrayed too. For fame, for ego!"

My home office is just off the master bedroom, and Linell could easily hear my end of the conversation grow more and more heated. Finally she could take it no more and came around the corner. "What's Cochran's problem?" she asked, not bothering to keep her voice down.

"Here," I said, handing her the phone. "You talk to him."

Linell had met Johnnie before he was involved in O.J.'s case, at fundraisers or law functions. He had always been cordial to her, and pleasant, as she had been to him. Now, however, that was about to change.

"Johnnie, this is Linell Shapiro," she said angrily. "I have to tell you, I've been listening to Bob's end of this conversation tonight, and I don't understand this. After what Lee Bailey did, why is there even a question in your mind about this? The man stabbed Bob in the back, and O.J., too. He was responsible for confidential stories about the case being leaked everywhere. This isn't about two men having a professional disagreement. This is about someone who's evil, who can't be trusted—by us or you or anybody else, but especially by O.J. Simpson!"

She didn't know Pavelic was still on the line. Later, he told me Johnnie's end of the conversation.

"Now, now, Mrs. Shapiro, I understand how upset you must be by all of this but it's important to put it behind us now. We're going to go on as a team, for the good of our client."

"How can this be good for O.J.?" my wife asked. "*None* of this is good for O.J. Come on, Johnnie, who do you think you're talking to? I've been a defense attorney's wife for twenty-five years, I know what the rules are. Don't you understand what's happened? Lee can't be trusted—why do you want someone working for your client who can't be trusted?"

From the look on her face and the sound of her voice, it was clear that Cochran was having none of it. She put her hand over the mouthpiece. "He keeps calling me 'Mrs. Shapiro,' " she said to me. "He's really being patronizing, like I'm a child."

"No, I *won't* calm down," she snapped at him. "Johnnie, Bob brought everyone together, he brought you into this case. If you can't understand what this has done to our family, why don't you at least see how bad it is for the case?"

I knew she would get no further than I had.

"Well, Johnnie, as far as I'm concerned, if Bailey stays, then Bob goes. It's just that simple!" And she handed the phone back to me.

"Bob, I know this isn't pleasant, and I really didn't understand that you and your wife felt so strongly about it," Cochran said. "But we have to work together, all of us, for the client. This isn't about you, or Bailey. It's about the client."

"That's the *point*, Johnnie," I said. "It *is* about the client. And this is bad for him."

"I don't want you to leave the case," Johnnie said.

"That's not your call to make," I said evenly. "O.J. Simpson hired me as his attorney. No one else changes that. Most especially Lee Bailey doesn't change that."

"I understand what you're saying," Johnnie said. "We will do what's best for our client."

When I hung up the phone, I turned around to find Linell standing in the doorway looking at me. "I don't believe Johnnie's attitude, why he doesn't see how serious this is. How could he think Bailey staying is good for O.J.?" Then she paused. "Bob, what are you going to do now?" she asked.

"I have no choice. I am committed to defending my client," I said to her. "You just told Cochran you know the rules. Well, one of those rules is that a lawyer cannot quit a criminal case once he's the attorney of record unless the client consents—and this client doesn't. I asked him at the jail if he wanted me out, and he was adamant that he did not. I'm staying, no matter how I feel about Bailey."

Almost a year later, Bill Pavelic told Linell he'd been a silent witness to that phone conversation. "I told Bob you reminded me of a lioness protecting her family," he said. "You really let Cochran have it. I respected you enormously for that."

Bailey stayed. Johnnie Cochran got the self-awarded Nobel Peace Prize for smoothing at least the appearance of troubled waters. Lee and I basically shook hands and went to our corners. There was no kissing and making up. Although he never admitted a thing and has repeatedly denied the charges of leaking, I never forgave him—and don't to this day. There were more leaks, more loose lips, and more tension to come. Why Johnnie and O.J. kept him on the team is a question for them to answer. All I knew was that six months before I had made a commitment to a client, and unless and until he decided otherwise, it was a commitment I meant to honor. We had a trial coming.

Chapter Fourteen

On January 9, Judge Ito announced to the jurors that they would definitely be sequestered. "This is something we all tried to avoid," he told them, "but it's become necessary." They would be staying in a very good hotel, he assured them, and they would be allowed family visits on Wednesdays and weekends. Additional arrangements would be made for their comfort and entertainment during the duration of the trial.

Oddly, this was the first experience with a sequestered jury for the prosecution, the defense, and the presiding judge. While the prosecution had wanted sequestration all along, the defense had taken longer to come around. During jury selection we'd seen and heard the results of the intense press coverage; our concern now was to keep them from hearing the evidentiary motions on domestic-violence evidence and the arguments over what would be admissible on Fuhrman. There was certainly no way to keep either of those issues off the television or out of the papers.

Before the holiday break, it had been my unpleasant duty to tell Dean Gerald Uelmen that after the hearings on the domestic-abuse evidence he would no longer be needed in court by the defense team. "We want a new look," Johnnie had said.

Often during the motion hearings, Uelmen would be criticized for not being forceful enough, for not being strong.

I would try to explain to O.J. that these were complicated legal arguments, argued primarily for the record. "The jury's not here for this, and Gerry isn't putting on a show. Ito's the only audience that counts here, and he respects this attorney." But a decision had been made. Uelmen would prepare the domestic-abuse motions but not present them in court. Maybe Bailey would do it, Johnnie said.

Uelmen was angry. "I'll be damned if I'll be a ghostwriter for Lee Bailey," he said. I agreed and took a firm stance that Gerry should argue these motions. Judge Ito respected him and called him "Dean" until Marcia Clark objected.

Johnnie then played the politician, persuading Gerry to reconsider. In mid-January, Judge Ito heard arguments concerning domestic abuse, and Uelmen appeared for the defense.

Like with most evidence of "prior bad acts," incidents of prior abuse are only rarely admissible in criminal trials because they can carry such a prejudicial weight to a jury. A defendant is only on trial for the particular crime he's been charged with, not for his history, no matter how unacceptable society believes that history to be. Thus Uelmen's motion to the court was to exclude everything the prosecution had asked for. "Where is there any similarity between a bedroom argument in which both parties had been drinking and the argument escalates into a slapping incident—and the slashing of two people's throats on a sidewalk?" he argued.

The prosecution had requested that evidence of fifty-nine separate incidents be admissible, and at one point deputy district attorney Cheri Lewis said the prosecution had added witnesses after reading Faye Resnick's book. Uelmen reacted strongly to that statement. "I find it very alarming that the Bible for the investigation of this case has been a sleazy tabloid book," he said. "My first reaction after reading it was that I wanted to take a shower."

Ultimately, Judge Ito allowed a number of instances into

evidence, including two 911 calls from 1993, a 1985 incident in which the police reported that O.J. broke a car windshield with a baseball bat, and the statements of two neighbors who had called the police to report seeing O.J. standing outside the Bundy apartment and walking back and forth on the sidewalk. When I later cross-examined those neighbors, I felt that we established it was O.J.'s color, not his demeanor, that had alarmed them sufficiently to call the police.

Ito excluded the material that he deemed "hearsay" evidence—in particular Nicole's own writings and what she had reportedly said to her friends—since she could not be cross-examined on these.

After arguing the domestic-abuse motion, Gerry Uelmen returned to teaching, although he graciously consented to come back to the Simpson defense team as needed. From the very beginning of this case, he had been an unsung hero, working in the background, logging in untold hours of research, and taking the majority of the motion work on his shoulders, with the brilliant collaboration of Dershowitz and Sara Caplan. The motions that we won on domestic-abuse evidence were brilliantly written and argued by the Dean. In fact, every motion presented in the case, except for those pertaining to DNA, was researched and written by Uelmen, Dershowitz, and Caplan. When Uelmen left the daily battles of the defense team, he did so with the affection and great respect of those who appreciated what a vital part he had played on O.J.'s behalf.

On January 8, Little, Brown publishers announced that O.J.'s book, *I Want to Tell You*, written with Larry Schiller, would be published in the next couple of weeks, with an initial printing of five hundred thousand. The book was composed mostly of the letters O.J. had received and his responses to them, along with some short autobiographical sketches.

The book had originally been the idea of O.J.'s psychologist, Burt Kittay, and the project had begun the previous fall.

When I first found out about it, I was adamantly opposed to it.
Anything O.J. said in the book, I argued, could open up lines
of inquiry by the prosecution. If he testified, he could be cross-
examined on material in the book, and I thought it might be
especially negative in the event of a second trial.

Skip Taft's reasoning, and he was in a better position to
know than any of us, was that O.J. not only needed the million-
dollar book deal to continue financing the case, but he also
emotionally needed a forum to express publicly what he'd been
telling the defense attorneys for six months. Those reasons notwithstanding, I didn't like it and I never changed my mind. I
saw it only as a significant potential threat to my client.

A few days later, Judge Ito severely limited O.J.'s visiting
privileges. He had abused them, the Judge said, by using the
time to write his book with Larry Schiller.

∞

On January 11, Judge Ito excused two jurors from the panel.
One was a Latina letter carrier who was reportedly in an abusive relationship; the other, the African-American man who had
worked for Hertz.

∞

On January 13, we experienced one of the most difficult and
emotionally charged days we had seen thus far, or would see
throughout the duration of the trial. The defense was arguing
its intention of questioning Mark Fuhrman concerning serious
allegations of racism. It was our contention that his documented
history of racially biased beliefs and behavior impeached Fuhrman's credibility as a key witness for the prosecution, and we
wanted the jury to know this.

Since the trial hadn't yet begun, the jury was not on hand
as Johnnie read aloud to Judge Ito and the prosecution lawyers
some of the background material we'd received on Fuhrman,
which contained repeated use of the word "nigger." Chris Darden, understandably, grew noticeably upset as he listened, and

made strong objection to the *n* word being used in the jury's presence.

"It is the dirtiest, filthiest, nastiest word in the English language," he argued. "It will upset the black jurors. It will issue a test: 'Whose side are you on, the side of the white prosecutors and the white policemen, or are you on the side of the black defendant and his black lawyer? . . . Are you with the man, or are you with the brother?' "

As a black prosecutor in Los Angeles, Christopher Darden had probably faced many difficult challenges, and being named to the Simpson prosecution may have seemed like a mixed professional blessing. Darden, a soft-spoken man, had a reputation for hard work and deep commitment to his job and his beliefs. But his courtroom demeanor, especially when he was riled, gave him the appearance of having a significant chip on his shoulder. He hadn't mastered (if indeed he wanted to) Johnnie Cochran's self-proclaimed adeptness at not ever letting people know what he was thinking and feeling.

Prior to the Simpson case, Darden had viewed Cochran as a role model. However, he had chosen not to emulate him. Once on the prosecution team, Johnnie Cochran claimed that Darden had become an outcast in his own community, and even in his church. Cochran took advantage of that, constantly baiting Darden for prosecuting O.J. Simpson, for being a "pawn" of the district attorney's office. That they should be adversaries in this case—and in particular concerning the use of the *n* word—struck many courtroom observers as a painful irony.

Cochran responded angrily to Darden's remarks about the jury being offended, saying, "African-Americans live with offensive words, offensive looks, offensive treatment every day of their lives. And yet they still believe in this country."

Then Chris Darden fell into the trap of trying to match Cochran's indignation. "O.J. has a fetish for blond-haired white women," he said, "but the prosecution won't bring *that* up at trial because it would inflame the passions of the jury."

At the counsel table, O.J. was teary as he listened, distressed about the use of the word he hated, and about the battle of words and emotions between the two lawyers. He was especially upset about Darden's reference to Nicole. To him, this kind of talk was race-baiting, and it didn't reflect the way he felt about race, or the way Nicole had felt about it. He was even more horrified that it was coming from two educated black men, over a word that typified everything he'd fought to get away from.

Said a shaken Judge Ito, "This is the one main unresolved problem in our society, and for those of us who grew up in the sixties and hoped this would go away, it's a big disappointment to still have to read this stuff."

We heard later that the pressroom had become very quiet after the argument. Although I congratulated Johnnie later on his ability to speak so passionately, I remained upset by the encounter between the two lawyers. I felt that it had somehow turned a legal issue, an evidentiary question, into a street fight. By baiting Darden successfully so early in the trial, Johnnie had established himself as top dog, unarguably a tactical advantage for the defense. Unfortunately, it set Darden and Cochran on a dangerous path that would run between them like a live electric wire throughout the rest of the trial.

On January 20, the judge ruled that he would not ban the use of the *n* word in front of the jury, saying, "When meritorious arguments are raised on both sides, the court must always remember this process is a search for truth and that it depends upon the sound judgment of our jurors."

Assistant district attorney Cheri Lewis had called our motion to examine Fuhrman on the issue of his racial bias a "fishing expedition." Lee Bailey answered, "This fish is hooked, gaffed, and in the boat."

∞

The opening day of the trial finally arrived on Tuesday, January 24, 1995, under a steady drizzling rain, gray skies, and the drone of press helicopters. It was gridlock hell in front of the court-house as everyone assembled for what writer Dominick Dunne had called "the Super Bowl of murder trials."

"This may be one of the most hard-fought legal battles ever," Judge Ito said in his opening remarks to the attorneys at the two tables in front of him. "I anticipate that both sides will spend a lot of time walking on the edge of the legal envelope. Believe me, I'll do everything I can to keep you from going over that edge. I expect to see a demonstration of some fabulous lawyering skills. I also expect to see absolute professionalism."

Chris Darden led off the prosecution's opening statement, almost immediately presenting their theory of an abusive, ob-sessed defendant. "If he couldn't have her," he said of O.J., "he didn't want anybody else to have her." Except for the 1989 incident in which O.J. had plead no contest, the prosecution didn't have much concrete domestic-abuse evidence and Dar-den struggled with weaving a convincing scenario without the facts on hand to support it. At one point during his remarks, O.J. leaned over to me and Johnnie and whispered heatedly, "That's a lie!"

If O.J. was this agitated this early, wanting to counter the prosecution, wanting to go on the defensive, how would he respond to what was to come? We had cautioned him about his demeanor in court, and he was trying to stay focused and calm, but he had received grim news just before we came to court. His friend Bob Chandler was dying.

Marcia Clark's two-hour opening statement was an excellent piece of work. She was calm, understated, and compelling. She told her story simply, using the facts as signposts to guide the jury, and although she made reference to the science, she didn't get bogged down in it. Just as Darden had done, she referred to Nicole as Nicole Brown and to O.J. only as "the defendant." When the pictures of Nicole and Ron's bodies flashed on the big video monitor, there was a collective intake of breath, and then the sound of quiet weeping in the visitors' seats behind us. O.J. averted his face, looking off somewhere in the middle distance. He had never seen the crime-scene photos and had said more than once that he intended never to see them.

Suddenly Ito stopped the proceedings, abruptly dismissing the jury from the courtroom before our opening argument had even begun. He had been told that a Court TV camera had inadvertently televised the face of an alternate juror. Angrily, he delayed the defense's opening, saying that he was of a strong mind to shut the cameras off for good.

I objected in the strongest possible terms, arguing that the prosecution had just spent four hours portraying O.J. Simpson as an abusive monster, and millions of people had watched as they did it. "It would be tremendously unfair for the world to see TV coverage of the prosecution and not our defense."

Saying that he wanted to deliberate, Ito recessed until the following day, when he would let us know his decision. At that time, Cochran would deliver the opening arguments for the defense.

Johnnie had gone over his opening with all of us, and there had been an immediate difference of opinion regarding how far we should go with an affirmative defense—to make a preemptive strike on the prosecution's case. I cautioned him to be careful to speak in general terms, especially when it came to events O.J. might be the only witness to, since the question of O.J. testifying remained open.

I was uncomfortable with some of the time line witnesses that Johnnie planned to mention, Rosa Lopez and Mary Anne Gerchas in particular. In high-profile cases, I've always been skeptical of witnesses who come in late with their stories. Something about Lopez unnerved me. She was a maid for the people who lived next door to O.J., and she was adamant about what she'd seen: O.J.'s Bronco parked out in front of Rockingham, at a time when the police claimed he was at Bundy committing the murders. But she was vague about everything before and after seeing the car, including the month or season her Bronco sighting had occurred. I felt she wouldn't be believable.

At least the next-door proximity made Lopez a natural witness, unlike Mary Anne Gerchas. Gerchas's story was that she'd seen men in knit caps running away from the Bundy crime scene. But when she saw them, she told us, she had been driving around the neighborhood looking at condominiums. In Brentwood at ten P.M. on a Sunday night? That would've been highly unusual. Besides, it wasn't our job to solve the murders, especially with anecdotal evidence from a questionable source.

I suggested that Johnnie be cautious when he raised the problems with the scientific evidence, especially with the invective he used against the L.A.P.D. I wanted him to use our CPA formula; that is, to describe the collection, preservation, and analysis of the forensic evidence and all the missteps along the way. However, Barry Scheck favored using "contaminated, compromised, and corrupted" and Johnnie liked that better. While there were certainly valid questions we could voice about the conduct of a couple of investigating detectives and the police lab personnel, I was against launching our relationship with this jury using a charge of blanket police corruption. "Just lay it out the way it actually happened, and let the jury draw their own conclusions," I suggested.

Johnnie's answer was a return to his now-familiar theme of "I've tried cases for thirty-three years and I know what I'm doing."

The next day, Johnnie delivered his opening statement. Ito had decided to turn the cameras back on, anchored in a fixed position, so that only the attorneys, the judge, and the witnesses could be seen.

O.J. had made a request to speak to the jury as part of the defense's opening statements; that request had been denied, but Ito did rule that he could show the scars on his knee, which would point to his physical inability to leap over the Rockingham fence, or kill two people. The pictures of O.J.'s body taken during Dr. Huizenga's examination, which showed no bruises or signs of a physical struggle, were also shown to the jury. Johnnie described O.J.'s longtime love for and generosity to the Brown family: He had secured the Hertz franchise for Lou, he steered clients to Juditha's travel business, and at one time or another he'd paid college tuition for two sisters and had given money to a third. He referred to this as O.J.'s "largesse."

Johnnie's statement was three hours long, and much of it was riveting. He's a natural-born storyteller, and the jurors were obviously listening carefully. However, he waded into the kind of trouble I'd been concerned about. He put too much emphasis on Lopez and Gerchas and used only fragments of the scientific evidence our experts had worked so hard to interpret and quantify.

He elaborated on the crippling nature of O.J.'s arthritis, in spite of the fact that we knew O.J. had shot an exercise video three weeks before the murders, which the prosecution could (and did) use to undermine that. And as we feared he might do, Cochran scrambled the timeline. When he gave a list of the witnesses the defense would call—witnesses, it turned out, that the prosecution knew nothing about—he made the normally calm Bill Hodgman ripping mad. Ultimately Hodgman objected thirteen times during Johnnie's opening.

"They can't rattle me," said Johnnie, "they can't stop me, and they can't shut me up."

California's reciprocal discovery law (which is relatively recent) mandates that each side turn over to the other any statements or interviews of witnesses that they intend to call. The job of making sure this was done on the part of the defense fell to Carl Douglas and Gerry Uelmen. Uelmen was winding up his daily involvement with the case; thus, the onus was on Douglas.

Hodgman was personally and professionally appalled at what Johnnie had done. We had given them "a myriad of issues" to deal with, he said. He was visibly angry.

As Judge Ito said to the defense attorneys, "How do you suggest I deal with the objections of the prosecution after I succeed in peeling them off the ceiling?"

Ever since the case began I had been criticized very often, especially by the ubiquitous attorney Vincent Bugliosi, for turning over too much material, some of which didn't need to be turned over at all. My reasoning had always been that we had nothing to hide, and our story wasn't going to change, so why not give the prosecution everything?

After Ito suspended the proceedings, I walked over to Bill Hodgman and put my arm around his shoulder, trying to find a way to address the way he was feeling. Hodgman is a great believer in the justice system, a man who truly embodies the expression "public servant," and at that moment he was rigid with anger.

"Bill, why don't you move for a mistrial, and we'll start all over again," I joked.

There was no cajoling him. "Bob," he said intensely, "we really have to sit down and talk."

"You've got to slow down with this," I said, alarmed at the look on his face. "If you don't take care of yourself, you're going to have a stroke."

That night, I was shocked to hear on the news that Hodgman had been hospitalized with chest pains. Earlier that evening, while he and the prosecution were reviewing Johnnie's statements, he was taken by paramedics from the Criminal Court building to Torrance Memorial Medical Center. It wasn't a heart attack, the reporter said; more likely, it was stress and exhaustion, exacerbated by anger.

When we assembled the next morning, I was thinking that we might request a short delay to give Hodgman a chance to recover and come back to court. But O.J.'s position was no more delays, and we supported him in that.

Marcia Clark requested a recess until one-thirty that afternoon. When she came back—the jury was still recessed—she launched the most vicious attack I've ever seen one lawyer hurl at another in a courtroom. On the record, she accused Cochran of activity that could (but would not) be reported to the bar, including deliberate misconduct and taking away forever the People's right to a fair trial. She and Darden said Johnnie had deliberately hidden evidence, was guilty of willful misconduct, and was deserving of sanctions from the court. In return, the prosecution wanted the judge to consider everything from not allowing defense witnesses to testify to reopening the prosecution's opening statements.

Johnnie immediately launched a counterattack, saying that the prosecution had withheld DNA reports and, furthermore, had stopped him from completing his opening statements, which had seriously compromised our case in front of the jury.

Without bringing the jury back in, Ito recessed for the weekend to consider the charges and countercharges. It was clear we were off to a rocky start, and nerves were frayed. Nevertheless, Chris Darden ended the day by saying, "I love the man. He's Johnnie Cochran, he's my idol."

"No offense to Chris Darden," responded Johnnie, "but I hope my wife doesn't love me the way he does."

The next day was a day of odd contrasts and wildly erratic emotions. Court was still in recess; Bob Chandler's valiant battle with lung cancer ended; O.J.'s book, *I Want to Tell You,* was published.

∽

On Monday, January 30, Carl Douglas came back to argue for the defense, and it was the beginning of a pathetic week for us. He began by saying that the discovery law was relatively new, and there was little familiarity with it, and that even though he acknowledged that the withholding of information was his fault—since he was in charge of discovery—exactly how much responsibility we were held to under the law was still being interpreted. The argument was not compelling. The fact of the matter was, we'd made a mistake.

When Ito issued his ruling, it was as harsh as it could be, and handed down in the presence of the jury. He said Cochran had deliberately withheld information, in violation of California law, and as a result Ito was going to allow the prosecution the unprecedented right of reopening their opening statement. It was as egregious an attack on a defense lawyer as I had ever seen by a judge, especially in a case that was being so closely watched all over the world.

When Marcia Clark came back the next day to make her second opening statement, she took Johnnie's statement apart point by point, weakening whatever impact his opening might've had with the jury. To add insult to injury, she refuted Johnnie's references to Mary Anne Gerchas, characterizing her as a "Simpson case groupie." Ultimately, we didn't call Gerchas to the stand.

Johnnie then began his whirlwind TV week, starting out his day on *Good Morning America,* continuing on *Entertainment Tonight,* and ending it with Ted Koppel on *Nightline.* The rest of the defense team got a call that there would be a photo shoot for a *Newsweek* cover at Johnnie's office, a project that O.J. had approved. I reluctantly went to the shoot—the photo was never used—but the reporter, Mark Miller, called me the next day to tell me he'd inadvertently taken our witness list showing which lawyers were going to examine which witnesses. He returned the list and to my knowledge never used the information.

∞

On February 1, Ron Shipp testified. He was a former L.A. cop and self-proclaimed old friend of O.J.'s. In my view, he was more of a hanger-on, a wanna-be. Shipp testified to two things: one, that because of his expertise on domestic abuse, he had counseled O.J. after the 1989 incident, and O.J. had admitted then that he had a tendency to be jealous of Nicole; and two, that on the night of June 13, he and O.J. had a conversation about a polygraph test.

According to Shipp, O.J. had expressed reservations about the test. "Would dreams affect it?" Shipp said O.J. asked. "Because I must tell you honestly, I've had some dreams about killing Nicole."

Shipp testified that he told O.J., "Well, that's something you have to talk to your lawyer about."

In fact, O.J. did talk to me about it and on his behalf, I offered a polygraph to the district attorney's office, on the condition that the results were admissible. They turned down the offer.

Contrary to what Shipp suggested, O.J. was never afraid to take a lie-detector test, although he, like anyone confronted with an unfamiliar science, had some understandable questions about how it worked. In his first statement to the police, he admitted as much. "I've got to understand what this thing is. If it's true blue, I don't mind doing it."

As Carl Douglas was cross-examining Shipp, O.J.'s concern was evident, as he kept turning to me and asking, "Do you like what's happening? Is it going well?"

"O.J., do you want to hear what you want to hear, or do you want to hear my honest opinion?" I asked.

It was a bad cross. Douglas was antagonistic and sarcastic, trying to destroy the witness by repeatedly asking questions—in a loud voice—about his being with a blonde in a Jacuzzi, when Shipp was black and his wife was sitting right there in the courtroom. He even accused Shipp of trying to launch an acting career by giving testimony in the Simpson case.

I didn't like what I was seeing, but Johnnie kept reassuring us. "Carl's doing fine, he's doing exactly what I want him to do. He's tearing him apart." To what end? I wondered. We had plenty of credibility witnesses to come—Fuhrman, Vannatter, the L.A.P.D. lab staff—and we had expert witnesses of our own. If we're going to attack the character of every one of the prosecution's witnesses, I thought, we're in for a very long day in court.

Gerry Spence was quoted in the newspaper as saying Douglas's disastrous cross of Ron Shipp didn't erode Shipp's credibility in the least. "If I was Douglas's father," Spence joked, "I'd take him out in the woods and spank him real good so he'd never do what he did again."

A lawyer must adjust an examination according to the witness's reaction. Put simply, Shipp wasn't believable, and a short and simple cross would've been effective. Had I done it, I would've begun with one question: "Mr. Shipp, have you ever had a dream that didn't come true?" The defense had to get it through to the jury as soon as possible that the prosecution's case was shaky indeed if the time of death was decided by a dog and the motive for murder was based on a dream.

That day, Ito adjourned court early so that I, along with Skip Taft and Bob Kardashian, could attend Bobby Chandler's funeral. We promised O.J. that we would go in his stead. We also did it on our own behalf, to honor Chandler and the kind of man and friend he had been.

∞

Monday, February 1, Brent had the day off from school. I had asked him if he'd like to go to court with me. I was pleased when his response was an enthusiastic yes.

As large as this story was playing in the rest of the country, it was even larger—yet somehow more personal—in Los Angeles. Everyone had an opinion. Linell and I frequently heard from our friends about marital battles occasioned by a husband being on one side and a wife on the other. It was no different for the city's kids, especially for the children of the attorneys. Brent had heard from some of his classmates that things had changed on the defense team. He was aware of the publicity and he was feeling a little protective toward me.

I explained how some of the changes affected me—that although I was responsible for overall strategy and had to be prepared for all the testimony, the real responsibility for the presentation of the evidence wasn't mine now that we were in trial, and I had to be realistic about what that meant.

"And I want you to be nice to Lee," I cautioned him on the way to court. "We're having a business dispute, but it's nothing to do with you. He's still your godfather."

"Oh, I have no problem with being nice to Lee, Dad," Brent said. "I really hate Johnnie Cochran, though."

"Oh, come on," I said. "Johnnie's a very fine lawyer and very important to the team. I want you to be respectful, Brent."

Brent was in a good mood. His hockey team had won the night before, four to one. As he had become more involved with competitive sports, he was learning to take hits, even to lose sometimes, to "play hurt," as O.J. would say.

"Okay," he said, a faint grin on his face. "I'll behave, Dad."

∞

In the weeks leading up to the trial, the other lawyers wanted to know what kinds of questions I was going to ask of the witnesses I would be cross-examining. The question a lawyer asks is dictated by the answer he gets on the question he *previously* asked. The process is somewhat like weaving, in that each thread is connected to the one that comes before it. I've learned that I have to be flexible enough to go with the ebb and flow of a witness, yet focused enough to bring the testimony back to the center.

A lawyer may have a list of specific questions, because of course he's looking for specific information. Even though a judge will instruct a jury that questions are not important, only answers are, it's clear that jurors focus closely on lawyers and their questions and the manner in which those questions are asked. You can't get lost in the narrative, you can't lose the thread, or you fall into the trap of getting an answer that surprises you. In addition, there's the Golden Rule: Don't open up anything in front of the jury that can be used against you in rebuttal.

To me, every witness is evaluated and approached as an individual, relative to his or her specific role in a case, like a piece of the puzzle. Memory is flawed, recollection changes in tiny increments with each telling: A witness whose story plays exactly the same with each telling, like a recorded statement, is often giving a carefully constructed story, not a memory.

Some lawyers use the take-no-prisoners approach, where every witness is an adverse witness and should be discredited. Sometimes it's appropriate; more often, in my opinion, it's not. O.J. was often uncomfortable when a defense attorney unnecessarily took a witness apart. "Why are we beating up on this witness?" he'd ask. "This is an honest person."

In fact, there's a great risk in attacking witnesses, although you'd think, by watching television, that it happens in every courthouse in the country. However, to the jury a harsh attack on a witness often reflects negatively on the lawyer and, by association, his client. When cross-examining a witness, lawyers must be careful to balance the need to impeach that witness with the need to bring out favorable information. A good cross can sometimes turn a witness for one side into a positive witness for the other.

When Johnnie's game plan looked like it was going to involve only attack questioning, I gave serious thought to not doing any of the examinations at all. Alan Dershowitz talked me out of that almost immediately. And so on Friday, February 3, I would be cross-examining the prosecution's star witness, Denise Brown, Nicole's sister.

A defendant sitting in a courtroom is definitely in a Catch-22 position. If he shows his emotions, he's accused of being manipulative. If he's resolutely poker-faced, he's accused of being heartless and cold. And now, with television in the courtrooms, there was an additional reason to be self-conscious. Just as when Shipp was on the stand, O.J. was obviously frustrated by not being able to respond directly and point out errors in the way Denise told anecdotes about his life. He tried to make eye contact with her, and he shook his head whenever she said something he disagreed with.

Under direct examination by Chris Darden, Denise was emotional and teary. Nicole's acquaintance Candace Garvey had testified that at Sydney's dance recital O.J. was talking companionably to his friend Ron Fischman. However, Denise testified that he was alone and angry and looked "scary." She also told of a night when she was with O.J., Nicole, and a group of friends, when O.J. grabbed Nicole's crotch and said, "This is where babies come from, and this belongs to me."

"That's a lie," O.J. said, loud enough to be heard by the visitors in the first row. "I would never say that. Nicole had C-sections."

Denise ended her testimony that day in tears, telling of how in the middle of a fight, O.J. had picked Nicole up and thrown her against the wall. It was a vivid and troubling image, and the prosecution had timed it well: The jury would have the weekend to reflect on it.

From watching her on the stand, I knew Denise was likely to cry at any opportunity, and I didn't want to bring those tears back. The prosecution suspected that I would be tough on her, and they hoped it would backfire on me. They guessed wrong. I didn't want to focus the jury's attention on me as the bad guy striking out at a vulnerable, grieving woman. Nor did I want to give her the opportunity to open a discussion of battered-woman syndrome, or outline her theory of these crimes. So my approach was deliberately soft, understated, respectful. There were some points I needed to make—for instance, that she herself had battled with a substance-abuse problem—but I didn't see a necessity to be cruel when I did it.

Before I cross-examined Denise, I handed the prosecution almost one thousand pages that we had compiled from a database search. The pages contained everything said by and about Denise Brown since her sister's death. I was under no legal obligation to give the material to the prosecution, and I didn't intend to use any of it, but I wanted them to believe that I might. Perhaps they would overprepare her; perhaps it would put them all a little off balance.

When I examined witnesses in the trial, I preferred not to use the center lectern but rather the same one the district attorneys used, an arm's length from the jury. When Darden had finished questioning Denise, he saw me head for the lectern. He turned and deliberately pushed it back against the prosecutor's counsel table and computer equipment, so that I couldn't get behind it and position it.

"Excuse me," I said evenly as we passed each other and the jury looked on, and then I moved the lectern forward again.

The cross-examination went well, as quietly and subtly as I'd hoped, although there was little question that this particular witness would have preferred to be at a beheading: mine. The questioning did nothing to disparage her character, but I managed to reveal factors that might have impaired or skewed her vision or ability to be objective about Nicole and O.J. Primarily, I wanted to emphasize that the physical abuse that Denise witnessed was limited, that at the time it didn't alarm anyone, even her sisters, and that often the incidents she witnessed were during times of considerable intoxication on the parts of all parties.

When I went back to the table, Johnnie said, "Bob, you went too easy on her. What about all the information in the file about her private life? We need to discredit her, and I need something concrete for the closing statement."

"Look," I said to Johnnie, "if you want to ask that kind of question, then you do the recross. It's a bad idea, and it'll open up stuff we don't want to open up."

"O.J.'s the client," Johnnie argued, "and you have to listen to the client."

"I'm the lawyer," I said, "and the client should listen to me."

"Don't be such a baby," said Cochran.

I had come to understand the fundamental difference in our philosophy of client representation. Johnnie always told O.J. what he wanted to hear. My position had always been that the client hired me to be the lawyer. Just as I insisted my client tell me the truth, I was determined to tell him the truth as well. It wasn't always happily received.

Johnnie didn't take me up on my offer to do the recross; I did it. Denise's testimony that O.J. looked scary at the recital, that he looked like a "madman," gave me the opportunity to show the home video that we'd received only two days before from the prosecution. It revealed a smiling and relaxed O.J. after the recital, warmly shaking hands with Lou Brown, hugging his son Justin, and being affectionately kissed good-bye by his former mother-in-law, Juditha, and by Denise herself.

When I got back to the table, I said to O.J., "Look, I'm sorry I got pissed at you, but I can't always make decisions just to please you."

"No problem, Bob," he said. "Sometimes you just have to get in my face."

Chapter Fifteen

On February 7, we lost another juror. That day, the prosecution presented crime scene photographs, including pictures of the two victims that had never been shown outside the courtroom and by court order could not be broadcast by the television cameras. Once again, O.J. looked away.

Police Officer Robert Riske, the first cop on the scene, testified that he arrived at 12:09 A.M. "I called my watch commander and told him we had a double homicide and that O.J. Simpson was somehow involved." He knew this, he said, because he could see a large picture of O.J. inside the house, and when he used the phone in the kitchen (without putting on gloves or dusting for fingerprints) he saw an envelope with O.J.'s name and return address. He then called the detectives.

On cross-examination, Johnnie Cochran elicited information from Riske that showed that the crime scene was improperly secured—no gloves and booties on officers, no dusting for prints. Although if they'd found O.J.'s prints, it would've been no surprise. In his initial statement to police, O.J. told them, "Oh, Christ, I've slept at the house many, many, many times, you know? I've done everything at the house, you know? Roughly, I was in her house maybe two weeks ago, ten days ago."

That day Bill Hodgman returned to work, as the out-of-court case manager of the Simpson trial, and still holding his position as district attorney's director of the bureau of central operations. We would see him in court only sporadically during the trial. I was sorry not to have had him at the prosecution table every day; he was a steadying influence not just to his own team but to all of us.

∞

On February 12, a Sunday, the jury went to view Rockingham and Bundy. Everybody went—the prosecution, the defense, Ito (in a car by himself), O.J. (in a car with deputies), more deputies, and the jury (traveling on a bus with blacked-out windows). This had to rank as one of the strangest field trips any of the participants had ever taken, using the bus and thirteen other vehicles to move from place to place, with citywide security rivaling that of a presidential visit. From beginning to end, the trip went without a hitch, impeccably planned and carried out by Judge Ito and the police and sheriff's departments. I couldn't imagine how much it must have cost to put the expedition together.

When we gathered at the courthouse before leaving, I was met by Gloria Allred, who walked up and handed me some kind of document. The cameras immediately started whirring. "Gloria, did you come all the way here on this Sunday morning to serve a lawsuit on me?" I asked.

It was a request on behalf of the Brown family that O.J. not go into the Bundy residence. However, this had been arranged before Allred's letter. It was not a photo op any of us wanted. Instead, O.J. stayed in the police car about a block away.

Dominique Brown was at Bundy as a representative of her family, and she stood outside, very forlorn and solitary as the jury went through the condominium for two hours. Walking through the rooms four at a time, the jurors were very solemn. They didn't make eye contact with any of us, and no one was allowed to talk, although some jurors took notes. The apartment was silent and empty, and it was difficult to shake off the feeling of melancholy after everyone had left.

By contrast, O.J.'s home was decorated with fresh flowers and family portraits and was filled with a sense of life. His Heisman trophy was on display, and the children's rooms were bright and cheerful, as though they'd just been there. It gave a radically different impression from the starkness at Bundy. "You might've made a mistake bringing them here," I said to Scott Gordon, one of the young prosecutors who'd come along.

O.J. was happy to be at Rockingham, in spite of the fact that his constant companions were members of the sheriff's department and the L.A.P.D. He went through the house in much the same way the jurors did, looking closely at the mementos, stopping occasionally to take it all in. "Who would give all this up?" he scoffed. "Who would jeopardize this kind of life, this kind of family?"

He pointed out the play area he and Nicole had designed for the children, with its swing set and a large sandbox. "That's where I practiced my golf swing," he said.

∽

On Monday, I learned from Carl Douglas that Johnnie had decided Lee Bailey would cross-examine Mark Fuhrman. I was surprised about this, telling him that surely nothing could've been more powerful than a black man asking a white officer whether he had any racial bias, or asking if he'd ever used the term "nigger."

But Carl said that Johnnie didn't want to examine Fuhrman because "he didn't want to have blood on his hands or get a negative reaction from the community." Cochran had had an uncomfortable run with publicity lately. There had been a rash of tabloid stories about his personal life and his relationships. He was cautious about making moves or taking steps that could be misinterpreted or exaggerated in the press.

I had the same response to headlines about Johnnie's private life as I did to headlines about mine: It was none of anybody's business who we were when we weren't in a courtroom. Let them hack away at our strategy or our presentation or even our wardrobes if they wanted. Our private lives should have been left alone.

∞

On February 16, O.J. talked all during Marcia Clark's examination of Detective Ron Phillips. Johnnie would do the cross the next day. Phillips testified that the police had spent the better part of an hour looking for O.J.'s phone number, when Nicole's phone had a speed-dial button clearly marked "Daddy."

There were many sidebars during that session, and too much off-the-record yakking, with Judge Ito steadily growing more impatient. I was wearing a pin on my suit lapel that said "sidebar" with a line drawn through it. I had little hope of it being taken literally. Each day seemed longer than the one before it, and we were still early in the process.

Typically, I'd arrive home a little before seven P.M., unless we had a meeting after court. If one of the kids had an ice-hockey game, I'd feel guilty for not being able to go; if they each had one, Linell had to figure out how to be in two places at one time and would head off in two different directions. If there were no ice-hockey or social obligations (and those had been severely reduced once the trial began), I'd try to take a quick nap, box from eight to nine-thirty, and have a light supper with my wife. Then I'd review the day, check my messages from my office, prepare for the next day's witnesses, and head for bed just after midnight. Luckily, I was able to go to sleep instantly during this time, because it was as close to a competitive training schedule as I've ever been on, and insomnia would've just about killed me.

When we came back for Ron Phillips's second day of testimony, I found that although he was present in court, he'd spent the previous night at the hospital, with chest pains. He'd had a bypass the year before, and even his cardiologist had advised him not to get on the stand this morning. Marcia Clark suggested that we all go easy on him because of his heart condition, and the fact that we'd basically put him in the hospital the night before.

"Marcia, you've had him on the stand for a day and a half," Johnnie said. "If you want him off, stop asking questions."

"Are you sure you're all right?" I asked Phillips.

"I'm fine," he answered. "I have to do my job, and this is part of it. I appreciate your asking, though."

Johnnie's cross of Phillips was relatively gentle. Although he'd been Mark Fuhrman's partner, and was with him during the crucial early hours of June 13, there was no point in telegraphing our strategy. We were willing to save the fireworks until later.

It appeared we were going to lose another juror, Michael Knox. When he'd worn a San Francisco '49ers' jacket on the field trip to Bundy and Rockingham, I thought that alone would get him kicked off the panel, but Judge Ito had found that he had been negotiating for a book, and reportedly had told someone on the jury that an acquittal would guarantee more money. In addition, there was some concern that he'd once been arrested for spousal abuse, which he hadn't disclosed on his questionnaire.

The judge had requested Knox's divorce file to see if it referred to this incident. When Marcia Clark said "I wouldn't want anyone to see my divorce file," Judge Ito quipped "It's too late, Marcia, they already have."

We'd heard that one or more television stations had hired lip-readers to watch O.J. in court and report on what he said at the counsel table. They reported that when the blue cap found at Bundy was entered into evidence, O.J. smiled. His friends had always joked about the enormous size of his head. "That cap wouldn't fit me," he said.

"No cap would," I joked.

The term for what fighters or ball players do when they bait each other during the game, using profanity and personal insults, is "talking shit" or "talking trash." In all my years in court—and all my hours at the gym—I had never heard more trash-talking than what constantly took place between Cochran and Darden, especially at sidebar conferences.

"You're an embarrassment, you'll never be allowed back in the neighborhood," Johnnie would say to Chris.

"I wouldn't even want to go into your neighborhood," Chris would answer.

"Can I get the rights to these outtakes?" I once asked Judge Ito.

"That's what I like about you, Bob," Ito said, laughing. "You're always thinking."

On February 22, Chris Darden examined Detective Tom Lange; for the following two days, Johnnie did the cross. Ito gave him a tremendous amount of leeway, allowing him to ask very detailed questions on police procedure. The jury heard two key details from Lange: that plastic bags weren't immediately put on Nicole's hands to preserve trace evidence, and that the coroner didn't arrive at the scene for ten hours.

At one point, Cochran asked Lange about Sydney Simpson's statement to the police that "Mommy was talking to her best friend and crying." We suspected this was a reference to Faye Resnick, who had been staying with Nicole recently and had gone into a drug rehab a few days before the murders.

Clark immediately went to a sidebar, saying, "The only witness for that is Sydney, and she's not on your witness list."

"Well then, I'll put her on," Johnnie said.

"You know you're not going to call her," Marcia scoffed. "O.J. would *never* let you call her."

"I'm running this case, I'm going to do what I want," Cochran snapped. "And if you people were real lawyers, you'd stick to trying your own case."

That got to Darden. "He thinks he's the only lawyer in the world, Judge," he said angrily. "Well, he's not."

"Mr. Darden, stop now," Ito warned him.

"He's out of line, Judge," argued Darden, "and you shouldn't allow this."

"I've warned you," Ito said carefully, "and I'll warn you again, Mr. Darden. If this continues, I'll hold you in contempt."

"Go ahead and hold me in contempt," Darden said.

Ito dismissed the jury. "Now take three deep breaths, Mr. Darden, and calm down," he said after they'd gone. "And then come back when you can make an appropriate statement to the court."

Darden adamantly refused to apologize. Marcia Clark came back to plead on his behalf, but Ito wouldn't hear it. "If you're his lawyer, fine. If he wants another lawyer, fine. But I invite him to settle this quickly with a simple apology, or he'll find himself in contempt. Those are his choices."

Everybody was always fighting for the last word, rather than the most effective one, and Clark was the worst offender. If a ruling went against her, she'd continue to argue, until Ito would use a version of his increasingly familiar "That's *enough*, Miss Clark!" This time even Bill Hodgman got involved, and the three prosecuting attorneys stood talking together for a few moments. Finally, Darden gave in and apologized to the judge; Ito, in turn, apologized to Darden. The press reacted like it was the most important moment of the trial so far. I assured the reporters that it had absolutely no substantive effect whatsoever, and we needed to move on.

We didn't get much more accomplished with Lange that day, since the prosecution was constantly interrupting. Cochran continued to bait both lawyers; Clark responded by trying to laugh him off, Darden by making more tense and angry objections. While Ito had made it clear that he wasn't going to tolerate disrespect for the bar, it looked like he was going to allow the defense as much latitude as the prosecution in dealing with witnesses. For a judge with a pro-prosecution history, that was a pleasant surprise.

Gil Garcetti had announced to the press that even if the jury came with an eleven-to-one hung jury for acquittal, he'd retry the Simpson case. I was sure that if that happened, the prosecution wouldn't want us all standing again in front of this judge.

∞

Rosa Lopez, constantly harassed by the press, kept saying she was going to go home to her native El Salvador. On February 23, the day before she was scheduled to appear, we discovered that she'd evaded the Pinkerton guard we had hired to keep an eye on her and was nowhere to be found. I never believed she was key to our case, and I didn't relish the idea of how we'd look if a much-touted witness simply evaporated.

For days, Lopez had alternately begged and threatened to leave. Judge Ito could have ordered her to stay, but the only way he could actually prevent her from leaving was to put her in jail, which none of us wanted to happen. On the scheduled day, Lopez arrived in court. Since she was a witness for the defense, her testimony would ordinarily not have taken place this early in the trial. However, it was agreed that she could testify out of order and that her testimony would be conditional—that is, it would be videotaped and not shown to the jury unless and until the defense attorneys decided it was strategically wise. This was very important for us, since it allowed Lopez to testify under oath, but absent the jury. We could evaluate her testimony, decide if it hurt or helped, and then make the determination as to whether or not we would put her on in front of the jury.

If it hadn't been such a difficult session, it could almost have been described as comical. Lopez didn't understand the adversarial nature of the procedure and became very emotional when she was being cross-examined by Chris Darden. One moment it appeared she understood English; the next moment she would fall silent and look to the Spanish-speaking translator for her cue. Although our investigator Bill Pavelic had worked with her, trying to help her understand and negotiate the process, she constantly fell back on a truculent "I don't remember" whenever she felt Darden was pushing her.

The cross-examination had to be continued through to the following Monday, since Marcia Clark said she had child-care problems that Friday afternoon. Lopez argued that she couldn't come back on Monday; she'd made an airline reservation to leave the country immediately.

While Lopez was still in the courtroom, prosecutor Cheri Lewis checked and found that no reservation had been made, at which point Chris Darden challenged Lopez on the lie. He had her on the ropes.

Lopez had contradicted herself numerous times, and her credibility was impeached. But the judge wanted to protect himself against reversible error and didn't want her to leave without being cross-examined further. Thus the continuation—which gave the defense the weekend to work more with Lopez. She came back on Monday with different clothes and, for a few minutes, a somewhat different attitude. Still her demeanor was a potential disaster, and we wisely never allowed her testimony to be heard by the jury.

We deserved to lose Lopez, and the prosecution was right to go after her the way they did. It turned out that Bill Pavelic had taped a session with Lopez, and we'd never turned it over to the prosecution in discovery. At this, Marcia Clark went completely ballistic. "Their conduct has become so egregious!" she stated angrily, and asked for the appropriate sanctions.

Since I was at the time of the interview the lead lawyer of the team, I took complete responsibility. I told Judge Ito, "I am responsible for everything that happened at that time." However, Ito found that Lopez had been the responsibility of Cochran and Douglas, who were each fined one thousand dollars for not reporting Bill's audiotaped interview with Lopez. When Johnnie pointed out that a fine of that size had to be reported to the state bar association, Ito reduced it to $950.

The Lopez episode concerned me greatly. It was becoming clear that Cochran and Douglas did not take as conservative a view of the discovery laws as I did. And it was rumored that Lopez had been paid money for her testimony, which I didn't believe was true.

Always in the back of our minds, from the very beginning, was the possibility of a second trial, either because of a hung jury or a conviction followed by an appeal. We had to be aware of the public perception not just of O.J. but of his defense lawyers. In a second trial, impaneling a jury would be harder than it was the first time, getting a favorable verdict would be tougher, and out-strategizing the prosecution would be daunting. Anything that made us look unprofessional would hurt us in the short run; it could do even more damage in the long run.

Ever since the debacle with Bailey, the press seemed to equate Johnnie's larger public role as a demotion for me. Whenever O.J. saw something regarding the situation in the papers, he said to me, "These guys don't realize that this was our plan all along, especially after we got this jury—that you were going to hand the ball off and Johnnie would run with it."

In fact, Johnnie was taking more control in strategy, and in the media. Had it been up to me, there would've been no statements, no television interviews, no print interviews, nothing to increase or intensify the white light of scrutiny we were already under. I raised objections where I could, and tried to pick my fights. As I watched Johnnie take over, I often remembered the football analogy. I'd thought that the quarterback—me—would run the team. But obviously, O.J. identified with the guy who was playing *him*—that is, Cochran.

∞

On March 1, Michael Knox was dismissed from the jury. The following day, the papers were full of the story that Marcia's ex-husband, Gordon Clark, had filed suit for full custody of their two little boys. At Marcia's request, the Superior Court judge ordered the records of the proceedings sealed. It was difficult not to feel compassion for her. She was working long and hard days on a case she was obviously committed to. At the same time, she had to undergo this personal struggle in public view.

∞

On March 9, Detective Mark Fuhrman took the stand as another star witness for the prosecution, and a suddenly charming Marcia Clark treated him like he was a poster boy for apple pie and American values. He had never been alone during the entire first morning of the investigation, he told her earnestly, except when he was taking notes. Bill Pavelic believed that he hadn't taken contemporaneous notes but rather had carefully—and neatly—crafted his report much later, to support his version of those events. Fuhrman had never planted evidence, he said, and he had never, ever made racist slurs. Everyone in the courtroom was aware that the eyes of every single juror were on Mark Fuhrman.

When Bailey cross-examined Fuhrman a few days later, he asked Fuhrman if he had ever, in the past ten years, used the *n* word. Fuhrman answered that he had absolutely never done so. Bailey reworded and repeated the question; Fuhrman answered it exactly the same way. Then Bailey went over the top. He vowed to call Max Cordoba, he told Fuhrman.

Maximo Cordoba, a black former marine, was ready to get on the stand and testify that Fuhrman had called him a nigger. "I've spoken to him on the phone, marine to marine," Bailey asserted. That night *Dateline NBC* broadcast an interview with Cordoba in which he claimed he'd never spoken to Bailey.

An angry Clark then asked Judge Ito to cite Bailey for contempt. "As an officer of the court he has lied to this court," she raged. "He was impeached by his own witness."

Bailey jumped up, red-faced and angry. "I object, Your Honor," he said. "Either put Cordoba on the stand or stop her from testifying."

Judge Ito told Bailey and Clark to make some apologies, ordering them not to "engage in gratuitous personal attacks upon each other." Even Lee's mother got into the act; she called him on the phone later and told him to "lay off Marcia Clark."

The next day, again talking to *Dateline,* Cordoba "remembered" that he'd talked to Bailey and that he recalled "in a dream" that Fuhrman had called him a nigger. Cordoba was never called; neither the prosecution nor the defense was interested in having a witness testify to more dreams.

I knew that O.J. always viewed himself as a gentleman, and he felt things should be done in a gentlemanly way. He had locked his jaw at the word "nigger" and he felt that Bailey's attack had been about ego, that discrediting Fuhrman seemed to be more about Bailey's needs than about O.J.'s. "I've got ten witnesses to refute Fuhrman!" Bailey kept insisting.

"Do we need that many?" O.J. asked him quietly. "Why not use one good one?"

The consensus seemed to be that Bailey did little or no harm to the prosecution's witness. In fact, by pressing as hard as he did, Bailey may even have made Fuhrman look sympathetic. As one reporter phrased it: "Fuhrman managed to elude capture."

"The last roar of the lion," wrote David Margolick of the *New York Times,* "was really more of a meow."

It was clear to me that when Mark Fuhrman said he hadn't used the *n* word in ten years, nobody on the jury believed him. Bailey's continued use of the word over and over did nothing but heighten racial tension both inside and outside the courtroom, and it was completely unnecessary. We knew we had several civilian witnesses who could damage Fuhrman's testimony; we didn't know at this point that there would come another witness who, with Mark Fuhrman's own words and voice, would make him and his testimony look absolutely grotesque.

On March 17, juror Tracy Kennedy was dismissed because it was discovered that he, too, was preparing a book. He had denied to Judge Ito that he had compiled a list of jurors' names. When the bailiffs, with Kennedy's permission, examined his personal computer and discovered juror information in the disk storage, Kennedy said, "Oh, I thought I got rid of that." In his book, published some months later, Kennedy reported that he'd suffered great depression both while on the jury and after his release, and in fact he'd attempted suicide.

He was replaced by Anise "Ann" Aschenbach, an alternate we had some uneasiness about. She had once sat on a criminal trial, was the sole jury member to vote for conviction, and had managed by sheer force of will to turn the whole jury around.

Earlier that morning, which was St. Patrick's Day, the police disarmed—i.e., blew up—what they believed to be a pipe bomb, which had been left in a newspaper rack outside the courthouse. Near it was a note reading "Fenians Arise," which pointed to some kind of link to Irish terrorists—a nice St. Patrick's Day touch.

Ironically, the explosive device had been discovered by my driver, Keno Jenkins, who spotted it when he went to buy a paper, and then alerted the police on the car phone. Some days truth really is stranger than fiction.

One day in court, I wore a blue-ribbon lapel pin signaling support for the Los Angeles Police Department. It had been given to me two weeks before by Dennis Zine, the president of the Police Protection League. I'd been wearing it off and on since I got it, but nobody noticed—or objected—until the day I cross-examined Detective Philip Vannatter.

Since the trial began, Vannatter's appearance had been scheduled and rescheduled, which gave me time to study everything he'd said so far. And he'd said a lot. There were his investigative reports, for one. In addition, he'd testified at the grand jury, at the preliminary, and at the hearing on our motion to suppress evidence, when Ito found on the record that Vannatter had "engaged in a reckless disregard for the truth."

Phil Vannatter was a seasoned detective as well as a shrewd, cagey, experienced witness. He liked to look jurors in the eye, to make a connection with them while he proved that he knew what he was doing.

No one does a job perfectly. People forget rules or they take shortcuts to get the job done. The best witnesses are those who acknowledge this and tell it like it is. "Did you make mistakes?" the lawyer asks. "You bet I did," says the smart witness, the implication being that everybody makes mistakes. The jury is full of human beings who understand that very well. It's when you try to justify a position that is not justifiable that you get into trouble.

I had no bombs to drop on Vannatter, no sweeping moment of impeachment. Just a few, simple questions, which he could not and did not answer to my satisfaction. Why was so much time spent at Rockingham, at the expense of the Bundy crime scene? Was there a rush to judgment, a decision in the early morning hours of June 13 that O.J. Simpson was absolutely, positively, irrefutably the murderer? And why, when O.J. Simpson's blood was drawn minutes away from the police laboratory on June 13, did Vannatter then carry it in his pocket for three hours?

The detective contended that he was following procedure by delivering the blood directly to the criminalist, Dennis Fung, at the crime scene. It was my hope that the jury heard his contention with some skepticism.

In contrast to Detective Tom Lange, whose demeanor had been stoic and whose answers had been direct, Phil Vannatter's attempt to outthink me—in combination with a visible reddening of his face when he was challenged—enabled me to present him to the jury as someone whose credibility was flawed. He was the kind of old-school cop who was too impatient to go by the book, who believed even as he shaded the truth that the end justified the means. He wasn't beyond adjusting or tailoring his testimony to make evidence, and his behavior, look better than it actually was, and I had to get the jury to see that.

That night, Linell told me she felt sorry for Vannatter and was disappointed in me for the way I'd cross-examined him. He was a decent, hard-working cop, she said, whom I'd made to look much worse than he was. Maybe he was an old school cop who bent the rules now and then, maybe he was a little loose with the truth. But he was hardly in the same league as Fuhrman.

As for Tom Lange, I always figured that he didn't take it personally. We both had our jobs to do, and like me, Lange had been around long enough to know that that's the way the system works. Actually, I liked him. In fact, Lange is the kind of man I could sit down and have a drink with. Whether he'd want to have a drink with me is another question.

Ever since the beginning of this case, my younger son, Grant, and his friends had been fascinated with Kato Kaelin. There was something benign and nonthreatening about Kato. Linell said he was kind of like a Barney for the preteen set.

She had tried to keep the more grisly information about the case from the boys, but now Grant wanted to come to court for my cross-examination of Kato. I assured Linell that there wasn't likely to be anything brutal either spoken or seen in the courtroom during that session.

Grant came to court on March 21, but Marcia Clark's direct examination went long, and my cross wasn't scheduled until the next day. I took Grant back to meet Judge Ito, who spent fifteen minutes talking with Grant alone in his chambers. When Grant told him he had to go back to school the following day, Ito said, "You should see your dad work, Grant." He then issued and signed a "court order" to Grant's teacher, requesting that he be given permission to take the following day off from school to attend court.

Back the following day, Linell and Grant sat next to Carmelita Simpson-Durio, O.J.'s sister. Carmelita, a warm, strong woman, had managed the delicate task of being supportive to her brother while still maintaining her close relationship with Nicole's family. During a break in court, she said to Linell,

"Don't think that Dale Cochran [Johnnie's wife] hasn't noticed how that Marcia Clark and Johnnie flirt. She told him to cut that out!"

As Linell sat there with Grant beside her, Lee Bailey turned around at the defense table, and they made eye contact. Caught off guard, Linell made a slight gesture of greeting. She told me later that he "stared a hole through my eyes," turned his back, and refused to acknowledge them the rest of the session. It was hard for Grant not to notice the snub. "Why is he acting that way to you, Mommy?" he asked.

"He's very busy, Grant, just ignore it," Linell responded.

I've always assumed that people have integrity and are worthy of my trust until I'm proven wrong. Linell is more cautious, more of a skeptic than I am, and she doesn't give her trust easily. Once that trust is betrayed, for her it's over. That day, she decided not to come back for any more of the trial. "I can't stand to sit behind the defense table anymore," she told me.

Chapter Sixteen

On Wednesday, April 5, juror Jeannette Harris was dismissed, because allegedly she'd once been shoved by her husband, which constituted abuse and which she hadn't disclosed on her questionnaire. Her replacement was Brenda Moran, the juror who would be so outspoken the day after the verdict was announced.

Jo-Ellan Dimitrius had been convinced that Harris was one of our most sympathetic jurors. In fact, when Harris spoke with the press, she told them that she didn't believe the jury would vote for conviction. To date, six jurors had been excused; of those, three were black, one Latina, one part Native American. With the jury sequestered, their names a tightly guarded secret, how could these anonymous tips keep coming in about their conduct or their history, some of it going back many, many years? After Harris was excused, we requested an evidentiary hearing. We wanted to know how the anonymous complaints about these jurors were being forwarded to the judge, and who the tipsters were. The hearing was denied.

A few days before Harris was dismissed, a female juror alternate asked to speak privately to the judge. The judge asked one lawyer from each side to attend. Cochran attended for us, Marcia Clark for the prosecution.

It turned out that the juror, an attractive woman with long blond curly hair and an air of glamour, felt she was being shunned by the black jurors and criticized for her fashion, for her attention to her appearance. Due to her answers in voir dire and the fact that she was married to a black man in the L.A. fire department, we had thought she would work well with the black jurors. Now, Jo-Ellan Dimitrius was speculating on the possibility that the jurors were unconsciously viewing her as a Nicole substitute.

Ito asked her to stay on, knowing that he would be excusing Jeannette Harris within days, and not wanting to lose her if he could help it. She said she would do her best.

Once Harris had been excused, she went immediately on television and reported what we'd been suspecting: There was a split in the jury. She hastened to add that she didn't mean in voting, because of course there was to have been no discussion of the trial itself. She meant in friendships, or tension in the absence of friendships. I didn't expect or welcome jury bonding at this point; this jury still had a lot of work and deliberation ahead of them. But a schism this early might be difficult to repair, and might influence jurors to vote for or against *each other* rather than for or against the defendant. In addition to the interjury tensions, Harris reported that some of the guards from the sheriff's office were being unkind to black jurors and showing favor to the white ones. Since we hadn't heard this from anyone else, we dismissed it.

The day after Harris was excused, we arrived to find there would be no court that day. Two jurors were sick with the flu, one of them actually hospitalized, on an intravenous line for dehydration. Later that day, a third juror fell ill with the flu. This trial seemed to have a penchant for sending people to the hospital.

∞

Since the heart of our DNA strategy was to attack the L.A.P.D.'s collection and contamination of the evidence, a key moment for the defense was Barry Scheck's cross-examination of criminalist Dennis Fung. I was amazed to remember that only months before, I'd been unenthusiastic about Scheck's pugnacious, hard-edged courtroom style. In short order, Scheck got Fung to admit that he actually hadn't performed many of the procedures he'd claimed to have done in the preliminary hearing; the trainee, Andrea Mazzola, had done them. Fung didn't want anyone to know that someone so inexperienced was handling key evidence.

This was only Mazzola's second case, and here she was collecting important DNA evidence at a critical stage in the "case of the century," making textbook errors that were caught on a news video. She didn't change rubber gloves between blood samples, and the video recorded her touching the ground with supposedly "clean" gloves.

Fung had other problems. Evidently Tom Lange had ordered that Nicole's body be shielded from press and onlookers, so it was covered with a white cotton blanket from the Bundy apartment. It may have been an act of consideration, but scientifically, it was a significant mistake. Since the blanket had been in her house, and had presumably come in contact with Nicole, O.J., the children, the animals, and any number of other people, there was now a serious question of cross-contamination. Scheck ran a video that showed Fung handling evidence with his bare hands, rather than with gloves, as he'd stated. "There, how about *that*, Mr. Fung?!" Scheck said with relish.

The challenge rang in the courtroom, and some of the jury members leaned forward to get a better look at the video. "Is that a question, Mr. Scheck?" asked Judge Ito.

There were a number of questions concerning the whereabouts of the vial of O.J.'s blood that Detective Vannatter had taken from downtown to the crime scene. Fung had previously testified that Vannatter brought it to Bundy in a gray envelope, whereupon Fung took custody of it. He later amended his testimony to say perhaps he could've carried it out in his hand, or put it in a paper bag, or put it in his lab kit, called a "posse."

However, when he saw the videotape, he realized that none of those three things happened. First Vannatter arrived, and moments later, Andrea Mazzola carried out a garbage bag. Without knowing the answer, the defense didn't want to ask, "What's in the bag, Mr. Fung?" Judge Ito asked the question for us, and after a moment's hesitation, Fung answered, "I think it's the blood vial."

Fung had asked the cops for a plastic bag, and they'd supplied it from who knows what sources. He put the blood vial in it, and Mazzola, without being told what was in the bag, put it in the front seat of the evidence truck, where it sat until Fung drove off.

If Scheck's cross had been a fight, it would have been stopped as a technical knockout. If it were a horse race, the animal would've been shot out of humane considerations. In fact, during a break, Judge Ito said to Scheck, "You'd better be careful, you're getting close to being reported to the Humane Society for cruelty to indefensible witnesses."

Like a good boxer, Scheck homed in one jab at a time, and the cross put a litany of errors into the record. The jury heard about the blanket error (covering Nicole's body); the fact that trainee Mazzola, not Fung, collected the blood samples; the possible degradation of blood samples left sealed in plastic baggies in the truck. Fung didn't see or record blood evidence found in the car; he didn't inventory blood samples, and he later left them vulnerable to tampering in an unlocked storage cabinet. He confirmed that Vannatter carried blood from place to place, which was unprecedented in his experience. He acknowledged the July 3 pictures of the gate, which showed blood that hadn't been evident on June 13, and conceded that he didn't see blood on the socks until weeks later, which raised the question: When did it get there?

Afterward, one lawyer commented, "They'll probably rewrite all of the L.A.P.D. lab procedures and call it the *Barry Scheck Memorial Manual.*"

During the Fung testimony, we were momentarily interrupted when frequent court visitor and cross-dresser Will B. King was removed by the bailiffs. He was screaming at another court visitor who had supposedly sat on his dress. Said an impatient Judge Ito, "Eject that m . . . wom . . . person!"

On April 17, Hank Goldberg was faced with the unenviable task of "rehabilitating" Dennis Fung. Goldberg was tall, lanky, pale, and all business. He and Scheck glared daggers throughout the whole examination, constantly objecting and interrupting each other. Ito grew noticeably angry with the constant back-and-forth on the redirect and the recross, with Goldberg at one point accusing Barry of trying to have "a Perry Mason moment." As effective as Scheck had been, after this session neither he nor Peter Neufeld was ever cut much slack by the judge.

After Fung's testimony, I offered a fortune cookie to writers Dominick Dunne and Joe McGinniss, joking that they were from the Hang Fung Restaurant. It was an off-the-cuff flip remark that showed up as a lead news story. "Shapiro is a bigot," was the upshot, and the bad reaction lingered for days.

I arrived at court one morning to be greeted by an Asian protestor in a black hat, with a sign in Chinese characters. I got out of the car and started to walk up to him, when Jim Amarino, the head of L.A.P.D. security for the courthouse, came running over to me, quite concerned. Amarino, his colleague Laurie Taylor, and the other L.A.P.D. officers responsible for my security had always gone out of their way to protect me and were especially considerate to my wife and sons whenever they attended the trial. This was ironic, given that while they were taking care of me outside the courtroom, inside I was attacking a couple of their L.A.P.D. colleagues. It was out of gratitude for their care that I continued to wear the blue police support pin on my lapel in the courtroom.

This particular day I told Amarino that I wanted to speak to the protestor. With a shocked grin on his face, he went over to the Asian gentleman and respectfully asked if he could pat him down for security. The man nodded. I then went up and introduced myself to him, apologized for my bad joke, and we spoke together for a few minutes. I invited him to join me for lunch that afternoon, but when I came down to look for him during the break, he wasn't anywhere to be found.

In the days to come, I learned that my fortune-cookie remark had done damage that I deeply regretted. I made a formal apology to Dennis Fung and his family in open court and published a letter of apology to the Asian community, which was graciously accepted. I later addressed numerous Asian groups and gave scholarship money and donations to an Asian charity. Cochran, who afterward quipped "We're having Fung now," never apologized to anyone, for anything.

By the time he'd been through a direct examination, a cross, a redirect, a recross, and, I think, one last round, Dennis Fung had spent a torturous eight days on the stand. We'd heard that before coming to testify, he'd told his colleagues that he'd been a fan of O.J. and hoped the football hero wasn't involved in this crime. Fung certainly couldn't have predicted what happened to him at the hands of one of the Simpson lawyers. When at last it was all over, one of the more bizarre moments in the whole trial occurred. On his way out of the courtroom, Fung stopped at the defense table and shook hands with O.J. and the whole team. It not only made the papers, it led to an immediate investigation of court security. The deputies were unnerved that in mere seconds, someone had come that close to the defendant.

∞

In mid-April, Cochran arranged a lunch meeting in the courthouse for himself, Chris Darden, Marcia Clark, and me. His purpose, he said, was "to find a way for us all to act more professional." Johnnie's wife, Dale, delivered lunch, setting up china and silver on the linen tablecloth and serving an excellent fish dish, with rice, peas, and potatoes.

It was an oddly wonderful hour. The four of us joked and talked; and the meeting was more like a gathering of old friends than a detente among adversaries. Whether we liked each other or didn't, whether our styles clashed or our views differed, we were all in this together. We agreed that we had to cooperate in finding ways to speed things up, cut the sidebars, and reduce the rhetoric. We had no way of knowing at that point, of course, that we were barely halfway through the trial.

∞

Judge Ito had decided, after Jeannette Harris's dismissal, to interview the remaining jurors, with both prosecution and defense attorneys present. He wanted to discover if the charges of racial animosity were true. It was clear that some antagonism was boiling up: We'd heard about a kicking incident, a hitting incident in the video room, and a tripping incident in the jury box. Ito wanted to do what he could to keep the panel intact, in good spirits and good faith, until the trial was over.

While Ito conducted these interviews, four of us—Cochran, myself, Marcia Clark, and Chris Darden—sat on a small couch in his chambers. Our quarters in court were close; these were even closer. The judge's clerk, Deirdre Robertson, was there also. She had become a good friend to all the jurors and had heard many of the negative stories directly.

The jurors, considering their living conditions, were faring better than I would have expected. The pressure of doing everything together and having nothing in common except the trial—and they couldn't even acknowledge that—had to be very, very difficult to bear. For more than three months, these people had been separated from their jobs and families, completely isolated from their lives and what was going on in the world. They were like astronauts, except astronauts train for this kind of isolation and have a pretty good idea about when they're going to land.

We came to the end of the interviews not as worried about what had gone wrong with them as we were in awe of what they were doing each day. It was clear, however, there were going to be more problems if the trial dragged on much longer.

∞

Immediately after the Dennis Fung testimony and the interviews with the jurors, we had some unscheduled time off, due
to the Oklahoma City bombing disaster on April 19. When we
returned, the security at the courthouse had been intensified,
and we were requested to come directly into court, not linger
outside with press or admirers.

We had had previous bomb threats at the courthouse. Each
lawyer, on both sides, had received threatening mail. But we
had dismissed those threats. "They're all just nuts," we'd say.
Now, all of those people so tragically murdered in Oklahoma
had been the victims of exactly the same kind of "nuts" we'd
been hearing from. It was a sobering, sorrowful thought.

∞

With the hits the prosecution was taking on collection and contamination of DNA evidence, they began to mount a broader
DNA argument. Rockne Harmon, the prosecution's DNA expert imported from Northern California, showed up as we prepared to head into the technical phase of DNA testimony.

Rock Harmon is a quintessential prosecutor. Even if he
wanted to, he probably couldn't function well as a defense lawyer. A graduate of Annapolis and a Vietnam veteran, he is a
true believer in absolute right and absolute wrong. To Harmon,
those on the side of right are prosecutors; the rest of us sit at
the right hand of the devil.

Harmon is known as an intimidating opponent to others in
his field of forensics, and has a reputation for attacking his peers
personally if their views differ from his—which by his lights
are absolutely, scientifically correct. His courtroom style, which
could be described as energetically abrasive, was effective. In
fact, as different as they seemed in background and style, Harmon was cut from the same cloth as Barry Scheck. The two of
them often went at it with their hands very close to each other's
throats. They didn't like each other, they didn't trust each
other, and the question of mutual professional respect was
moot. Their antagonism made the DNA wars in this trial more

hard-fought, more energy-sapping, and ultimately more tedious than anything we could've anticipated. Except, of course, for Harmon and Scheck, who were in their glory.

∞

In my experience, a client's participation can be pivotal to a case, and every day, O.J. was more and more integral to the defense. He had a great recollection of every event that had taken place in his life, and everyone he'd ever known. He insisted on getting copies of every motion and memo, and he studied them all, from Ito's rulings to the DNA textbooks. He would be on the phone late into the night with Dershowitz, with Uelmen, with me and with Cochran, going over details, refuting and arguing with testimony that had been presented, anticipating what was going to come up the following day. He was especially critical of any lawyer when the subject at hand was one he knew about, especially anything having to do with the Brown family, Nicole's life, and their friends and neighbors. "You guys gotta talk to me," he'd insist. "You sometimes don't know what you're talking about."

∞

April 21, a Friday, was supposed to be a half-day session, but early that morning I heard a news item on the radio that surpassed almost anything I'd heard in my twenty-five years of law practice. The Simpson jurors—eighteen in all, including the remaining six alternates—were refusing to come to court and were demanding that Judge Ito come instead to their hotel.

The week before, echoing one of ex-juror Harris's remarks, a juror had complained to the judge that three of the sheriff's deputies were giving preferential treatment to white jurors. Since this was the second time he'd heard this complaint, which involved the same three deputies that Harris had singled out, Judge Ito reassigned them, and put new deputies in their place. It was this action that precipitated the jury "strike," which, it turned out, wasn't so much a strike as it was an expression of solidarity with the removed deputies.

Ito refused to meet with the jury at the hotel. Instead, he pledged that he, along with attorneys for the prosecution and defense, would willingly hear their complaints in chambers. When they arrived, we were startled to see that thirteen of the jurors were dressed in black.

What I feared was happening—that the jury was dividing down racial lines—was in fact *not* happening. True enough, there was a division, but it appeared to be between the older, more conservative jurors and the younger, more outgoing ones.

The consensus was that when Judge Ito dismissed the deputies, without explaining to the jurors why this was done, their sense of safety, of security, was somehow damaged. They were wearing black, they said, because they were in mourning. Members of their "family" had abruptly disappeared. "These guys were an integral part of our life here," said one juror. "They were our link to the world. They took care of us. We cried with them when we had family emergencies, or when we had the blues." What these jurors wanted, it was clear, was some control over their personal destiny.

Their litany of complaints wasn't surprising. The pace of the trial was too slow, the pressures too enormous, and the separation from their familiar lives and loved ones was becoming unbearable. Some jurors were asking flat out to be allowed to leave. Small quibbles had become huge battles. Who sat with whom at meals, who was in control of the video clicker, whether they came back from a shopping trip in an hour or in an hour and a half—these had become make-or-break issues.

Ito now found himself in an untenable position. If after two complaints he hadn't dismissed those deputies, he would've been criticized for not being sensitive to jurors' feelings and needs. But taking the action he did had made him, in the press's eyes, a judge who'd lost control of a jury. The sheriff was mad at him, *Time* magazine now named him a "Loser of the Week," and worst of all, the trial had come to a screeching halt.

The real question was one of philosophy. What were the responsibilities of the deputies? According to Judge Ito, first and foremost was providing security for the jurors, to make sure nothing happened to them. Their second obligation was to accommodate jurors' needs. The job description seemed to fall somewhere between guard and flight attendant, with some psychological training thrown in.

As with the deputies, a judge at trial can't be all things to all people. Ito's failing was that he was too kind, too considerate, for the unprecedented challenge of long-term jury sequestration. There were too many agendas here: the immediate legal concerns of prosecution and defense, the needs of the Browns and the Goldmans, the welfare of the jurors. How could he possibly have made everybody happy—if, in fact, making people happy was part of *his* job description?

We decided we needed to make a few adjustments. The first task would be to pick up the pace. Testimony would begin promptly at nine in the morning. Lunch breaks would be only an hour. As for the individual jurors, Ito would continue to hear and heed their complaints. More outings would be arranged for them, so that they weren't tethered only to the courthouse and the hotel. It seemed, for the time being, that the jury storm had blown over.

∞

On May 1, juror Tracy Hampton, one of the jurors who had insisted on the ouster of the three deputies, was dismissed. She had been fragile and emotional for some time, and Jo-Ellan Dimitrius had predicted that Ito would let her go. A few days after she left, Hampton was taken to the hospital for what was reported as severe stress; we heard later that it was a suicide attempt. She recovered and was featured in a *Playboy* magazine layout in March 1996.

∞

During the trial, I attended only one Lakers game, although normally I would've gone more often. On this one night, I was sitting midcourt, in the sixth or seventh row, and Linell and the boys were with me. Up on the big video screen, they flashed pictures of celebrities in the audience. Magic Johnson's image drew cheers from the crowd, as did Jack Nicholson's. When my face appeared, I heard some scattered boos for the first time, along with a couple of voices in the crowd shouting "Guilty, guilty!" The man sitting next to me leaned over and said, "Don't worry, Bob. When this is all over, they'll be cheering."

Moments later, the screen televised the face of Los Angeles Raiders owner Al Davis, who had recently announced that he was moving the team back up to Oakland. Davis drew an immense chorus of sustained boos. I wondered if he or the athletes on the floor ever grew used to them. I wasn't sure that I would.

Chapter Seventeen

In the spring, Kato Kaelin's book deal with Marc Elliot was announced; sixteen hours of taped interviews that Kaelin had done with Elliot were turned over to the prosecution by the author. I saw Kaelin some time later, at an engagement party for Larry King. I made a deliberate point not to talk to him.

Marcia Clark could have recalled Kato after the news of the book deal came out and impeached his earlier testimony that there was no book in the works. For whatever reason, she made a strategic decision not to do so.

On May 1, L.A.P.D. criminalist Gregory Matheson took the stand for five days of blood-evidence testimony. The prosecution's DNA strategy had become defensive: Every single issue that we'd raised in opening arguments or shown in our charts, which were required by the new rules of evidence, they immediately tried to counter. It was as if we had presented the case and they now had to rebut it.

One of the issues raised in Matheson's testimony was the finding of Nicole's blood on one of O.J.'s socks, which had been retrieved at Rockingham.

When the socks were initially examined by the crime lab

personnel immediately after the murders, no blood was present. They countered this with, "Well, this was a dark sock, and blood couldn't be seen." However, twelve items of evidence, including a shirt, gloves, and a scarf, were collected from Rockingham and tested for blood traces, in a procedure called a phenothaline preliminary test. However, the thirteenth item, the sock, was never tested. Two weeks after the evidence collection, our experts, Dr. Michael Baden and Dr. Barbara Wolf, along with Michelle Kestler from the L.A.P.D. lab, had looked at the same sock, and no blood was noted. It wasn't until two months later that blood was found.

There were other questionable factors as well. For example, the sock was found on a pale Oriental carpet. If the sock was wet with blood when it was dropped there, why was there no trace of blood on the carpet? The blood was on the ankle of the sock, having seeped from one side of the sock to the other; if someone had been wearing the sock when the blood got on it, that seepage couldn't have happened.

∞

As the prosecution heated up the DNA wars, Rock Harmon had reportedly been calling and talking to some of our expert witnesses, trying to get information from them beyond what we'd presented in discovery. We prepared a motion asking for sanctions against him; Barry Scheck was low-keyed and understated as he presented the argument. Harmon, however, was absolutely obnoxious, referring to the defense as the "rogue's gallery, not interested in the truth."

"They had a great April," he said, "but now they're afraid of a bad May." Although Ito didn't sanction Harmon, he did call his behavior reprehensible, which gave us a nickname for him: Reprehensible Rock.

∞

When you have a blood test, the standard-size tube into which that blood goes holds ten ccs. There are thirty ccs to an ounce, so the amount in the tube is about a third of an ounce.

In the preliminary hearing, during my cross-examination of Thano Peratis, the L.A.P.D. nurse, Peratis testified that he drew 7.9 to 8.1 full ccs of O.J.'s blood at the police lab on June 13. I then asked him how he knew he'd drawn that precise amount. His answer was, "I looked at the tube"—which was calibrated. The prosecution was adamant that after being used in standard serology tests, there wasn't enough of O.J.'s blood (and DNA) remaining to be planted anywhere. However, Bob Blasier, Scheck, and Neufeld had prepared a chart illustrating that after the amount of blood used for lab tests had been subtracted, approximately 1.5 ccs of O.J.'s blood was unaccounted for. We wanted that chart admitted into evidence for when Peratis testified in the trial.

Consulting with Harmon, district attorney Hank Goldberg set up a pattern of objecting to almost every sentence out of Blasier's mouth, throwing off his tempo and irritating Ito in the process. "You've made the same point about eight times, Mr. Goldberg," Ito said. In the jury box, jurors were nodding off.

Ultimately, the chart was admitted into evidence; we planned to use it a few weeks later, when questioning Peratis again.

∞

Early in May, we had a defense team meeting with Skip Taft, and one of the items on the table was my continuing lack of cooperation in signing photographs, specifically one of O.J., Johnnie, and me together. Taft estimated that he could realize between sixty and eighty thousand dollars per thousand autographed pictures, which were sold to a wholesaler in Florida.

Cochran had asked for an opinion from the state bar, which said there was nothing unethical about it; he and O.J. had already signed a thousand. The argument, of course, was that it was one way to get a few of our bills paid.

I was more than willing to respond to requests from charities, who frequently auctioned off the trial memorabilia. I had sent autographed copies of O.J.'s book (with signatures from

Johnnie, O.J., and me) to at least one hundred of them, and sent signed photographs and ties that I'd worn in court as well. However, I believed that selling signatures during the course of a trial was unprofessional, and I simply refused to do it. "If you want to make us into whores," I told Taft, "don't make us streetwalkers."

∞

Early in May, I finally went to one of Grant's Little League games, at Roxbury Park. In the third inning, Kevin Upton, another player's father, turned to me and said, "Ronald Reagan's here." I waited to hear what the joke was, and he said, "No, he's really here."

I turned and there he was, wearing a baseball cap and a red, white, and blue jogging suit, walking between two Secret Service men. He went behind the home-plate screen and stood watching the kids for almost an inning. No one approached him.

I went into the dugout and told the kids that the President was there watching the game, that this was a historic moment for them. I wanted to greet him, and I wanted my boys to have this opportunity to shake hands with an American president, and perhaps to understand how unique a moment this was. I asked the Secret Service if we could speak with him, and they said yes.

I'd seen President Reagan before; his office is in the same building as mine in Century City, and before his illness, he was often in, coming and going through the halls with one or two Secret Service men, waving as he got into his car at the end of the day. But this was the first time I had spoken with him. It was not long after Reagan's public announcement of Alzheimer's, yet he seemed in great shape, robust and clear-eyed, with color in his cheeks and a firm handshake. He stood perfectly erect, as though at attention, and was graceful and patient as the boys and their parents came up to be introduced. Grant stood right next to me, shaking hands with the President and smiling up at him.

It was the first time I had ever seen or talked to a president outside of an organized political setting, and it was with a certain awe that I spoke with him. Even though I hadn't agreed with his policies, I had great respect for him and for the office he'd held for eight years. He had shown great courage in surviving a serious assassination attempt, and in spite of great criticism, he had never wavered about his beliefs or convictions. That, I said, was truly admirable. "Thank you very much," he said, and smiled the legendary smile.

I watched as he and the Secret Service men continued on their walk. It's one thing to argue politics. It's another to actually meet a president. He had been the most powerful man in the free world, and there he was, on a Sunday afternoon, watching boys play ball in the park. I thought it was quite remarkable.

∞

On May 8, the People called John Meraz, the tow-truck driver who had taken the Bronco from Rockingham back to the impound lot. It was Meraz's testimony that the car had been locked when he towed it. Cochran did the cross, and O.J. was concerned, as he always was with the civilian witnesses, that Johnnie was pressing too hard on Meraz about the car being locked.

"Do we have to attack everybody?" he asked.

We needed to know if Meraz saw blood either inside or outside of the Bronco, so Cochran asked him. Given my rule about how dangerous questions are when you don't know the answer, I tensed up for a moment. But we got the answer we wanted: No, Meraz didn't see any blood.

∞

Each member of the defense team had an ergonomically designed chair that had been donated by a company in Los Angeles called Relax-the-Back. One day during court, while

Johnnie was trying to adjust his, he hit the wrong button, released the back support, and nearly fell backward out of the chair. Then, in an effort to bring the back up, he pushed the middle button (which controls the seat height), and crashed to the floor. I started laughing and had to turn away, literally biting my cheeks. No one in the audience had noticed except the bailiff and Detective Vannatter, and Vannatter had gone red-faced with laughter, fighting to keep from making any noise. O.J. was looking down at Johnnie like he had just arrived from another planet.

I thought, I have to get a grip here or I'll explode. Concentrating as hard as I could on getting Johnnie up, then helping him to readjust his chair, I finally conquered my overwhelming desire to giggle. Vannatter and I studiously avoided eye contact the rest of the day.

∞

Larry Schiller, O.J.'s book collaborator, had worked with Norman Mailer on the research for *The Executioner's Song*. When Mailer came to Los Angeles to launch the book tour for his new novel, Schiller invited Linell and me to attend a small dinner party at Spago in Mailer's honor. Johnnie was there with his wife, Dale, and Bob Kardashian and Barry Scheck also attended. It felt a little like we were all out on a school night.

I've always been a fan of Mailer's, and we share a love for boxing. He told me that he'd become interested in it later in life, as I did, although he had boxed a bit as a kid. We had both boxed with our own kids. Mailer said he thought there was probably something very tribal in that.

My boys, on their own and with little encouragement from me, had begun to develop an interest in boxing, especially Brent, who was talking about getting involved in Golden Gloves. He was going through a growth spurt, getting tall and leggy, and becoming tough as nails. The competitive instinct was there between him and Grant, and between them and me. I didn't mind giving them the advantage when we were sparring—I didn't need to boost my ego by beating my kids at sports.

Once I told Brent he could hit me as hard as he wanted, as long as he hit below the neck. I'd be defensive, but I wouldn't hit back. He obligingly pounded away at my stomach, and then without warning threw a right to my face. Instantly, almost as a reflex action, I came back with a short jab, and connected. His nose bled, his mouth was cut, and I ended our session washing the blood off my son's face with a hose in the yard. I felt absolutely horrible about what I'd done. And I knew that I wouldn't be able to keep up with him much longer.

One of my dinner companions that night at Spago was the actor Martin Landau, who'd won an Oscar that spring for *Ed Wood*. When he asked how the trial was going, I made a crack about *Mission: Impossible*. I was rewarded with a smile from my wife, who was used to my Hollywood faux pas and had been holding her breath in case I didn't know to whom I was talking.

"How are you doing with all the celebrity stuff?" Landau asked.

"I'm mixed about it," I said. "I like being acknowledged for being good at my job. And we all know that this has more to do with O.J. than it does with any of us as individuals. The tabloid stuff is pretty hard to take for my family, though."

He nodded. "I can imagine," he said. "Actors put our hands up for celebrity. We want people to know who we are, and losing privacy is the trade-off. But it's different for you guys." He was watching Barry Scheck across the room, surrounded by a circle of admirers.

Later in the evening, Warren Beatty came in. Beatty is known as something of an expert on reluctant celebrity. His private life has been the subject of intense press scrutiny for three decades.

Beatty's also a student of the American political and legal system, and our conversation about privacy included his acknowledgment of the right of the press to "get the story."

"There's a downside to it, though, Bob," he said. "Once you forfeit your right to privacy, you never get it back."

∞

On May 8, we got our first look at George "Woody" Clarke, who had come from San Diego to work through the prosecution's DNA analysis testimony with Cellmark lab director Robin Cotton. It was immediately apparent that Clarke had poise and style, and his presentation with Cotton was well prepared. Good graphics, easily understood questions, and an easy manner on both their parts made the dense material somewhat easier on the palate.

If I had been one of the prosecutors, I would've been beaming all through Cotton's testimony, she was that good. Highly educated, warm and affable, she was the high school teacher you hoped you'd get. If she didn't know something, she readily admitted it. What she did know, she did her best to make understandable to the jury, rather than boost her own ego by staying with esoteric or indecipherable scientific technology.

However, DNA isn't inherently fascinating to the lay audience, even in this case, and thus the effective Clarke-Cotton team lost their audience. By the third day, the most diligent note-taking jurors had put their pencils down, Cochran and I were both fading, and O.J., who had only his cell to go back to, was nevertheless gazing longingly at the door.

∞

I had been talking with Dr. Henry Lee about how much blood can come from a nick or a scrape, and how a drop of blood expands upon contact with the ground. I started doing experiments at home with water in an eyedropper, dropping it on different surfaces from different heights. I was surprised to find that a drop from three feet would end up between the size of a nickel and a dime. I then tried it with cooking oil, and got the same result. But I wanted to see what would happen with blood.

While shaving, I took the razor and made a little slice in my chin. I was immediately rewarded with blood—far more than I had expected. Even hitting what I thought was the right pressure point, I couldn't shut the blood off with a hand towel, and in minutes there was blood all over the tile on the bathroom floor. Minutes after that, the towel was soaked through.

Once the bleeding had finally stopped, I made sure I took the towel in the car with me. I picked Johnnie up on the way to court and showed him the towel.

"Bob, you'll do anything for a client, won't you?" he said, laughing.

I put the towel into my briefcase and took it into the courthouse. I showed it to Judge Ito and the prosecution team, telling them I would have liked to be able to show it to the jury. No one was amused.

Perhaps the greatest misconception in this case is the prosecution's "mountain of evidence" versus the amount of blood that was actually found. At the Bundy crime scene, the blood from the victims was of course enormous, as large an amount as the police had ever seen. But the amount there that was not the victims' that was available for analysis—the drops of blood leading away from the Bundy crime scene—amounted to four blood drops inside the walkway, and one outside the walkway, each the size of a dime. If these were all left there at the same time, as the prosecution contended, each should've had relatively the same amount of human DNA. A drop of blood will contain approximately fifteen hundred nanograms of DNA. However, the four drops inside the walkway had amounts varying from two to ten nanograms, much less than anyone would expect, even with degradation. The drop outside the walkway contained thirty-five nanograms. The blood on the sock found in O.J.'s bedroom contained upward of one thousand nanograms of DNA—ten times more than all the other blood samples combined.

Bacteria causes degradation, and degradation causes a loss

of sample. The blood on the gate behind the Bundy residence wasn't seen by any of the detectives or technicians until three weeks after the murders, long after everything had been washed down. Yet that blood had more DNA than the samples found on the ground, and was less degraded than the blood on the ground. How was this possible?

It was not the obligation of the Simpson defense to prove how the blood got there, when it got there, why it got there, whether it was planted there, whether it had been there for some period of time, whether it was contaminated, whether it came from sloppy techniques in the lab, or whether the reference samples of O.J.'s blood, when they were opened in the lab, spewed out onto other samples. This was not our job. Our job was to ask the questions, point out the improbables. For every single item—sock, glove, knit hat, blood—we were able to show doubt, reasonable and real.

Early in May, Gerry Uelmen and I met with the judge and the prosecution away from the jury to discuss the admissibility of the autopsy photographs. Uelmen had been teaching full-time but had agreed to return for motions whenever we felt we needed him in court.

The assistant district attorney who would be arguing for the prosecution was Brian Kelberg, a medical/legal specialist who had attended medical school before law school. He would be examining the deputy coroner, Dr. Golden, and trying to diminish the impact of his performance in the preliminary hearings.

Kelberg wasted no time in telling us how he was going to present Golden as a witness. He was first going to go through the mistakes that Golden had made during his career as a coroner, and then the specific mistakes he'd made on the autopsies. His tactic was to show that this doctor had made mistakes throughout his professional life; that in fact mistakes were endemic to his career.

Kelberg's strategy called for the prosecution to take the lead in destroying Golden, so that we could not. And they would argue that the autopsy photographs had to be admitted into evidence, in order to show Golden's errors. There were wounds that he said existed that didn't exist; there were others he'd referred to in his report that weren't evident in the photographs.

The photographs were as unimaginable as any I had ever seen, and Ito agreed. The close-up shots of the cleaned wounds, especially the ones in the neck areas, were simply incomprehensible. There was a hole in Ron Goldman's throat large enough for a fist, and Nicole's throat seemed open from end to end.

I argued that the photographs were such that anyone seeing them would have such a visceral reaction, such rage, as to seriously prejudice the defendant. It simply wasn't necessary to introduce them at all; Golden could testify to cause of death, we would certainly stipulate to that, and the jury didn't need to see these photos to establish that information.

The defense lost that round; at the end of May, Ito ruled that the jury could see the photographs. Later, of course, it became obvious that Dr. Golden was a Trojan horse to bring the autopsy photos into the trial. Dr. Golden was not asked to testify by the prosecution.

∞

On May 10, I took a break from court, and went down the hall to see Michael Baden, who was in town with Barbara Wolf testifying as a key prosecution witness in another criminal case.

For nearly a year, I'd been the only lawyer who sat in on each and every hearing and session in the courtroom. I had become a desk lawyer, captive at the end of the table with my computer, listening as O.J. commented on every piece of evidence, hearing Cochran respond with "We'll look into that" or "Carl's on top of it." I'd sprained my back sparring with Grant the weekend before and couldn't find a comfortable place in my chair. Taking a walk down the hall for a strategy session with Baden and Wolf seemed like a good idea.

After Michael had completed his testimony in the other case, he and I and Barbara went into another room to watch the live television feed of the trial. Since the trial had begun, I hadn't seen any of the television coverage; I had deliberately avoided anything except the evening news recap. Seeing the way the camera editorialized what was taking place in that courtroom, especially the actions and reactions of the lawyers, was a revelation.

There was an alert Peter Neufeld, looking intently at the witness he was examining. Scheck, who had been the DNA point man for days, looked less focused, his clothes disheveled, his hair badly in need of a trim. Blasier was hunched over his computer, probably in-putting some esoteric data or creating graphics for the next day's use. Cochran was agitated and restless, slumped down in his chair. O.J., who had a tendency to throw his head back and look up at the ceiling when he was thinking, was, said Barbara Wolf, "looking scornful."

"I needed to see this," I said to my two friends. "I need to tell them about this, especially O.J. We've forgotten the cameras, or gotten used to them. If we look like this to television viewers, we must look like this to the jury."

∞

The rule of the court is that when an objection is made, the brief legal explanation—it assumes a fact not in evidence, is hearsay, irrelevant, or whatever it may be—is made, and any detailed or further explanation is given at a sidebar conference. Otherwise the jury hears remarks or observations from either prosecution or defense that will poison their ability to deliberate fairly. In this case, although there was certainly no shortage of sidebars, Ito had warned lawyers for both sides numerous times about "speaking objections" in which we continued to argue or explain our reasons for objections in full hearing of the jury.

In mid-May, Judge Ito sanctioned Peter Neufeld and Woody Clarke each $250 for specifying their objections during Cotton's testimony within the jury's hearing. He ordered them not to bill their clients for the charges.

"Thank you, Your Honor," said O.J.

"You're welcome, Mr. Simpson," said Ito. Later, we heard that Clarke's colleagues in San Diego took up a collection to pay his fine.

As the first anniversary of Nicole's death approached, O.J. became angry when he saw his kids on the cover of *Life* magazine, and he called Lou Brown to tell him so. He thought the Browns were being naive about the press's intentions. "They don't care about you," he told Lou. "They care about themselves, about how much money they make off this stuff."

He wanted his kids protected, out of the spotlight, so that they'd be able to make their own choices. "I taught Sydney to play chess when she was only seven," he said proudly. "She's going to be able to be anything she wants."

In mid-May, the jurors sent Judge Ito a letter, signed by a majority, asking to extend the week—full days on Friday and half days on Saturday. They were willing to forego the outings Ito had been arranging for them in order to put in more court time. Cochran was against it, I was mixed, and O.J. was strongly in favor. The judge said he couldn't open the courtroom on Saturdays, but extending on Friday afternoons was a realistic possibility.

Marcia Clark and Johnnie were back to being flirtatiously friendly with each other; O.J. dogged Johnnie about it, especially when it happened in front of the jury. "Don't do that," O.J. repeatedly said to Cochran.

On the way into court on May 18, a reporter called out to me, "What will O.J. say to his kids on Nicole's birthday?" She would've been thirty-six. I told O.J. later that it had to be the stupidest question I'd heard since this all started.

"What do they think, that I've got this thing scripted?" he asked. "She wouldn't have hung around for a party with her family, she didn't like that stuff," he said. "We would've taken the kids and our friends and gone to Cabo."

∞

Someone sent cans of black spray to Cochran and me, for the bald spots on our heads. The gift giver said that he was being blinded by the reflection of my pate on television. I was impressed with the gesture—the guy actually went to the trouble of having the spray cans personalized with our names.

∞

When Barry Scheck cross-examined Gary Sims, the senior criminologist for the California Department of Justice, he used Sims's testimony for defense purposes, as an example of excellent procedure, in contrast to that of the L.A.P.D. crime lab. Sims couldn't say for sure whether the socks found in O.J.'s bedroom were tampered with before the technicians in the lab got them. Sims also testified that there was no way for him to say for sure that the police did not tamper with the crime scene.

The prosecutors clearly weren't happy with Sims. He was straightforward, giving scientific interpretations as clearly as he could, and doing his best to avoid showing favoritism to either side. Rock Harmon had done the direct on Sims, and he objected constantly during Scheck's cross. If Ito didn't sustain Harmon's objections, Harmon would remain standing until Ito would finally say "Sit down, Mr. Harmon."

As careful as the court had been with screening newspapers, the jurors had seen in *USA Today* that Harmon had cracked a joke about the DNA analysis of O.J.'s blood excluding everyone except the San Antonio Spurs. "Not exactly a world-class comedian," grumbled O.J.

"Harmon bought new clothes to be on TV," he speculated. He was always giving Johnnie and me a bad time about our ties. He preferred a more conservative style, saying that it was more businesslike. When O.J. first went to USC, John De-Lorean hired him as a product spokesman for Chevrolet. The Chevy people took O.J. to Carroll's, a conservative clothing store in Beverly Hills, stressing to him that this was how a businessman should dress. "People should say 'you look good,' " he said, "not 'that's a great suit.' "

During Scheck's cross of Sims, the witness couldn't immediately locate one piece of information in his notes. Scheck had the data in front of him. Scheck said, "Well, would you agree if I told you that . . . ?" and then recited the data. Responded Sims, "Mr. Scheck, I'll take your word for anything."

Both men were clear speakers; they knew this was a tough audience. But the testimony was dense, confusing, and the jurors obviously bored. Scheck raised the possibility that someone not identified in the case left blood at the scene, but there was no way of knowing if the jury picked up on this. Two days later he was able to get into evidence that the tissue and isoenzyme found under Nicole's fingernail was type B; her blood was type AB.

Scheck was impressive, both in his knowledge of the science and the dogged way he cross-examined a witness until he got what he wanted. But he was constantly worried that he was falling short, that the jury wasn't getting it. "I don't like to do anything less than my best," he said. "And I'm not sure this is my best."

Chapter Eighteen

As was our custom, Johnnie and I, along with Bob Kardashian and other members of the defense team, often met with O.J. for a few minutes before he was brought out of the lockup in the morning. While we were there on May 24, Guy Magnara, the sheriff's bailiff, came in and announced forebodingly, "The judge wants to see everybody in chambers."

"What is it?" I asked.

"More jury problems," he said.

Johnnie and I looked at each other in alarm. When we went into the judge's chambers, it was a stone-faced Judge Ito who greeted us.

"I've just received this letter," he said.

It was a handwritten, five-page letter on a secretarial steno pad, sent anonymously by someone who described him- or herself as a twenty-year-old German receptionist for a book agent. The letter-writer had seen Judge Ito on his television interview with Tritia Toyota and been deeply moved by the story of the judge and his family being interned in the camps during World War II. This person's family had suffered too—we assumed in German concentration camps—and because of this shared connection he felt with Ito, he believed that he had an obligation to bring a certain matter to the judge's attention.

This person claimed to have it on very good authority that a female juror, who had once been an alternate, was negotiating for a book. The juror's husband had been doing the negotiating, an agent had met with both of them at the Intercontinental Hotel (thus correctly identifying the location where the jury was sequestered), and the book even had a title: *Standing Alone: A Verdict for Nicole.* The letter-writer provided other details that only someone with firsthand knowledge of the case and the jury's travails this far could have known.

In the presence of the prosecution and defense lawyers, Judge Ito spoke with the jurors one by one. After a couple of days of questioning, he narrowed things down—after all, we knew from the start we were looking for a married woman—until he finally felt certain that the subject of the anonymous letter was juror Francine Florio-Bunten.

In spite of adamant denials that she was putting together a publishing deal, Florio-Bunten was removed from the jury.

Florio-Bunten's consistent denials in the months since she was excused, coupled with rumors that there was a concerted effort to get her off the jury, have resulted in continuing speculation that someone affiliated with the defense was actually responsible for the anonymous letter that kicked off Judge Ito's investigation. Subsequent to the verdict, she gave interviews in which she said she would have voted guilty and hung the jury. Whether or not that actually would have happened, there's no way of knowing.

Soon after Florio-Bunten's departure, Ito also excused Willie Cravin, the juror who had caused some conflict as king of the video remote control, and Farron Chavarria. The panel that remained, made up of nine blacks, one Hispanic, and two whites, would be the jury that would ultimately deliver the verdict.

∞

Collin Yamauchi, a forensic scientist with the L.A.P.D. crime lab, did the initial collection and testing of the reference blood samples of O.J., Nicole Brown, and Ron Goldman. Young, inadequately trained, and very defensive, Yamauchi proved a poor follow-up to witnesses like Sims and Cotton. Barry Scheck's cross-examination of him came perilously close (for the prosecution) to opening up a very nice door for the defense.

While under direct examination by Rock Harmon, Yamauchi had to refer to his notes for his answers. The defense was given the opportunity to examine the notes, and Scheck quickly spotted the words "alibi—Chicago."

When Scheck asked Yamauchi what that referred to, he answered, "Yes, I heard on the news that he's got an airtight alibi, he's in Chicago, and you know, it's his ex-wife and this and that, and he's probably not related to this thing."

Ito immediately barked "Sidebar!"

Section 356 of the California evidence code says that if one side introduces material contained in a statement, the other side may seek to have the entire statement placed in evidence so that nothing is presented out of context. What Yamauchi had done was open the door to allowing O.J.'s first interview with the police—and the audiotape of that interview—to be introduced to the jury, without subjecting O.J. to cross-examination.

California law allows statements of a defendant to be introduced only if the prosecution chooses to introduce them. In this instance, we believed O.J.'s statement would be beneficial to his case; evidently the prosecution agreed, since they'd fought long and hard to keep it out. Now we jumped on the opportunity, and Johnnie immediately demanded that the tape be admitted into evidence.

"But it only goes to Yamauchi's state of mind!" Marcia Clark argued heatedly, insisting that it was not the alibi itself, or O.J.'s statement about having an alibi, that Yamauchi was referring to.

Judge Ito responded that it was more complicated than that, that Yamauchi, a prosecution witness, had actually raised the existence of an alibi in front of the jury.

Clark exploded, with angry and harsh language aimed directly at Ito. It was my belief that if any of the defense team had used that tone (and decibel level), we would've been strongly sanctioned.

However, as I suspected would happen, Judge Ito found that the jury hadn't heard enough from Yamauchi that would mandate the introduction of O.J.'s statement, and he ruled that it couldn't be introduced.

∞

In an interview in the Sunday, June 4, issue of the *Los Angeles Times,* Chris Darden said, "The case has shaken my faith in the system. . . . The intense scrutiny of our personal lives is unfair. I don't know if I ever want to try another case . . . or practice law again."

∞

When O.J. heard that Judge Ito was going to allow the autopsy photos into evidence as part of Dr. Lakshmanan's testimony, he grew very morose and depressed. He had never seen the pictures, nor had he ever let us describe them to him. Now he knew he'd have to sit in court and listen to the descriptions. Judge Ito called us in and told us that the deputies were very concerned at O.J.'s appearance and behavior, so they'd put him on suicide watch again.

Hearing of the deputies' concern, O.J. turned to Guy Magnara and said, "I'm not suicidal! The last time they did this, they woke me up every fifteen minutes around the clock. They turned the lights on and off all night. If I look awful, it's because these guys aren't letting me get any sleep!"

Over the Memorial Day weekend, I had worked on strategy with Michael Baden and Barbara Wolf, who had come into town to help me prepare for cross-examining the coroner. We read his reports repeatedly and carefully examined the autopsy pictures. "Look for the unexpected," Michael instructed me. "Sometimes the more important things are the hardest ones to find." It reminded me of Sherlock Holmes telling Dr. Watson,

"I don't know what I'm looking for, but when I find it, I'll let you know."

We'd learned that the prosecution had decided to sacrifice Dr. Golden; he would not be testifying. Dr. Lakshmanan, the chief medical examiner, would testify instead. Brian Kelberg would be doing the direct examination. I would be doing the cross-examination.

I was disappointed that I wasn't going to get another chance at Golden. An analysis of Golden's errors and the testimony he'd given under my cross-examination at the preliminary hearing had led Michael Baden to believe there was a possibility that we'd be able to get Golden to state that the time of death was shortly after eleven o'clock on the night of June 12. Lakshmanan, however, couldn't be counted on for that.

Lakshmanan is a highly educated skilled professional who prided himself on being board-certified in several different areas of medicine, including geriatrics, infectious diseases, and internal medicine. Michael Baden told me that certification in each area required at least three years of specialized study. "If Lakshmanan had spent those years studying pathology instead," he said, "he'd be a much better medical examiner."

Since we didn't have to go after the hapless Dr. Golden for his errors, the defense was prepared to stipulate to the cause of death. But we knew the prosecution wanted something more dramatic. They were going to showcase Lakshmanan in order to get a crime-scene narrative and the autopsy photos in front of the jury.

Brian Kelberg got Lakshmanan to perform a physical demonstration illustrating the prosecution's hypothesis of how the two murders might have been committed.

"Now, Doctor," Kelberg would say, "could a six-foot two-inch, male African-American have caused these injuries if he was standing behind an individual?" Then he would proceed to outline a scenario that fit solely within the assumption that O.J. Simpson was the only possible killer.

I objected. Kelberg's scenario, I said, was assuming facts not in evidence. Ito overruled the objection.

Lakshmanan then answered, "Yes, this is consistent with—"

Interrupting, I objected again. What did "consistent with" mean? As Michael Baden would later say, Kelberg's scenario could also be consistent with a five-foot midget standing on a ladder. Ito overruled me once more.

At sidebar, I reminded the judge that whenever Scheck had tried to get "hypotheticals" in, Ito sustained the prosecution's objections, which were the same as mine were now. Why couldn't my objections be sustained as well?

"I didn't sustain all their objections," Ito answered.

"You sustained most of them, Your Honor," I said.

"Well, I'm not sustaining yours," he said.

The jury reaction to the photos was reported as being very dramatic, but I noticed something the reporters perhaps did not. When the photos of Nicole were introduced, many individuals were clearly disturbed and saddened. But when Ron Goldman's photos were shown, the level of emotional reaction went sharply higher. One gentleman took his glasses off and began to cry; two of the women had tears running down their cheeks.

It would be foolish to try to weigh one victim against the other, to say that one person was less or more vulnerable than the other. However, the press had often tended to treat Goldman's death as secondary to Nicole's, as an afterthought or a footnote. It was clear inside that courtroom that the jury saw him as an equal victim.

During Lakshmanan's testimony, O.J. was obviously distraught and tearful, breathing heavily, rocking back and forth in his seat. Bob Kardashian had returned to the defense table, positioning himself not just to comfort O.J. but also to shield him from the camera.

We adjourned early one afternoon, as the jurors were overcome by the photographs. Two actually left the jury box before officially being excused. I had seen the pictures often enough to believe I would be immune when they were actually put on the screen. However, the obvious grief in the room combined with the images on the screen was overwhelming. I grew lightheaded and dizzy, and my chest hurt. At one point I even took my watch off and checked my pulse. I thought of asking Ito for a recess or an early adjournment, but knew that if the request came from me, the press would've announced that Shapiro had gone out with a heart attack.

Dr. Lakshmanan's testimony tied with Dennis Fung's for marathon length: eight days. As I prepared to cross-examine him, I felt the jury had been bored by too much detail, some of it painfully numbing. My mission was to hammer home our major points. I went to the far podium so I wouldn't be distracted by O.J.'s comments, or Johnnie's. Neither one claimed expertise in forensic pathology, and their suggestions were distracting, throwing my rhythm off.

Lakshmanan admitted under my questioning that in his entire career he had never testified in place of—nor heard of anyone else testifying in place of—the coroner who had actually performed the autopsy in question, especially when that coroner (Dr. Golden) was available to testify. I hoped that this would make the jury wonder why Lakshmanan was on the stand.

Lakshmanan had been asked on direct examination about possibilities—vague medical possibilities. I wanted instead to narrow the focus. "Reasonable medical certainty" is a term doctors use to describe conditions or opinions, rather than speculation. I had no doubt that any question I asked about reasonable degrees of medical certainty would be answered in a way favorable to the defense, since I believed Lakshmanan was an honest witness. Even though he was appearing for the prosecution, he wouldn't risk ridicule by others in his profession by saying he could make an absolute determination when he clearly could not.

"Can you tell us with a reasonable degree of medical certainty how many people are responsible for these homicides?" I asked him.

"No," he answered.

"Can you tell us with a reasonable degree of medical certainty how many different weapons were used to accomplish these homicides?"

"I already opined, saying that a single-edged knife could have caused all the knife wounds," he said. "But with reasonable medical certainty, I cannot exclude a second knife."

Assistant district attorney Kelberg had taken eight days to convince the jury that a guilty verdict could be built upon speculation, conjecture, and theories that were "consistent with" his hypotheticals. Dr. Lakshmanan's answers to my cross-examination reminded them of the need for *proof without doubt*. The only hypothesis about which there was no doubt was that these two people had died by virtue of having their throats cut. By what, by whom, by how many—no one could say.

Until that day, I'd believed that my cross-examination of Irwin Golden in the preliminary was my career best; in the trial, I was proudest of the work I did with Lakshmanan. Afterward a reporter wrote, "Within ten minutes, Shapiro destroyed eight days of testimony."

As the prosecution moved toward closing its case and we began to work on presenting the defense case, everyone was getting a little punchy. Serious legal debates and fights at sidebars were often punctuated with bad jokes, knowing insults, or the kind of humor you might see at summer camp.

Even though the jurors had become legendary for their impassive facial expressions, they were each very different. Some took notes, others didn't. Some stayed alert and awake throughout even the most daunting scientific testimony; others struggled, and even dozed. Over the months we felt we'd come to know them, their individual moods and reactions. So, instead of referring to them by their numbers or seat locations, we'd often call them by the nicknames we'd given them.

"Foo-Foo Lemieux took a lot of time with her hair today," someone observed of one juror.

"The Demon is in a bad mood today," someone else would say. "I don't think she likes us much."

"Touchy-Feely isn't paying much attention," a third would notice. "Neither is Horsehair."

"I wonder how Two Tons of Joy will vote when this is over," another would say, looking over at two of the heavier women in the jury box. And we all knew which way Grampa would vote.

It wasn't that we didn't take them seriously. It was more that we took them too seriously, and if we thought too much about who they were and what they were thinking, we wouldn't be able to get through the rest of the trial.

Chapter Nineteen

That glove has holes in it, and worn spots. If they knew anything at all about O.J. Simpson, they'd know the man doesn't own anything that's worn, or with holes. He barely tolerates the wrinkles in his jail uniform. They say they've convicted hundreds of people with less evidence than this. If they've put people away on less than this . . . I'm worried.

—Bill Pavelic

In mid-June, Richard Rubin, the former vice president of the Aris Isotoner Company, had flown out from New York to testify about the brown leather glove. During a break, while O.J. was in the lockup, Chris Darden told Judge Ito at sidebar, "I'm going to ask O.J. to try on the gloves."

"That's completely inappropriate," Johnnie said. "We'll object."

"We're going to take this up on the record later," said Ito.

Rubin walked over to the evidence table, put on a pair of thin latex gloves, and began to examine the leather gloves as if they were ancient Egyptian tapestries. Gingerly, he picked the right one up, looking first at one side, then the other. After he put it down, he picked up the left and conducted a similar inspection. After he'd put both gloves back down again, I looked over to the prosecution table and asked Chris Darden and Cheri Lewis if they objected to me examining the gloves myself. "Go right ahead," Lewis said, reminding me to put latex gloves on first, which I did.

And then I did something that to my knowledge no one else

had done. In front of everyone, I put the leather gloves on. Yet nobody seemed to be paying any attention to me. I then very quickly took the gloves off and headed for the lockup.

I walked up to O.J. and said, "Show me your hand. Palm up." He put his hand against mine. Each finger was a half-inch or more longer than mine; his palm at its widest was at least an inch wider than mine.

"You're not going to believe this," I said to him. "But I just tried the gloves on. They fit me, although they're a little loose at the wrist. But there is no way they'll fit you."

"I told you!" he exclaimed. "Those gloves are not mine. Bob, I've been telling you guys that all along! Thank God!"

"Juice," I said, "when the jury comes back in, Darden's going to ask you to put the gloves on. We're going to object, for the record, but I know Ito's going to allow it. I want you to walk in front of the jury, put the glove on, try as hard as you can to get it on—because believe me, it's not going to fit—and then hold your hand up in front of them like you're carrying the Olympic torch."

When I left the lockup, I walked over to Johnnie. "Try the gloves on," I said quietly. "You're in for a surprise." After he'd done it, we just looked at each other. Our case was at a turning point, and Chris Darden was going to take us through the turn, just like the engineer on a train. He was going to break The Rule and ask a question he didn't know the answer to.

The demonstration took place exactly as I'd expected. Cochran and O.J. and I, escorted by a bailiff, approached the jury box. As O.J. was putting the gloves on, Darden instructed him, "Pull them on, pull them on." O.J. did as he was told, turned to Darden, and said, "They don't fit. See? They don't fit." And the jury heard him. He'd spoken to them, and he wasn't going to be cross-examined on it.

The prosecution tried to scramble. They argued that the gloves didn't fit because of the latex gloves that they'd insisted everyone wear underneath. Maybe it was because the gloves had shrunk, because of the blood on them. We countered with the results of a test showing that blood could not have shrunk the gloves. Maybe he was exaggerating or acting—although then the joke became that he'd never been a very good actor to begin with, why would that change now? Rubin would testify about the special stitching and the glove lining, which might have shrunk. Extra-large should fit O.J., Rubin said. But it didn't matter. The gloves didn't fit.

For months, critics had been lambasting the "Dream Team," saying that the whole trial came down to how much money O.J. was prepared to spend to buy himself a defense. Well, if anything showed what the defense was up against, it was Bill Bodziak, and the FBI's investigation of possible shoe patterns found at the crime scene.

The FBI had examined the L.A.P.D. photographs of the blood patterns at Bundy. Among those patterns was what appeared to be a shoe sole. They sent that pattern around the world to determine the manufacturer of the sole, tracing it to a small factory in Italy. The manufacturer traced the sole to two companies that had bought the piece to be used in their shoes. Bruno Magli, one of the shoe companies, had used the sole on two limited styles and estimated that only 300 pairs had been made in size twelve. The FBI traced when and where the shoes were sold retail in the United States and went through every receipt in Bloomingdale's in New York City to see if they had been purchased there; they had not. They contacted additional retailers throughout the country in an effort to show that the shoes could have been purchased by O.J. Simpson. They were unsuccessful in this unprecedented investigation.

Then they brought in what they believed to be a duplicate pair of the shoes that fit the pattern. When we took them into the lockup under Magnara's supervision, O.J. took one look and said, "I'd never wear those ugly-ass shoes. They went through my closet. They know what kind of shoes I wear."

Bodziak, an expert witness who had been with the FBI's forensic laboratory for ten years, came into court on June 19 to testify about the sole pattern. He looked every bit the part of an FBI agent: short dark hair, lean fit body, and an air of discipline that I suspected would be hard to break.

Bailey was going to do the cross on Bodziak, in spite of my objections. Scheck and Neufeld were equivocal, and Bob Blasier was cautious. "We've worked with him, brought him up to speed," Blasier said. "But I'm not sure he's done the work."

Between the direct examination and the cross, Bailey went into the back room with a clothing bag and changed suits. He'd been wearing a gray suit in the morning; when he began his cross-examination, he had on a blue pinstripe.

Bailey's cross was all over the place, going off on tangents. He misstated the evidence that was brought out on direct examination, calling the shoe a twelve and a half when it was a twelve, and a European size forty-six and a half when it would have been a forty-six. He was frantically trying to embarrass a witness who was calm, cool, articulate, and professional. And Bailey was breaking his own cardinal rule: Unless there's something to accomplish on cross-examination, less is more.

During the break, O.J., Johnnie, Carl, and I went into the lockup together, and Johnnie jumped all over Lee.

"I told you to stay on point," he said. "You promised you would. You're trying to show how smart you are, and all you're doing is showing how smart *he* is."

To his credit, Lee was chastened, and he went back to conduct a more focused, to-the-point cross.

Nevertheless, O.J. was livid at Bailey's performance. "That's it, I don't want to see him up in court again. The man will do no more witnesses." It was something I'd been hearing for months, but it was a pledge nobody would stick to.

∞

On June 21, Cochran and Darden were each fined $250 for trash-talking at a sidebar. Darden had only $112 in his wallet, and Ito ordered him to turn it over immediately. The judge then reduced both fines to $100. I offered to pay half of Cochran's fine, saying, "We're a team."

∞

On June 23, Peter Neufeld cross-examined Dr. Bruce Weir, a respected population geneticist. The issue at hand was the possibility or likelihood of people sharing the same DNA characteristics. Neufeld had done his homework and was able to discover mathematical errors in Weir's calculations—errors that worked against O.J.

Weir was dumbfounded. "I've made a mistake," he said. "I'll have to live with this the rest of my life." At 10:30 there was a brief recess. "I've heard so much of this stuff," O.J. said, "that by the end, I'll know more about DNA than Johnnie Cochran does."

During the break, as often happens, Weir went out, conferred with the prosecutors, and came back to court a somewhat better witness. Although he'd improved, he had not recovered. I suggested then to Peter that he wind up his cross and just leave it alone.

I had been watching the jury's faces as the scientific witnesses paraded on and off, giving their jargon-filled testimony and statistics. I didn't believe for a minute that they understood the specifics of what they were hearing. Occasionally, just to check my theory, I'd talk to the reporters, to see if *they* understood the scientific testimony. If they had problems, if they had questions, if they didn't understand, it was clear to me that the jury wouldn't understand either. The reporters could bring on experts to explain; the jury would have to rely on themselves. And I frequently found that the reporters were confused. But nobody would forget Dr. Weir, a prosecution expert, saying, "I made a mistake. I was wrong."

During Weir's direct examination, Neufeld was once again sanctioned, for talking too loud at a sidebar conference. He was fined two hundred and fifty dollars, and he was furious. Throughout the whole trial, Ito was tougher on Peter Neufeld than on any of the rest of us. In spite of my continued reassurances that it wasn't personal, that Ito actually respected him, Neufeld was adamant. "No judge has ever treated me this way," he said. "I'm not paying the money. I'm going to jail."

I talked to Johnnie, and we agreed that it wouldn't look good for one of our lawyers to land in jail for contempt. Since I had paid Peter's last fine, Johnnie would pay this one.

∞

Mid-morning on the day Weir testified, Kardashian faxed us asking for a late-lunch meeting at Martoni's on Beverly Drive. Johnnie, Carl, Skip Taft, and I met with Kardashian. Bailey, who'd already had lunch, stayed at the courthouse.

"We're all very unhappy with Bailey," Skip Taft told us. "We don't want him participating in the courtroom anymore." Bob Kardashian concurred with Taft. Lee's work on the case had ceased to be about O.J., or on behalf of O.J.—it was about his own reputation, his own ego. He was going to solve the case, he was going to be the hero.

The immediate problem of taking Bailey out of the courtroom was that he'd been assigned to argue a motion to prevent the prosecution from introducing certain hair and fiber evidence. "When am I going to argue my motion?" Lee kept asking Johnnie.

"See Carl," Johnnie would tell him. Once again, Carl was the designated hatchet man. He did all the dirty work. In fact, he did all the clean work. He did *all* the work.

Ultimately, after discussions with Neufeld, Blasier, and Scheck, it was decided that it was okay for Lee to do hair and fibers. Blasier would go through the science with him and be at the table when he did the cross.

When we told O.J. that contrary to his expressed wishes, Bailey would be back in court, Johnnie wasn't in court that day. He'd gone to San Francisco for an interview and also to visit O.J.'s mother. This was typical of the way Johnnie would let us know about his side trips. "I'm going to go up and see O.J.'s mother," he'd say. "And by the way, while I'm up there, I'm going to do an interview."

∞

The Demon was reading a John Grisham novel, *The Rainmaker*. We had seen her walk out with it; somebody said that it dealt with a sports hero who was a wife beater. Cochran called the book to Judge Ito's attention. Ito called the juror to a sidebar and told her he'd have to take the book away. She was mad and sulked the rest of the day. When Ito returned the book to her a few days later, she looked over at the defense table and gave us a caustic smile.

∞

The prosecution's FBI hair-and-fiber witness, Doug Detrick, testified in late June and into the first week of July. At one point, Bob Blasier got a look at Detrick's notebook and found an important report that had been sent to the D.A.'s office. We had not received it in discovery. Information from this report was incorporated in a prosecution graphics board exhibit, and specifically mentioned an exclusive kind of fiber that was standard in the Bronco. Blasier objected strongly to the introduction of this material and asked that it not be admitted.

Ito had been getting more and more concerned about discovery violations as the case went on, and he found this one to be particularly egregious. He decided to bar the evidence completely, saying that it was too late for the prosecution to introduce it.

In the world of scientific analysis, hair and fibers carry only limited weight. That's because experts cannot conclude absolutely that a hair or fiber from a sample is the same as a hair or fiber that is randomly found. The best they can say is that one is "consistent with" the other. Marcia Clark was well aware of this; however, she kept using the word "match" when talking about the hair and fibers. Bailey, properly, kept objecting. Clark apologized, said it was a slip of the tongue, and then did it again. And again. Bailey objected again, his hands and his voice both shaking. Finally, Judge Ito had had enough.

"Ms. Clark, you're flirting with contempt," he said. "If I hear you use that word again, you're gonna spend the weekend in jail."

In answer to Bailey's final question, Detrick finally admitted, "The courts have never recognized hair examinations as a positive means of identification," and he paused slightly before he continued, "and we don't either."

∞

Marcia Clark was back to flirting regularly with Johnnie Cochran, and he was back to responding. Once at a sidebar conference, she said to him, "You just call these sidebars so you can stand next to me."

The flirtation was obviously galling to O.J., who didn't see it as being the harmless pastime Johnnie kept claiming it was. If the jury was noticing, it was a confusing message for them to get.

I told Johnnie his behavior wasn't going over, at least not at the defense table. "You do this cutesy shtick with her, and walk out of the courtroom with her, and every time you do, O.J. gets pissed," I said.

Cochran just smiled. "I'll handle O.J.," he said.

∞

The prosecution was preparing to rest its case, and the defense team was trying to decide whether or not to make what's called a 1118 motion. This is a motion to dismiss because the prosecution has not proven its case to a degree that an appellate court would uphold a conviction in the event there was one. The defense generally makes this motion for the record, knowing that it won't be granted but that it will protect appellate remedies.

"There's no chance of the motion being granted," I said. "Ito won't dismiss this case without letting it go to the jury. And then the press will have 'Defense Loses Motion to Dismiss Case' as a headline tomorrow morning. There's no upside to it for us."

Ultimately we made a very perfunctory motion, not a written argument, and it was, as expected, summarily denied. On July 6, after ninety-two days and fifty-eight witnesses, the prosecution rested its case.

Chapter Twenty

One of the most important factors in a defense case is the demeanor of the defendant around the time of the crime. How did he look? How did he behave? Witnesses who can testify to these questions from their firsthand knowledge are called "demeanor witnesses."

Fortunately, the way O.J. had appeared near the time of the murders was one of our strongest points, and key to that was the video from Sydney's dance recital, which went so far to contradict prosecution witnesses who testified that he was out of sorts, angry, hostile, and preoccupied. This was a genial man, who had a relaxed and affectionate relationship with his former in-laws, and was obviously comfortable sharing this family event with them. Witnesses on the plane flight to Chicago would testify that they saw nothing out of the ordinary; witnesses on the flight back would testify that his behavior—the phone calls, the agitation—were in tune with what they would've expected, given his situation. Close family and friends would talk about his behavior at home, before and after the funeral.

O.J. Simpson had prided himself on discipline. It took discipline to sit in court day after day and not crack, and to maintain his sanity as he returned to his cell alone each night. I'm sure there were days he was tremendously sad, or depressed, or angry, but he wouldn't want anyone to see this. It wasn't how he had been brought up, and as best he could, he stayed "up," at least in public.

When the prosecution finally rested its case, the emotions O.J. had worked to keep under control hit him. This was what he had been waiting for. Their turn was over, and his turn was coming. As he reviewed our demeanor witnesses and we discussed the kinds of questions we would ask and the information we wanted the jury to hear, he grew very emotional.

"If we could guarantee a hung jury, would you rest the case now?" I asked him.

"No!" O.J. said adamantly. "No, absolutely not. I want to win. I feel like I could cry. But I'm not going to cry in front of this jury."

∞

Shortly after the Fourth of July weekend, our investigator Bill Pavelic informed me that a friend of mine, a lawyer from San Francisco, had called him several times about Mark Fuhrman.

This lawyer was someone Bill had worked with before, on my recommendation. The lawyer was aware, as anyone paying even mild attention to the case would have been, that Mark Fuhrman was of key concern to the defense team.

"A lawyer in Los Angeles is offering to sell audiotapes of Mark Fuhrman that will blow your case wide open," our contact told Bill. He had heard this from two tabloid reporters, who were as curious to hear the tapes as one might expect but who were also concerned about being victims of some kind of scam.

The Los Angeles lawyer's name was Matthew Schwartz, and he represented someone named Laura Hart McKinney. She was a screenwriter and had recently interviewed Fuhrman as part of a film project she was trying to develop about Los Angeles cops. Schwartz stated that the tapes contained many, many examples of clear perjury on the race issue, and the use of the *n* word in particular. Furthermore, they were a police "textbook" on framing blacks and planting evidence. There were fifteen hours of tape, approximately three hundred transcript pages. The bidding price of these tapes was slated to start at $250,000.

A licensed attorney making these representations would expose himself to major criminal liability if he was trying to perpetrate a scam. I tried to maintain my own skepticism while hoping all the while that Schwartz and his tapes were for real. I instructed Bill to pursue whatever avenues he could to find out if the tapes existed, and if they actually contained what the lawyer and Schwartz said they did. Bill Pavelic needed to act as fast as he could. If what the lawyer was telling us was true, I figured we had about one day to stay ahead of a tabloid bidding war. I didn't intend to meet or match anybody's price; I wanted the tapes subpoenaed.

Pavelic was told how to contact Matt Schwartz and Laura McKinney. In turn, Bill instructed the lawyer to call Carl Douglas and investigator Pat McKenna. Douglas would prepare the subpoena; McKenna was supposed to serve it. However, Gary Randa, Cathy Randa's son, got the subpoena assignment instead. When he went to Matt Schwartz's office, he was told that Schwartz was "on vacation." The person who told him this, we later discovered, was Matt Schwartz, who evidently wanted to keep the bidding war open.

The television tabloid show *Hard Copy* knew about the tapes; so, suddenly, did a lot of reporters. It was time to go directly to the source—McKinney—and to do that we had to go to North Carolina, where she now lived.

While the drama of the tapes was going on outside the courtroom, the defense team was considering whether or not O.J. should testify. He thought he was ready. He wanted to tell his side of the story from the beginning. But the advice that we would give him would be the most difficult decision a lawyer must make.

Early on, both Cochran and Lee Bailey had taken a public

position that O.J. should and would testify. But as the defense began its case, that decision still hadn't been made.

Jurors expect people who aren't guilty to testify and explain themselves, correct the misapprehensions, tell their story. No matter how many times the jurors are instructed and reminded that a defendant has no obligation to testify, our voir dire and focus groups showed that almost everyone wants to hear a defendant testify.

We had seen some of the world's best witnesses, both scientific and police, people who testify on a day-in, day-out basis, who have been on the witness stand hundreds of times. Yet, when put under the microscope of cross-examination, they were shown to have made inconsistent statements that lawyers later argued were a basis for disbelieving the witness or outright impeaching his credibility totally. But how do you tell a strong-willed man who has proclaimed his innocence for fifteen months that he should not testify?

For his part, O.J. was concerned about the jury's stamina. "I don't think they can take much more of this," he said. "They're exhausted. I'm afraid we might lose them."

Ultimately, the defense lawyers unanimously decided that O.J. would not testify, and he concurred with that decision.

∞

As we were preparing the defense case, O.J. was quoted in the *New York Daily News* as saying, "I ran two thousand yards in the snow, I can handle Marcia Clark."

"He said that in the lockup. How did it get out?" Johnnie asked. How do you think? I wanted to say. Bailey was back in town.

∞

The gears shifted considerably once the trial went to the defense part of the case. It seemed less frantic, less formal. Judge Ito, for the first time, was wearing jeans and sneakers under his robe. Witnesses would now come to the stand on behalf of O.J., not against him.

From here on, the defense strategy was to present credible demeanor witnesses to undo the prosecution's "demonization" of O.J. and timeline witnesses to refute the prosecution's theory of when the murders took place. Drs. Baden and Lee would then further counter the prosecution's forensic witnesses, arguing that errors in procedure and judgment had created a scenario that was possible, but not provable. Meanwhile, outside the courtroom, we would continue to pursue the Fuhrman tapes, with the intention of using them to impeach a key witness in what I hoped the jury would see as a hopelessly contaminated case.

On July 10, Arnelle Simpson was the first witness on behalf of the defense. A beautiful and charming young woman, she radiated the love and trust she had for her father, and he beamed across the room at her as she testified. She spoke very movingly about his shock and sadness at Nicole's death. She was a perfect, unimpeachable witness. The prosecution knew that and left her alone on cross-examination.

The next witnesses were O.J.'s sisters, Carmelita Simpson-Durio and Shirley Baker. They had been totally supportive of him, spending each day in the courtroom while keeping their jobs at night. They each gave a chilling view of what it had been like at O.J.'s house the night he came back from Chicago—sorrowful, depressing, everyone crying, looking for an answer. They effectively disputed Ron Shipp's testimony, testifying that they'd kept a very close eye on their brother that night, and O.J. had never been alone with anyone.

It wasn't so much what O.J.'s sisters said or even how they said it, but their presence was a powerful endorsement of their brother. "He was always there for us," they said.

And finally, there was O.J.'s mother, Eunice Simpson, who, in spite of advanced age and failing health, had sat patiently in her wheelchair for days at a time in the courtroom. While there, she had often been warm and affectionate toward the Brown family, as they had been to her. The families, after all, shared their grandchildren in common.

Mrs. Simpson looked elegant, dressed in shades of yellow, conveying serenity and faith in her son. Kardashian and Cochran opened the low swinging "bar" doors that separated the lawyers from the spectators, and helped her out of her wheelchair. Like the stoic she was—and like she'd taught her son to be—Mrs. Simpson would not allow anyone to help her, using her cane to take minuscule steps to the witness stand under her own strength and power.

She talked with great dignity about her son's life, his upbringing, and her special moments with him. She evoked a palpable love and empathy in the courtroom, and a sadness that she had seen her son go from the championship field to being a defendant in a murder case.

∞

We began our timeline witnesses with a young man named Dan Mendel and a young woman named Ellen Aronson. They had been on a blind date the night of the murder and had walked past the Bundy residence at 10:30, only a few minutes after the prosecution said the murders were being committed and the dog supposedly began wailing. Both testified that they neither saw nor heard anything unusual as they passed. Their testimony was simple and unequivocal.

Denise Pilnak, a Bundy neighbor, was another timeline witness. Pilnak was so time-sensitive that she usually wore two wristwatches, she said. Yes, she'd heard the dog barking, but not until 10:35. Until then the neighborhood had been quiet.

I had some reservations about Robert Heidstra, the next timeline witness, who was also a Bundy neighbor. I was concerned about his credibility. According to Lee Bailey, who had talked to him extensively, Heidstra didn't hear the dog barking until precisely 10:37. He'd heard men's voices as well, raised in an argument in front of Nicole's apartment at that time. I was worried about that kind of absolute precision, which is easy to impeach. Bailey assured us that Heidstra would be a good witness.

Heidstra, of French birth, had a very thick accent. Either he had trouble understanding the attorneys or they had trouble understanding him. Whatever the reason, his testimony came across as halting, equivocating, and confused. He further complicated matters by stating that he had seen a light-colored sports utility vehicle speeding away from Bundy. He couldn't say what exact make of car it was. However, he stated that it drove *down* Bundy when it left, which would mean the driver was going away from, not toward, O.J.'s house at Rockingham.

It's hard to say who won the Heidstra round, but I regretted that he'd been a witness for us. We should have known more about him, more about his background, and more about what he was going to say. During the next break, we were livid with Bailey. He had vouched for Heidstra's credibility; clearly, his judgment was off.

While Chris Darden was cross-examining Heidstra, the witness at one point agreed with Darden that, yes, one of the voices he'd heard was a "black" voice. Cochran immediately objected to what he called Darden's "racist" questioning.

"It was the witness's word," said Darden. "If it's racist, then it's the witness that's racist, not me."

Cochran continued to argue, and so did Darden.

"This is what created a lot of problems for myself and my family," Darden said angrily, "these statements that you make about me and race, Mr. Cochran."

I thought Ito was going to physically come down from the bench and break it up. "We'll take a recess," he said, "because right now I'm so mad at you guys, I'm about to hold you both in contempt."

I always thought that Darden had the second-toughest job in the courtroom. As a black man working for the prosecution—in a case that increasingly focused on race—he was caught in an almost constant bind. Johnnie's incessant baiting just intensified things.

But the most difficult job in the courtroom was Judge Ito's. Each lawyer had the benefit of a team of researchers and the advantage of having studied the evidence for more than a year. He had a research assistant and a couple of volunteer law students. As he heard the evidence for the first time, he had to make his rulings spontaneously from the bench, with the whole world watching him. When the criticism of him came, as it invariably did on an almost daily basis, the rules of judicial conduct prohibited him from doing what the rest of us did: walk out into the hallway and explain what had just happened in the courtroom and why.

∞

That night, Johnnie and I met with Matthew Schwartz, Laura Hart McKinney's attorney. He outlined the material contained in the tapes of Fuhrman. "They're important, and we know you're going to get them," he said. "We just want the opportunity to try to sell them first."

Once we'd heard about the existence of the tapes, both Johnnie and I immediately began to fear they'd be destroyed—which could lead to an obstruction of justice. Schwartz understood our concerns. His client was honorable, he said, and wouldn't do anything to undercut our case. She just wanted to explore the financial possibilities before the tapes became public and ceased to be of any value. We pledged that we would try not to subpoena them for a week, and in the meantime they would be kept in a safe. The safe was in McKinney's home, in North Carolina.

∞

While the Fuhrman discussions took place offstage, the trial continued. For three days in mid-July, Dr. Rob Huizenga testified to O.J.'s physical health. His osteo- and rheumatoid arthritis was quite serious, Huizenga said, and seriously limited his ability to move back and forth—laterally—even if O.J.'s appearance belied that.

"He looked like Tarzan," Huizenga said, "but he moved more like Tarzan's grandfather."

Once again Brian Kelberg performed one of his physical demonstrations to illustrate a hypothetical—this time holding Huizenga in front of him and making slashing motions—to show the jury that even someone with restricted lateral motion could have performed the physical actions necessary to slash a victim. Indeed, Huizenga had to admit that he could not say absolutely that O.J. was physically incapable of doing so.

In order to rebut Huizenga's claim that O.J.'s arthritis was serious, the prosecution played the exercise video O.J. had made just a few weeks before the murders. The video showed that O.J. could indeed raise his arms and move up and down, but he was quite limited in his capacity to move laterally, as Huizenga said he was. In fact, O.J. was working hard in the video to show he wasn't impaired by the disease that had so crippled his mother. "He did not want to see himself as arthritic," Huizenga testified. Richard Walsh, the physical trainer who directed and produced the video, would confirm Huizenga's view.

The press reported that Huizenga's testimony and the video were setbacks for the defense, but I wasn't so sure of that. Although O.J. appeared in high spirits on the tape and exuded great energy, there was a plodding quality to his movements, an absence of quickness and flexibility. I wondered if the jury tried to imagine him leaping over the back fence at Rockingham, dropping the glove, running into the wall, sprinting into the house, and making his limo in time to get to the airport. From the tape, I couldn't see it. I didn't think that they would, either.

∞

We were at the bench, and the court reporter needed to change the paper in her transcribing machine. "Don't let Marcia Clark talk," she said. Ito responded: "Would that I could prevent it."

∞

I was always interested in the mail that came to me via the courthouse. Often there were tips and information; just as often, I was fascinated and interested in what the "real" people were thinking, as opposed to the pundits and self-appointed experts. Throughout the summer, the letters to the defense team had been running about half in favor and half against. And then I opened a letter from Canada.

A man identifying himself only as a "Canadian citizen" said it was obvious that I was the only person O.J. Simpson would listen to. It was my duty, therefore, to make him plead guilty immediately. If I did not do so and O.J. walked, the man would find us, follow us, and approach us with twelve sticks of dynamite attached to his body. Dying didn't matter to him, he said—he had terminal cancer anyway, and no heirs. And if the dynamite didn't work, the one hundred thousand dollars he had in the bank would be used to hire a hit man. Shaken, I gave the letter to the sheriff's deputies.

Later that day, in an entirely unrelated matter, we heard that one of the deputies had been killed. At home and off-duty, he had gone to investigate a burglary in his own neighborhood and was shot. The news rocked all of us. The minutiae of a trial can sometimes distance you from the very reality that brings you there. You're in a courtroom, people in uniforms have guns, and the whole adversarial procedure is focused on crime—the people who commit it, and the people who try to prevent it. As in a morality play, the drama focuses on the good guys versus the bad guys. I am always jarred to realize that a courtroom is still an artificial, reconstructed reality. Every now and then the real pain of the streets intrudes.

Shortly after this, Johnnie Cochran began to show up at the courthouse accompanied by young black men from the Nation of Islam, Reverend Louis Farrakhan's organization. They were his bodyguards, he said in response to my protests. I couldn't have been more dismayed. I didn't want them anywhere near this case or my client. Their presence sent the wrong message.

∞

Early on in our investigation, we had learned that there was a concentration of a chemical called EDTA found in some of the blood evidence from Bundy and the sock found at Rockingham. EDTA is a preservative used in reference samples of blood; that is, samples of blood taken from individuals to be used later for comparison with samples from the crime scene. As was customary, O.J.'s blood reference sample in the lab had been treated with EDTA. If traces of EDTA were found in the blood evidence, that blood had either been confused with or planted as real evidence.

Here the hubris of the prosecution surfaced in an ironic fashion. Their attorney Rock Harmon was so sure that there was no EDTA in this blood evidence that he issued a challenge. "If they're so interested, let's send this blood to the lab," he said. "If EDTA is found on these items, then this is a case that shouldn't be prosecuted, and we'll dismiss it. If there's no EDTA present, then we'll know we're right, and the defendant should change his plea to guilty."

Samples were sent to the FBI lab; the reports came back positive for EDTA. The prosecution then tried to backtrack, arguing that EDTA is a naturally occurring substance present in everyone's blood, preserved or not. We countered with testimony that the amount of EDTA found on the sock and the back gate exceeded the amount one would normally expect to find. We wanted the jury to hear our basic question: Why was a blood preservative found where it seemed questionable?

Our witness Frederic Rieders, a forensic toxicologist, acknowledged that his review confirmed the existence of EDTA preservative in the sock and on the back gate at Bundy. In answer to a challenge from Marcia Clark, he said, "If you hear hoofbeats, it's more likely to be horses, not zebras. So it's most likely that the source for EDTA in a blood sample is that it was EDTA blood to begin with."

Due to a scheduling conflict, Marcia Clark couldn't continue her cross until a few days later. When she got Rieders back on the stand, she'd had some time to do further background checking and proceeded to relentlessly attack the witness on errors he'd made in another case seven years prior to the O.J. trial.

Ito grew very short-tempered with her line of questioning. "Let's wind this up," he snapped. "Let's try the Simpson case sometime today. In fact, that's it for this witness, we're through."

I suspect the whole discussion, like much of the blood wars, was beyond anyone's comprehension, including the jury and many of the lawyers. But the general effect was to undermine the jury's perception of police procedure.

∞

In the middle of July, we informed Judge Ito of the existence and substance of Laura Hart McKinney's taped interviews with Mark Fuhrman. Based on the brief excerpts we'd heard and the information we'd given him, the judge agreed that they were material to the case and immediately issued a subpoena for their return to his jurisdiction.

At the end of July, Johnnie Cochran went to North Carolina armed with the subpoena. There a local judge blocked our attempt to get McKinney's Fuhrman tapes, ruling that the tapes were only collateral, not material, to the question of O.J.'s guilt, and therefore the defense had no right to them.

It was a major setback for us. Shocked and frustrated by the ruling, Cochran announced our intention to appeal. At this point the news was out. From one end of the country to the other we heard the question: What is on those tapes?

On August 7, the North Carolina appellate court overruled the lower court and ordered that the McKinney tapes be turned over to us.

The prosecution team was now fully aware of the tapes, and what they reportedly contained. Now that we had obtained them through our own efforts, our money, and our fight with the North Carolina court system, Marcia Clark decided that they belonged to her. None of us among the defense team had heard the tapes in their entirety, and the prosecution hadn't heard them at all. And who "owned" them wouldn't keep them from being evidence in the case; they would have to be shared with the other side in discovery. So her move to claim them for the prosecution was, as far as I was concerned, an ineffective power play.

To complicate matters further, Judge Ito himself was indirectly involved in the contents of the tapes. They contained material pertinent to Captain Margaret York, Ito's wife, involving confrontations Fuhrman had had with her. If this was true, it would contradict Captain York's earlier statements that she'd had no dealings with Fuhrman—and that therefore there had been no need for Ito to remove himself from the case. Thus we faced yet another ironic encounter with the prosecution. The tapes that were our salvation were quite possibly also the potential source of a mistrial.

Chapter Twenty-one

I was looking forward to presenting Michael Baden's testimony on behalf of the defense. "There are great limitations on what medical examiners can do in our reconstructions," he had said when he agreed to testify. "We can't, for example, go to an arson scene, examine the ashes of the deceased, and tell if that person had a mustache." But there was solid information to be obtained, provided that you didn't have to contend with such factors as incomplete investigations, an incompetent laboratory staff, and a ten-hour delay while you waited for the coroner to arrive at the crime scene. By the same token, there are 1400 homicides in Los Angeles County each year, and no one had questioned the collection of blood evidence in the microscopic way that we had in this case.

In August, Michael Baden testified that when he was at the L.A.P.D. crime lab two days after the murders and examined the socks that were removed from O.J.'s home, neither he nor Dr. Wolf nor the L.A.P.D. lab's Michelle Kestler had seen blood on them.

Dr. Baden's testimony was intended primarily to show that testimony delivered by the prosecutor's medical examiner went far beyond what can be learned from an autopsy examination. This was expecially true in the case of Dr. Lakshmanan, who had substituted as a witness for Dr. Golden, the original coroner. For instance, when Dr. Lakshmanan described the attack on Ron Goldman as having been committed from behind, by a single assailant who was right-handed, of athletic build, with a height and weight similar to O.J.'s, he was over-reaching what he had any ability to know with a reasonable degree of certainty.

Baden also challenged the prosecution's contention that the attack on the two victims could've been accomplished within one or two minutes. There had been a protracted struggle, as evidenced by Ron Goldman's hugely swollen right hand, which led Dr. Baden to believe he'd hit his attacker quite hard, probably inflicting considerable damage. He explained that Goldman had died as the result of slow seeping of blood from veins in the neck, and that it would have taken at least five or ten minutes of blood loss in this manner for death to occur. He knew this, he said, because the wounds in the lungs had produced very little bleeding.

On Kelberg's cross, he asked Dr. Baden what explanation O.J. had given for the cuts on his fingers when Baden first examined him at the Kardashian residence on June 17, 1994. Baden explained that Simpson had told him he first cut himself while searching for his cell phone in the Bronco in the dark on the night of June 12, and then cut himself more deeply on the broken glass in the Chicago hotel room, thus resolving prosecution allegations of alleged inconsistent statements by the defense about the cut fingers.

Although Baden could not say with a reasonable degree of medical certainty how many killers there were, his opinion was that one person could not have murdered both Nicole and Ron without incurring significant injuries, as well as being drenched by a tremendous amount of the victims' blood. As we reminded the jury, our immediate physical examination of O.J. the day after the crimes, and the photographs taken at that examination, reflected no injuries from such a struggle.

∞

In mid-August, the battle in Judge Ito's chambers over who "owned" the Fuhrman tapes threatened to overshadow whatever trial proceedings were going on in the courtroom on any given day. Once the tapes arrived at Judge Ito's office, he decided that by rights they belonged to the defense. In a meeting with both sides, he gave them to Johnnie Cochran.

At one point Marcia Clark said heatedly, "We will object to the playing of these tapes!" Barry Scheck shot back at her, "How can you object without even hearing them?" Marcia looked directly at him and snapped, "Shut up, Scheck."

Scheck turned red with anger, and something seemed to snap. Thereafter he was much less tolerant of Marcia's behavior. As a man of real moral principles, Scheck was appalled that the prosecutor was determined to protect her witness even if it could be proved he had perjured himself.

In the portions of the tapes we'd heard, Fuhrman was an equal-opportunity bigot, expressing the same poisonous hostility toward blacks, Hispanics, and women—including his former superior, Captain Margaret York. As the defense feared might happen, Marcia Clark cited a conflict of interest on Judge Ito's part and quickly moved to request that the judge recuse himself from the trial.

It was clear that the prosecution had lost any desire to be fair about either evidence or this judge. It was bad enough that they had refused to call the coroner, Irwin Golden, to the stand because he had clearly bungled the autopsy. Now they were fuming because the judge was losing patience with their antics. There was an air of desperation in the prosecution's actions. Henry Lee had informed us that they were frantically shopping around the country for additional experts to try and rebut defense evidence. Now in Fuhrman's tapes they were faced with a potent weapon that would destroy a witness they had made the center of their case. They had been warned about Fuhrman and chosen to ignore those warnings. If this judge didn't go along with squelching the tapes, the prosecution would simply try to replace him with a judge who would.

Both the prosecution and defense had been aware of the potential conflict posed by Captain York from day one. And both sides had agreed to take a waiver allowing Judge Ito to hear the case. The very reason for taking a waiver was to acknowledge potential problems down the line, since York was an important police official.

Judge Ito was upset by the prosecution's bid to disqualify him. He saw no choice but to make some accommodation to their concerns, even though it raised the specter of a mistrial. In a session held outside the presence of the jury, he said, "I love my wife dearly, and I am wounded by criticism of her." He was on the verge of tears, but continued: "I therefore recuse myself on the matter of the tapes themselves, and on the decision as to whether or not Margaret York will testify."

That wasn't enough for the prosecution, however. Clark wanted a complete recusal, and a new judge.

The following day, because of the prosecution's actions, Judge Ito had packed up all the case materials in his office. He seemed resigned, indeed relieved, at the prospect of leaving the case and having another judge take over.

However, a somewhat subdued Clark came back willing to accept Ito's offer of a partial recusal. I suspect the prosecution was sobered by the idea of a mistrial caused by their loose-cannon witness. Perhaps cooler heads had prevailed, or the district attorney had decided to take a chance with things as they were.

Judge Ito would rule on the admissibility of the tapes; Superior Court Judge John Reid would rule regarding Margaret York. Within a brief two days, Reid decided that York's testimony would be of no benefit or import to this trial, and the matter was once again put to rest. Judge Ito would continue to preside as the sitting judge at the trial.

∞

In the lockup, O.J. passed the time by doing one of two things: playing solitaire, hand after hand, or reading a book. Every other day, it seemed, there was a new book that he'd consumed and wanted to talk about.

During the week he had court every day. The weekends, however, were particularly hard for him. Officials had reduced his telephone time, and they'd even cut back on his "freeway" time, when he was allowed to walk back and forth in a narrow corridor without anyone to talk to. It was like being in solitary confinement. On one rare occasion, he blew up at the deputies. He was watching a ball game on the television just outside his cell, and at a crucial point they switched to a local program that featured former police chief Darryl Gates—talking about the O.J. Simpson case. It seemed that no matter where you were, you just couldn't get away from it.

Barry Scheck's anger at Marcia Clark had been simmering ever since she'd ordered him to shut up in Judge Ito's chambers. He couldn't believe that she would argue to keep the tapes out just to maintain the integrity of her witness, Mark Fuhrman. "The man lied under oath!" he said. "How can they suborn his perjury?"

Scheck's DNA work in particular had always been focused on undoing the damage caused by prosecutors in falsely convicting innocent defendants. Scheck's indignation naturally spilled over whenever he felt prosecutors were being given unfair advantage in a courtroom they viewed as their home court, with a judge they thought should be a "home referee." That kind of arrogance was a natural outcome of the Divine Right of the Prosecution. However, I believed that while Judge Ito was a pro-prosecution judge, he would be fair. I believed that not only would he allow us to impeach Fuhrman's testimony about the use of the *n* word, we would be given license to show broader police misconduct as well. Naturally the prosecutors were going to fight that as long as they could. They had no desire to see the Simpson trial turn into the Fuhrman trial.

"He found the glove, he didn't plant it," said Gil Garcetti.

"He lied," was the defense response. Meanwhile a restive jury was sitting in isolation outside the courtroom, while Ito decided if they'd ever hear about Fuhrman's lies. As Ito had warned us, "I'm very concerned about the durability of this jury."

Nevertheless, the very existence of the tapes gave us a tactical advantage we didn't have before. Our colleague Bob Blasier said that in each of his trials there had come a point when he would become convinced of the outcome. "I think this is it," he now told me. "I think we're going to win."

∞

In late August, with the jury still waiting in sequestration, Gerald Uelmen presented his impassioned motion to admit the Fuhrman tapes, and Marcia Clark responded with an equally impassioned plea that they not be admitted.

The argument began with the screenwriter who had recorded the tapes, Laura Hart McKinney. Clearly, she was not a witness who could be impeached on any level. Her credibility had nothing to do with whether the jury would or would not hear the tapes. All she was going to testify to was that she had recorded the tapes herself, and that it was Mark Fuhrman's voice on them. Her testimony would be given without the jury present, since it was relevant at this point only to the admissibility of the tapes. The prosecution, and in particular Chris Darden, nevertheless tried to make McKinney look like a liar.

On August 29 the tapes were played in the absence of the jury, in order to decide what portion of them, if any, the jury would hear. For two emotional hours, the judge, the attorneys, and the courtroom observers sat and listened for the first time to this torrent of obscenities. Fuhrman used the word "nigger" more than forty times, and that wasn't the worst of it. As our original contact had reported, the tapes were a textbook for police brutality and witness intimidation, all stemming from hatred so profound it was like a physical, toxic presence in the courtroom. Fuhrman talked about beating people and breaking their bones, about pounding their faces into mush, about how "every word out of a nigger's mouth is a lie," about how he'd planted or manufactured evidence to "set niggers up." He preened about his importance as a key witness in the Simpson case. "If I go down, they lose their case. . . . The glove is everything. Without the glove . . . bye-bye," he said. It went on and on, becoming more and more obscene, until finally the only possible human response was nausea. Or a desire to crawl out of your skin.

Johnnie Cochran was uncharacteristically silent after the tapes had ended. So were the prosecutors. I was speechless. In twenty-five years as a lawyer, I'd seen and heard a lot behind the scenes, but this was beyond anything in my imagination. These were the words of a deeply disturbed man. How could he have remained on the police force?

Chris Darden looked agonized and shaken. When Gil Garcetti arrived for a private conversation with his courtroom team, Chris was obviously struggling to focus on his boss's words.

The reporters in the room were silent as well, and completely stunned. Later I learned that Linda Deutsch, the AP reporter, glanced over at Dominick Dunne and they discovered they'd written exactly the same words in their notebooks. *It's over.*

Outside the courtroom, Ron Goldman's family expressed their outrage that the trial had, in their estimation, now become the Mark Fuhrman trial. I remembered turning around one day in court to see Ron's sister, Kim Goldman, watching me. "You son of a bitch," she mouthed silently.

On the last day of August, in a ten-page ruling, Judge Ito stated that the bulk of what we'd all heard in the courtroom would not be admissible. He would, however, allow two incidents to be played to the jury. The two admissible references were relatively innocuous, and they would go only to substantiate Fuhrman's use of the *n* word. It seemed a crushing rejection for the defense. The jury would hear nothing from Fuhrman about beating up witnesses, nothing about planting evidence, nothing about his behavior, which to my mind was clearly pathological.

On September 5, a quietly attentive jury heard the admissible portions of the tapes. On September 6, outside of their presence, Fuhrman was recalled to the stand, and he proceeded to exercise his right of protection against self-incrimination. It was his intention, he stated, not to respond to any and all questions, from either the prosecution or the defense. He would, instead, assert his Fifth Amendment privileges.

Judge Ito ruled that he would not call Fuhrman back to the stand in front of the jury, saying that it would be incorrect to call a witness knowing in advance that he would answer with the Fifth. The defense was understandably disappointed in this decision. Would he *tell* the jury, then, that Fuhrman had taken the Fifth? Ito turned down this option as well. The defense then offered a possible compromise. We proposed that he inform the jurors that Mark Fuhrman was now "unavailable" for further testimony, and the jury could use that information to make their own evaluation of his credibility as a witness.

Ito agreed to offer this softer instruction, but the prosecution immediately appealed it. When the State Appeals Court overruled Ito's decision, assistant district attorney Cheri Lewis was reported in the *New York Times* as being seen happily skipping out of Judge Ito's courtroom.

Without the tapes, we still offered several witnesses to impeach Detective Fuhrman's credibility to this jury. One, Kathleen Bell, a white woman, reported Fuhrman having said that he routinely stopped couples if the man was black and the woman was white, even if he had to manufacture a reason to do so. "If I had my way, they'd gather all niggers together and burn 'em," he told her.

Another witness, Roderic Hodge, was once arrested by Fuhrman, who told him, "I told you I'd get you, nigger."

Yet another, Natalie Singer, repeated what Fuhrman had once told her was his motto: "The only good nigger is a dead nigger."

And finally, Laura Hart McKinney informed the jury that she had recorded these tapes. She confirmed that Mark Fuhrman had used the *n* word forty-two times. Even more damaging, she said the limited portions that had been played for the jury were the least offensive, the least inflammatory, of the entire fifteen hours of tapes. I suspect that leaving the other forty references to the jurors' imaginations was a powerful "piece" of evidence in and of itself.

∞

Near the end of August, as the Fuhrman drama began to play itself out, the esteemed Dr. Henry Lee again came to testify for the defense. Barry Scheck conducted the direct examination, and an increasingly agitated Hank Goldberg did the cross.

The focus of Dr. Lee's testimony was to point out the errors in the district attorney's crime-scene reconstruction. Among these was Lee's identification of what he thought might be a shoeprint on Ron Goldman's jeans—a print that came not from a Bruno Magli shoe, he said, but possibly a second killer. This finding was not a definitive one, he was quick to say, it was only a possibility that had been overlooked by the coroner.

As Dr. Lee spoke, the jury members were as focused and attentive as I had seen them, even while he did some painstaking but tedious blood-spatter demonstrations. One pays extra attention to Henry Lee, and not just because of his careful if occasionally fractured English. The presentation, the precision and forthrightness of his manner, make him the epitome of the credible witness.

He challenged the integrity of some of the blood spots removed from the crime scene and testified about the swatches of blood samples he was allowed to examine in the L.A.P.D. lab. They were damp, he said. If they had been properly stored, they should have been dry by the time he looked at them. "Only opinion I can give under these circumstances— something wrong," he said.

Like all good witnesses, he tried to reduce scientific testimony to a metaphor that the jury could readily grasp. He compared the lab contamination to finding a cockroach in a plate of spaghetti. "All you need is one . . . and you know it is contaminated."

When Hank Goldberg foolishly tried to challenge him, Dr. Lee again responded firmly, "Something is wrong."

On September 11, the defense had come to the end of its presentation. It was our decision to refuse to rest our case, however, until the California Supreme Court had ruled on Judge Ito's instruction to the jury regarding Fuhrman. Judge Ito, in an unprecedented move, then directed the prosecution to go ahead with its rebuttal case.

With a concerned eye on the flagging jury, Ito gave firm instructions that court would begin at precisely 8:30. One morning Marcia Clark had not yet arrived at the appointed time. The jury was seated, and Ito was growing steadily more angry. When Marcia Clark arrived, a half-hour late, the judge fined the prosecution $250. She became a little sarcastic, and Ito upped the ante to $1000. Gil Garcetti reacted like an angry basketball coach whose star player had just been given an undeserved technical foul. "I've told my people not to pay this fine. It's vindictive, petty, and not called for," he fumed. At the end of the day, Ito brought the fine back down to $250. Garcetti still wasn't pacified. "Outrageous," he said.

As the trial moved to its close, I sweated through my thrice-weekly boxing sessions in my garage with Jason Rossi, the gifted athlete and trainer whose arduous twelve-round workouts had kept me going. At twenty-five, Jason often seemed to have more maturity than men twice his age. All during the trial, he had constantly arranged and rearranged his schedule to accommodate mine. On one level his coaching was directed toward honing a physical skill; he also taught me to focus completely on one thing, to the exclusion of all others. Contrary to what one might've expected, I was rarely exhausted after a session with Jason. Instead, I was sharper, quicker. Whatever anger or frustration I had accumulated during the day was left in a sweaty puddle on the garage floor.

∞

Prompted by Judge Ito's impatience, the prosecution responded with a hurried series of rebuttal witnesses. On September 14, Gary Sims, the senior criminologist from the California Department of Justice, was called back to testify again that DNA tests of the blood found in the Bronco showed it to be Ron Goldman's. However, Barry Scheck's cross elicited evidence that the car, in spite of being a major piece of evidence, wasn't very well secured through the entire time it was in police custody.

"From June 14 until August 26, there were no records kept as to who entered and left the tow yard," Scheck said. "Unauthorized personnel were in and out of the car, in the seats and so forth. Would you consider that an appropriate way to preserve biological evidence?"

Sims answered honestly. "No, I don't think that should be allowed." After the trial was over, the investigation into the police lab procedures became so intensive that Gerald Uelmen quipped, "They closed the barn door after the Bronco was out."

Another prosecution witness, L.A.P.D. nurse Thano Peratis, was admitted on videotape rather than in the flesh, despite our objections. Peratis, who had drawn O.J.'s blood on June 13, 1994, had suffered a heart attack and was advised by his physician not to come to court. The prosecution wanted Peratis to appear on tape. We objected because we wouldn't be able to cross-examine him, or make our case that there was a percentage of O.J.'s original blood sample unaccounted for.

The issue of admitting the Peratis tape grew somewhat prolonged as Marcia Clark continued to spar with Peter Neufeld and Judge Ito about its importance. "You're warned in no uncertain terms," Ito told her. He did agree, however, to admit a portion of the tape.

When Hank Goldberg asked Peratis, on the video, how much blood he drew from O.J., the technician's answer was significantly different than it had been almost a year and a half earlier. "I came to the conclusion," he said, "that I didn't draw eight ccs. I drew about six to six and a half ccs." The defense team all agreed that Peratis's recovered memory was convenient indeed, especially since the district attorney thought it answered the question of the missing 1.5 ccs. Ironically, after the video-tape was played to the jury, we decided that it probably did more harm than good for the prosecution. The fact that a witness was adjusting his story at this late date couldn't help but give rise to a jury's suspicions.

Even at this tired time in the trial, there were a few light moments. For instance, there was a question about nighttime visibility at the Bundy crime scene. Judge Ito talked about phases of the moon affecting the available light. "Had it been waxing or waning?" he asked.

Marcia Clark requested that he explain the two terms to the jury. Ito was irritated, and said, "Everybody knows the difference between a waxing and waning moon!" And then he polled the courtroom to see who knew the difference between waxing and waning. I didn't. For once, Marcia and I were in accord.

On September 16, continuing the prosecution rebuttal, FBI shoe-imprint expert Bill Bodziak testified that Lee erred in iden-tifying a "second footprint." Of course, Dr. Lee had never "identified" a second footprint; rather, he said there was the possibility of an unidentified pattern imprint being that of a second shoe.

Richard Rubin, the glove expert, was asked at his court re-appearance by Bob Blasier, "Have you tried to be impartial?" When Rubin assured him that he had, Blasier read a postscript that had appeared at the end of an earlier letter to the prosecu-tion from Rubin. "Maybe I can make it to the victory party," he wrote.

On September 18, the prosecution conditionally rested their case.

∞

As our final rebuttal, we called two FBI informants to squeal not on the mob, but on Detective Vannatter. Craig and Larry Fiato, two ex-mobsters, were FBI informants currently in the Bureau's witness protection program. They and their FBI "minder" had been in the L.A. courthouse some months previous on another murder case where the Fiato brothers were witnesses for the prosecution. While smoking cigarettes in a designated area on the eighteenth floor, they met and talked with Detective Philip Vannatter. They had also spoken with him at another time, in a hotel room where they were waiting before they gave their testimony.

They were now prepared to come and testify that Vannatter had told them that on the morning of the murders the L.A.P.D. detectives "didn't go to Rockingham with the intention of saving people," as he'd testified, but rather because "the husband is always the suspect." If Vannatter had said it, this admission would go toward impeaching all the early testimony about why Fuhrman went over the wall and why the police had been roaming the property and looking for evidence without a warrant. But there was a risk here: Our witnesses were not without a few blemishes of their own.

Craig Fiato, also known as Tony the Animal, looked like what you might get if you put in a request to Central Casting for a wanna-be mobster. He sported an odd blond dye job on top of what was obviously dark hair, a dark goatee, and a large gold hoop earring in one ear. To season the mix even further, he testified to having had an intimate relationship with Denise Brown, Nicole's sister.

Craig and his brother Larry testified in a blacked-out courtroom. The television camera had been turned off to protect the Fiatos' identities. It was a true Hollywood moment. Then later that night Craig Fiato appeared on Larry King's show, in full view of the camera. "To think, he could've been my brother-in-law," O.J. joked.

Next, Detective Vannatter was recalled to the stand. I asked him, "Is there any doubt in your mind that O.J. Simpson was not a suspect when you first went to Rockingham?"

As affable as he'd been in his court appearances to date, Vannatter was clearly angry at being recalled. The fact that his return visit had been occasioned by two mob informants hadn't improved his disposition. "Mr. Simpson was no more a suspect at that point than you were, Mr. Shapiro," Vannatter said, in another memorable overstatement.

L.A.P.D. Commander Keith Bushey was then called by the prosecution to rebut the Fiatos' testimony. He testified that as commander of the L.A. West Bureau, it had been his decision to order the four detectives to Rockingham, in order to tell O.J. about the murders before he heard it on the news or from any other outside source. At sidebar when Cochran announced, "I'm gonna do this witness myself," and that he was going to be very tough on him, Ito gave him a look. The judge had admitted earlier that he was tired, that he was looking forward to the final arguments and not having to make any more rulings.

"I wish more people would ask questions like Mr. Shapiro does," the judge said. "That includes you, Mr. Cochran."

"I'll try, Your Honor," said Cochran.

By now, O.J. was as ready as anyone for it all to end. He told us that he'd talked to his son Justin the day before on the phone. Justin had asked him, "Daddy, why doesn't Dita [Juditha Brown] bring you home to have dinner with us?"

∞

Judge Ito was going to present his instructions to the jury prior to the closing statements of the prosecution and defense. Gerry Uelmen and Brian Kelberg argued back and forth over what Ito would be able to instruct the jury.

When the judge said that the jurors would be told they

should disregard Ron Shipp's dream statement if they found either that it wasn't made, or that it was expressing "unconscious thoughts," Kelberg objected. Ito asked if he was objecting because "Shipp happens." Everybody in the courtroom laughed.

The defense wanted Ito to instruct the jury that they would be allowed to reject all of Mark Fuhrman's testimony if they decided he testified falsely about anything. As to the specific murder charges the judge would instruct the jury to consider, Gerry Uelmen argued for a charge of first degree murder only. Kelberg asked for an instruction for both first and second degree (unpremeditated) murder, because he didn't want the jury faced with what he called an all-or-nothing Hobson's Choice of either sending O.J. to prison for life or setting him completely free.

Ito denied our motion on Fuhrman and informed us he would instruct the jury that they could find for either first- or second-degree murder. He then called a recess for lunch and left the bench. As he did, Barry Scheck slammed his legal pad to the table. "How many ways can we get fucked?" he said under his breath, and walked out of the room. He later apologized to the judge, who had heard the remark. Seeing the end in sight, Ito said only, "We'll take it up later, Mr. Scheck."

On Friday, September 22, O.J. Simpson was given a chance to address the judge outside the presence of the jury. We had been in chambers, and the judge had indicated that since O.J. had decided not to testify in open court, he needed that waiver on the record.

The defense indicated that O.J. wished to make a statement to the judge. When Judge Ito came out on the bench to hear that statement, Marcia Clark pleaded with him. "Please, don't do this, Your Honor. I beg you, don't do this."

She believed that any statement by Simpson that was not subject to cross-examination was inappropriate. She suggested that it was being done deliberately by the defense in hopes that whatever he said would eventually leak to the jury, perhaps via conjugal or family visits.

Ito overruled her objection and indicated that he was ready to hear the defendant's statement. O.J. rose to his feet and said, "As much as I would like to address some of the misrepresentations made about myself and Nicole concerning our life together, I am mindful of the mood and stamina of this jury. I have confidence—a lot more, it seems, than Ms. Clark has—of their integrity and that they will find as the record stands now that I did not, could not, and would not have committed this murder. I have four kids, two kids I haven't seen in a year. They ask me every week, 'Dad, how much longer?'"

As Judge Ito began to interrupt him, O.J. quickly finished. "I want this trial over. Thank you."

"Mr. Simpson, you do understand your right to testify?" the judge asked.

"Yes, I do."

"And you choose to waive that right?"

"Yes, Your Honor," O.J. said. "I do."

The defense rested.

Chapter Twenty-two

∞

Judge Ito assured the jury that after they heard his instructions, the prosecution and defense closing arguments would proceed as quickly as possible, without any breaks. There were scattered smiles among them, exhaustion mixed with anticipation, as though they had been on a long ocean voyage that was coming to an end.

At the prosecution table, Chris Darden and Marcia Clark were joined by Brian Kelberg. For the defense, in the front row sat myself, Cochran, O.J., Bob Blasier, Peter Neufeld, and Gerry Uelmen; behind us were Carl Douglas, Robert Kardashian, and Barry Scheck.

Looking very stern, Judge Ito addressed the jury. "It is now my duty to instruct you on the law as it applies to this case. . . . You must accept and follow the law as I state it to you, whether or not you agree with the law. You must not be influenced by pity for the defendant or prejudice against him. You must not be influenced by sentiment, sympathy, conjecture, passion, prejudice, public opinion, or public feeling. You must weigh the evidence, apply the law, and reach a just verdict regardless of the consequence."

The jury was tired. Juror number one, our odds-on favorite for foreman, was the only one taking notes. When Ito read the instruction that the defendant had no obligation to prove who committed these crimes, she carefully wrote it down.

Number two was clearly exhausted, with heavy eyes and mussed hair, looking like a student who had just finished her last final. Number three determinedly showed no change in her expression. Number four looked sleepy, with bags under his eyes and the youthful smile fading. Number five had looked exhausted for weeks; we'd heard the day before that she was taking pain medication for an infection, and I wondered about her ability or even her willingness to concentrate.

Juror number six had his right hand under his chin, looking stoic, ready to decide. Number seven seemed angry, as though she had no interest in the closing statements. "Why are they doing this?" her expression said. "I'm ready to deliberate *now*."

Juror number eight was very focused and seemed the least weary. Number nine had routinely shown more expression than anyone else and often seemed to wear her heart on her sleeve. Number ten was sitting up ramrod straight, looking directly at Ito.

Number eleven was the least expressive and most anonymous. Youth has its advantages, and throughout the trial, she had rarely showed any stress. Number twelve looked resigned, somehow pragmatic, as though thinking, "Life goes on. Let's get on with it."

The two remaining alternates were clearly ready to go home. The man looked sharp, the only one in a suit and tie on a Friday when everyone else wore jeans and a T-shirt. The woman seemed downcast, isolated from the others now that she knew she was not going to be deliberating after months of hearing evidence.

As Ito delivered his instructions, O.J. was fingering the family Bible on the table in front of him. Ito's clerk, Deirdre Robertson, kept opening mail at her desk. It was so quiet in the courtroom, you could hear the paper tear.

Fred Goldman was leaning forward, his eyes on Ito. His wife was sitting back in her chair. They were holding hands and silently praying, their hands clasped so tightly the skin looked like marble. Their daughter Kim looked like she would burst into tears any minute. It was almost over for us, yet for them, it must have seemed endless. When I caught Goldman's eye, he looked back with pure hatred. And I understood it. I wanted to reach out to him, to tell him I was sorry. I knew I would never, never be able to do that.

Arnelle was the only Simpson family member in court that day. She was rubbing her head, a clear sign of stress and fear, and halfway through the judge's instructions, she began to cry. When Ito began, I noted the time: 10:20 A.M. and fifty seconds. At the finish, it was 11:57 A.M. and thirty seconds. Except for the sound of Arnelle weeping, the room was totally silent.

September 25, the night before closing statements were to begin, was Rosh Hashanah, the celebration of the Jewish New Year. We attended services at Stephen Weiss Temple. Rabbi Zeldin gave me the Torah to hold throughout the entire service, announcing to the congregation that "Bob Shapiro has the honor of holding the Torah because he's going to need this blessing in the new year more than anyone." It was an astonishing gesture of faith and support on his part, and one for which he would be roundly criticized in the days to come. I was profoundly grateful for it.

On September 26, the prosecution began their closing statements. Marcia Clark would speak first.

That morning, I arrived at the courthouse to the largest crowd since the beginning of the case. O.J. and I met in the lockup briefly. My adrenaline was pumping. I turned to O.J. and said, "I can't imagine how you feel."

He was hyper, his words coming faster than usual. He was upset about his clothes. "They took the tie I usually wear with this," he said distractedly. As we walked in, he said, "Marcia Clark's going to do a great job."

We would get only one chance in front of the jury; the prosecution, since they were allowed to rebut, would get two. "We're ready," Johnnie said, reassuring O.J. "We're ready."

Before court started, Juditha Brown and Eunice Simpson, in her wheelchair, were whispering out in the hall, their heads close together. They may have been sitting on opposite sides of the courtroom, but the most important thing to them was always that they were grandmothers to the same children. Juditha later came into the courtroom with Tanya Brown; neither Denise nor Lou was there. Arnelle and Jason Simpson weren't there; O.J.'s mother and two sisters were. The three Goldmans were there.

Behind the families were the friends. From where I sat at the end of the defense table, I could see them all. Steve and Candace Garvey. The musician David Foster and his wife Linda, formerly married to Bruce Jenner. Bruce Jenner with his wife, Kris, formerly married to Bob Kardashian. In spite of their differences and personal histories, all of these couples had raised children and stepchildren together, going to O.J. and Nicole's for birthdays and barbecues. Since the murders, many of the friendships had ended. Now they were sitting uncomfortably close, waiting tensely as the story moved to its conclusion.

As Marcia Clark began speaking, Tanya Brown dropped her head into her hands and sighed audibly enough to be heard. O.J. was breathing heavily. The jury was completely riveted on Marcia. She was almost matter-of-fact, yet soft.

She knew that she had to separate her own credibility from Mark Fuhrman's. She came down hard on him. "Did he lie about the *n* word?" she asked, and then answered, "Yes. Do we wish no such person belonged to the L.A.P.D.? Yes. Do we wish no such person were on the planet?" she asked, and again answered in the affirmative. She was eloquent in her dismissal of him, and in the dismissal of the planted-glove theory. But I wondered: Is this good enough to get the sound of his voice on the tapes out of the jurors' memories?

She weakened a little at the motive, and what she called the planning, noting that O.J. borrowed cash from Kato. However, as she moved to the murders themselves, O.J. and Tanya Brown started crying at the same time. Fred Goldman had his jacket off. Arnelle sat with her head buried in her hands, her aunt's hand on her back.

Suddenly there was an interruption. A camera had focused on O.J.'s hand as he wrote something on the legal pad in front of him. Judge Ito stopped the proceeding, saying that what had happened was a clear intrusion on the attorney-client privilege. He was thinking of ending the camera coverage, he said. Soon, however, he relented, and once again, Clark continued her closing.

"These are not efficient murders," Clark said. "They are slaughters." As she spoke, O.J. and Tanya again started to cry. I could hear Fred Goldman breathing heavily behind me, and as his son was mentioned, he too began weeping. "Open up the windows," Clark said. "Let the cool wind of reason come in."

Chris Darden's closing came after Marcia's, and it was his best lawyering of the entire trial. He was passionate, straightforward, and spoke from the heart, with complete conviction.

When he talked about Nicole's move to Bundy, O.J. leaned over and whispered, "He's got the dates wrong, what's he talking about?" When he talked about Simpson being a time bomb ticking away, O.J. said, "That's wrong. I gave it a year; we broke up, we agreed it was best. Why is he saying I was angry at the recital? He's stretching like I can't believe. All anybody has to do is look at that video. I wasn't mad." Judge Ito gave me a now-familiar look. He could hear every word O.J. was saying.

We were haunted by Johnnie's opening statements. Darden and Clark hammered on Rosa Lopez, on Mary Anne Gerchas and the four men running away from Bundy. These were all witnesses we never called. "I'm just the messenger for Nicole,"

Darden was saying. "She wanted you to know, she left you a road map."

We recessed for the day before Darden had completed his statements, so he finished the next morning when we all returned to court. He attacked Aronson and Mendel, our two straightforward, credible timeline witnesses. I would've ended with the 911 tapes. Darden made an error, closing by trying to rebut the defense case.

For our side, Cochran began his close by taking direct aim at the L.A.P.D., calling it "an infected investigation by a corrupt detective and a bumbling cesspool of a lab." He challenged the mountain of evidence, especially the so-called blood trail. "If he had bloody clothes, bloody gloves, bloody shoes, then where's the blood on the doorknob? On the carpet?" Yet Cochran also lapsed into phony histrionics. He put on the knit cap, asking, "Who am I? I'm Johnnie Cochran, with a cap on. If it doesn't fit, you must acquit." He took a swipe at Chris Darden's "messenger" reference by recalling Mark Fuhrman's message. "The message can't be trusted," he said.

The next morning, Cochran came back to continue his close. At first, he talked from his heart, he talked from his soul, he talked from the Bible. It was almost as if he was preaching. His rhythm would get going, and you almost expected the jury to fall into a call-and-response pattern. "If you're untruthful in small things, you cannot be believed in large things," he said.

It was a musical style, a cadence that had served him well throughout his career, especially with black jurors. My concern was that the majority of the black jurors were already in our camp and that Johnnie's arguments now should be addressed to those who we'd felt were pro-prosecution. We needed to woo those who might be on the fence. How would they hear what Johnnie was saying?

And then he made a terrible mistake. He linked Fuhrman, a banal, petty, mindless racist, with the most monstrous murderer of all time, Adolph Hitler. In less than a minute, he accelerated from a corrupt Los Angeles cop to the Holocaust itself, suggesting to this jury that they could stop Fuhrman, as the Germans had not stopped Hitler. "Maybe this is why you're sitting here, the right people, at the right time," he said. It was gratuitous, inflammatory, and just plain wrong. Worse, as far as this case was concerned, it was completely unnecessary.

Barry Scheck's portion of the closing statement went a long way toward restoring my faith. "Ladies and gentlemen, as you've heard, my partner Peter Neufeld and I are from New York. More specifically, we're from Brooklyn," he began, and then proceeded, point by point, to rebut the prosecution's forensics evidence.

Using Dr. Lee's example of cockroaches in the bowl of spaghetti, he pointed to Nicole's blood planted on O.J.'s socks, and O.J.'s blood showing up after the murders on the rear gate at Nicole's condominium. "How many cockroaches do you need?" he asked.

"Every explanation that they're desperately trying to come up with is a highly improbable influence," Scheck said. "The most likely and probable explanation is the one that is not for the timid or the faint of heart: *Somebody played with this evidence!*"

That's what this case is all about, I thought. Ito had told the jury from the beginning that a defense team has no burden— they don't have to prove anything. But we *had* proved something. We'd proved reasonable doubt.

"That's a reasonable doubt for this case," Scheck continued. "Period. End of sentence. End of this case."

Johnnie then came back to finish. He defined reasonable doubt for them, with a simple emotion and articulation that surpassed Ito. He quoted Abraham Lincoln, he quoted the philosopher Cicero, he once again quoted the Bible. "You can't trust their message," he told the jury. "If it doesn't fit, you must acquit."

∞

The following morning, the prosecution came back for their rebuttal arguments. Chris Darden spoke first, briefly confusing the Constitution and the Declaration of Independence but nevertheless acquitting himself reasonably well. But he was tired, as we all were, and could not bring back the emotion of the day before.

When Clark followed him, she, too, made mistakes, only this time it was because she went too far with her emotion, leaving simplicity and logic behind. She pleaded for the jury to believe her. "You can trust me that this evidence is good evidence," she said. "I wouldn't bring this case before you if I didn't believe that it was a good case."

Johnnie Cochran and Barry Scheck interrupted Clark's second close with more than sixty objections to her personal assurances to the jury that all the prosecution's evidence was solid and reliable.

Objecting during closing arguments is a matter of style. The general rule is that people don't interrupt the other side. Not only is it discourteous, but jurors tend to hold it against you. They don't like it when you're rude. Lawyers will generally hold or reserve an objection until the very end, unless it is something that is so harmful and inappropriate that it must be addressed immediately by the judge. That was the case here. Ito sent the jury out of the room, and then he strongly cautioned Clark not to use her personal opinions in the case. "We're close here, Counsel," Ito said.

"Your Honor, this has been highly improper," said an agitated Scheck, still standing from his last objection.

"Sit *down!*" the judge told him. And then he repeated, "You're close, Miss Clark."

"When Counsel takes off the gloves," Clark argued, "saying basically that we're criminals, then we have the right under the law to correct that misimpression."

"But this is way, way over the line," Scheck said. "I mean, I've been teaching law for eighteen years, and I've never heard this kind of stuff."

Finally Ito said, "Miss Clark, I don't want to hear any more 'I's.' "

"Right," Clark answered.

When closing arguments had been completed, Judge Ito at last sent the jury out to deliberate. As he did, he reminded them, "You are not partisans or advocates, but impartial judges of fact."

As I watched them leave the courtroom, I began to replay the last sixteen months in my mind. We gave him the best we had, I thought. Every area of reasonable doubt had been explored, examined, and exposed. I truly did not expect a conviction. The worst-case scenario was that it would be a hung jury; Garcetti had already said if that happened, he'd retry the case.

I expected the verdict to come in two, maybe three weeks. Johnnie needed to make a business trip east, so he asked that we be put on twenty-four-hour call. Ito denied that, saying that everyone had to be available immediately. He simply was not going to inconvenience this jury one more day.

Three minutes after the jury left the courtroom, the buzzer from the jury room sounded: They had picked a foreman. It was their first unanimous decision. As we'd expected, they had selected juror number one, Armanda Cooley. From the very beginning of the trial, juror number one seemed to take everything in stride. Whenever there was a crisis, she came into meetings with a smile on her face, willing and able to make suggestions that found agreement from the judge, the lawyers, and the rest of the jury. Whenever hostilities came up, her name was never on the list of transgressors. For months, she had been the center of warmth and common sense toward which the other jurors seemed to gravitate.

On Monday, after one more sequestered weekend, the jury would begin to deliberate.

Chapter Twenty-three

The reward for winning is to be tossed right back into the pit.
GERRY SPENCE

Aside from the judge's instructions to the jury, which are pertinent to each case, there is no primer, no rule book from the American Bar Association or the Supreme Court, no words from the judge, that tell a jury how to do its job. There are only two basic directives: The first is to elect a foreman, the second is to keep an open mind. There is no set procedure that dictates what follows.

The jury had spent 266 days in sequestration; only half of those had been spent in court. The rest were spent in limbo, wondering what it was that had sent them out of court this time, and destined not to know until after they'd completed their deliberation and delivered a verdict—unless, of course, conjugal visits had delivered contraband information. There was no way for any of us to gauge what effect the enforced isolation would have on them, or on their deliberation process.

The lawyers, their families, and their staffs spent that weekend knowing there was nothing else that could have been done, and nothing else to do. For months, we had all led our lives inside that courtroom, and the first order of business was housekeeping. Pack it up and move it out. Files, computers, fax machines, more files. And all the while, the random thoughts kept coming into my head. Second-guessing myself. What will the jury do? And after they do it, what will I do? What will O.J. do?

I suspected that we were going to get a hung jury and the case would go back to court for a second trial.

"What will you do if that happens?" Linell asked one evening. It was easy to read her face, to see that she was anxious, afraid of what she might hear from me. I knew that if she didn't like what she heard, she was ready to put up a fight.

At first, I wasn't sure how to answer her. For the past eighteen months, I had worked on nothing but this case. I went to sleep thinking of it, woke up thinking of it, and often dreamed about it in between. Although I worked on one civil matter that fortunately was settled without a trial, I hadn't accepted any new clients, nor had I appeared on any other case. I hadn't read a book, other than judicial books or DNA books. I saw only three movies. Oh, sure, I'd spent time with my wife and kids and done things with them, but my mind was always someplace else, and they knew it. Unwittingly, I'd become a kind of silent member of my own family.

Had I been single, had it been earlier in my career, there was no question that I would have stuck around for the retrial if O.J. had wanted me, and he'd already said he did. But at this time in my life, things were not so cut and dry.

Linell, for one, had had enough. For her, the previous eighteen months had been alternately embarrassing, painful, or lonely. My career had always been a matter of pride to her, something we planned and built together. The unprecedented demands of this case, both public and private, had stretched us both to the breaking point. Ever since the trial itself had begun, she had been focused on the *end* of it, and the resumption of our lives as a family.

The kids, however, couldn't imagine that I wouldn't readily go back for a second trial. As badly as they wanted it to be over, they couldn't believe that I could ever quit without a final victory. Knowing my competitive nature, Brent just assumed I'd climb right back into the ring and start swinging again. And

Grant said, "You're his lawyer, Dad. You can't just leave in the middle of a case, can you?" Fortunately, I never had to make that decision.

∞

It seemed to me that the jury could have chosen one of two ways to begin. First, the foreperson could direct a very deliberate, point-by-point discussion on all the witnesses, key areas of testimony, motive, intent, opportunity, review of the physical evidence, or any combination of any of them. If that was the case, my guess was that they'd want to resolve any credibility questions of key prosecution witnesses. If there was any doubt after that, they'd move on to the expert witnesses and look at DNA issues last.

Or the jurors could, for the first time since they'd been impaneled months before, simply look at one another and ask, "Well, what do you think?" By taking an early straw vote, they could shortcut the process if most jurors were in agreement one way or the other. This, we discovered later, was exactly what they did.

Once their first vote was taken, and ten jurors were found to be in agreement for acquittal and two for conviction, they quickly moved to the next question. Just what was it that pointed to reasonable doubt for ten of them? And what pointed to a conviction for the other two? They requested an immediate playback of Allan Park's testimony. In retrospect, they wanted to hear the prosecution's most "damaging" witness to see how conclusive that testimony actually was.

On Monday, October 2, four hours after beginning their deliberations, the jury announced they had reached a verdict. A stunned Judge Ito announced that the verdict would be delivered at ten the following morning.

∞

Before court began on Tuesday, October 3, I spent an hour with O.J., who looked drawn and exhausted. "I slept at least twenty minutes," he said with a half-smile. "I kept telling my-self it was in their hands now, there was nothing more I could do."

As the jury filed in, I tried to gauge the jurors' mood, tried to read their eyes. True to their history, they held their poker faces to the last. None of them made eye contact with me, or with anyone else that I could tell. When the verdict was passed to the clerk, and then to Ito, I again looked at their faces but still couldn't read anything there.

We all stood in preparation to hear the verdict. The judge's clerk, Deirdre Robertson, then read it. As she said the words "We, the jury," there was a collective inhalation of breath in the room. And then she said, twice in a row, "find the defen-dant, Orenthal James Simpson, not guilty." It was all anyone at the defense table could do to remain upright.

Instantly, it seemed as though the entire room behind me was in tears; on one side, the Goldmans and Browns in grief and anger; on the other, the Simpsons in relief and gratitude.

Someone said later that in the moments after we received the verdict, I appeared to literally, physically, step back from the table. And in fact, I did. To me, a trial is a sober, somber event, and a courtroom is second only to a church. There may be wisecracks and insults at sidebars, and bad jokes in the judge's chamber, but it's serious business overall. And no mat-ter the outcome, no matter the verdict, I've always tried to maintain some measure of dignity and decorum in the first strange moments after a verdict is announced. Cheers and high fives are inappropriate; it's a courtroom, not the NBA playoffs.

I felt, and I still feel, that the jury had reached the right conclusion in this case. It was a victory, a legal victory, and people could certainly congratulate each other for the long months of hard work and effort that had produced the result we'd hoped for. Nevertheless, two people were still dead. It wasn't the time for a celebration. It wasn't New Year's Eve.

∽

At the courthouse press conference afterward, the mood was oddly jovial, almost giddy. Bailey introduced himself as Cochran, and vice versa, as though we were at a celebrity roast.

I called Johnnie aside and told him I was going to do an interview with Barbara Walters immediately afterward, at the Century Plaza Hotel near my office. It was the first of two on-the-record interviews I would give after the jury verdict. With the exception of Peter Neufeld, I was the only lawyer on the defense side not to have given an interview during the entire case. Now, although I'd been given several opportunities, I chose two: one to be taped—the Walters interview—and the other live, on Larry King's show.

For sixteen months I had promised Larry King that when the case was over his would be the first live interview I'd do. Immediately after the jury verdict I called him and told him I was ready to speak my mind. His response was, "You kept your word."

The Walters interview would be taped and have to be edited for time constraints. On King's show, I would have the chance to expand on my views, to express all the feelings that I couldn't address while the case was proceeding.

I told Cochran that I was going to be frank on these programs. "You've got to know what my feelings are about this. It wasn't necessary, what you did, what you said. The Holocaust reference, the Nation of Islam guards, raising the issue of race to ask for jury nullification."

He just nodded as he listened to me. "Johnnie, it could have backfired," I said. "We had reasonable doubt walking away, from the very beginning. You didn't have to play that card."

"I appreciate your candor, Bob," he said. "And you're entitled to your opinions. It's just that I don't share them."

Although I was hardly in a mood for a party, I did go to Rockingham to see O.J. and his mother and sisters. I had become especially fond of Carmelita, who dearly loved Arnelle and Jason and had worried so much about them. I had great empathy for the positions they had all been in throughout the sixteen-month ordeal, positions that they'd occupied with a certain grace, especially Arnelle.

As Keno turned the car up to Rockingham, it was, as Yogi Berra would've said, déjà vu all over again. There were the throngs of cameras on both sides of the street, making it nearly impossible to get in the driveway. Johnnie hadn't yet arrived, and I didn't intend to stay long. That evening was the beginning of Yom Kippur, and I knew that Linell was waiting at home for me so that we could go to temple.

Although things may have grown livelier later that night, while I was there the mood was not festive as much as it was quietly happy, and relieved. I greeted the members of O.J.'s family, some of whom were still in tears, and spent a few moments with Arnelle, telling her that she had demonstrated incredible strength throughout her father's trial. In all likelihood, she would continue to need that strength as the family began its transition into the next stage of a story I suspected wouldn't be over for a long time.

I joined O.J. and a few friends out on the balcony. He was wondering what the days ahead held in store for him. I told him that I suspected that for some time, his life would be very difficult. "I'll manage," he said, looking out at the garden. "It's just so great to be home. And you were here from the very beginning, Bob. I'm grateful for everything you did."

I said that I'd spoken with Johnnie about what was in my mind and heart about the race issue and his use of the Holocaust image in his closing remarks to the jury. I also told O.J. that I had been equally candid with Barbara Walters, and that the interview would be on that night. O.J. just shrugged his shoulders and smiled. "I'm not surprised. You always say what's on your mind."

Before I left, I called to thank Alan Dershowitz for all his work, for making his keen legal mind and diplomatic skills available to us day or night throughout the entire sixteen months. In turn, he thanked me for bringing him aboard, reminding me that as difficult and conflicted as the recent weeks

had been, he firmly believed that the groundwork for the verdict had been laid during the first two weeks of the case. "You
shut down a grand jury, Bob, and you wouldn't waive time,"
he said. "They never recovered from that."

More people were arriving as I left Rockingham, with even
more reporters and cameras out on the street then there had
been when we drove in. There were news helicopters circling
above, reminding me of the day of the Bronco chase. I wondered how and when the people in the house behind me would
ever return to anything approaching a normal life.

∞

That night at temple, I was glad to see that Rabbi Zeldin would
be officiating at our service, accompanied by Cantor Nathan
Lamb, one of the great singing voices in the country, and a
teacher and coach of many professional singers. Rabbi Zeldin
had told Linell that he had taken a lot of heat from members of
the congregation for giving me the Torah to hold during the
Rosh Hashanah services. "I don't regret it, though," he said.

As we took our seats, the tension in the room was palpable.
This was clearly a congregation that had sided with the percentage of the American public that believed O.J. Simpson to be
guilty. To them, I was the symbol of lawyers using the system
to gain an acquittal. The Barbara Walters interview would run
at ten that night, right in the middle of services. But it would
be reported, and shown again in news segments, over the next
twenty-four hours. I could only hope on this, the highest and
most sacred of holy days, that the members of my temple would
learn of my feelings about race, and later share what I considered to be one of my proudest moments: "Not only did we play
the race card, we dealt it from the bottom of the deck," I told
Barbara Walters. I hoped they'd understand how angry I had
been when Cochran compared Fuhrman to Hitler and the Holocaust. I could feel their eyes on my back as the service went on.
Linell sat beside me, her back very, very straight.

What a difference a day makes. When services continued at

the temple the next afternoon, the Walters tape had aired and been picked up by virtually every television network. There was a much greater understanding of my role as O.J.'s defense attorney and my disassociation from the language and symbolism that Cochran had used to make his argument. However, while I felt somewhat more welcome than I had the night before, there was still a strong negative response to the verdict itself. How ironic, I thought, that the trial should culminate with the Day of Atonement, and that in this place of spiritual awareness and awakening, I should be the focus for the conflict and anger the case had provoked.

Chapter Twenty-four

Cab drivers now ask me questions about the Fourth, Fifth, and Sixth Amendments.

—PROFESSOR PAUL ROTHSTEIN
Georgetown University Law School

A few days after the verdict, I went for my annual physical—which was two years overdue—and as I stepped off the elevator, a well-groomed man in his fifties, in shirtsleeves and tie, walked up to me and said, "I've just gotta tell you, that was the dumbest jury on the face of the earth."

"Excuse me?" I said. "Who . . . who are you? And if you don't mind, may I ask what do you do for a living?"

He gave me his name, and said, "I'm a surgeon."

"Well, Doctor, that's a very interesting comment you just made," I told him. "How many juries have you served on?"

He looked at me with astonishment, shaking his head. "I've got overhead," he said.

"Well, what do you do when you get a jury summons?" I asked.

He said, "I've never been called for jury duty."

"Surely you've received some notices at one time or another?"

He nodded. "Oh, absolutely, but I just send them to my attorney."

"Well, the system only works if everybody participates in it," I said.

Protesting, the surgeon told me how many people worked

351

in his medical practice, what a heavy workload he dealt with, how many patients he had.

"Don't you take a vacation?" I asked. "Don't you ever take any time off? I know the Simpson jury went on forever, but that's not the case with most juries, and sequestration is highly unusual. Couldn't you find one week? Two weeks?"

He was still shaking his head. "I've got too many responsibilities."

"Are you suggesting that some citizens are too important to serve on juries?" I asked him. "If you are, then I think you completely forfeit the right to criticize verdicts you don't like."

I deliberately made him uncomfortable. But I've always felt that jury service is a duty and privilege of American citizenship. It's right up there with voting. Unfortunately, many Americans don't do that, either.

The prosecution says to a jury, "Look how it all fits together." It's the job of the defense to then say, "Look where it all falls apart." In this case, the prosecution immediately concluded that O.J. was the suspect, the only suspect, and guilty of the crime. Then they tried to build the case around that. Whereas the defense asked, What do they have that establishes this, and where are the inconsistencies? Frankly, it's much easier to pick a case apart than it is to put a case together.

The prosecution made two errors: They built the case on Fuhrman—and with him, Vannatter and his "reckless disregard for the truth"—and they built it on an endless defense of DNA as well. In terms of Fuhrman, they knew about his history when, or even before, we did—possibly as early as the preliminary hearing, but certainly before the trial. They could have pitched him over the side then and not left his trial testimony (and thus their whole case) open to dissection and doubt. For whatever reason, they chose not to do this.

In terms of the science of blood, I think the prosecution overtried the case. They attempted to prove not only the science but everything behind it, and not only lost the jury, but bored them. When you lose a jury, you're in trouble; once a jury is bored, you're in *big* trouble.

Against their "mountain of evidence," where did reasonable doubt come from? Their mountain of evidence collapsed under an avalanche of incompetence, contamination, and lies. On one hand, there's evidence of blood in a Bronco. But the first witness who said he found that blood was found to be, demonstrably, a liar. In addition, there's ample evidence that for three months that car was wide open and available to anyone who wanted to climb into it.

Then there's the glove. If a bloody glove is found at a crime scene, and the prosecution theory is that the person who dropped it there was in a hurry and bleeding, or had blood all over him, there should be evidence of that leading to and from the glove. Yet the ground around and beneath it was completely undisturbed. There were no blood or tracks or leaf-and-dirt disturbances leading up to it, none leading away. Fuhrman described the glove when he retrieved it as "wet and sticky." Eight or nine hours after it was used in a murder? Why wasn't it dried out? Had it been stored in a moisture-retaining bag and taken from one place to another?

How did O.J.'s blood get to Bundy? By his own statement to the detectives, he'd been there often in the previous year and a half, to visit and play with his children, their friends, and the dogs from both houses. How did it get on the foyer floor in Rockingham? Well, why wouldn't O.J.'s blood and DNA be at Rockingham? That's where he lived. How did the blood of the victims become intermingled with his in the Bronco? I don't know. But with the initial questions to Mark Fuhrman and ample evidence of lax police security for three months, we demonstrated how it *could* have happened. What about the blood and EDTA on the sock? What about the blood found on the Bundy fence that wasn't seen two weeks before? It had EDTA traces and extraordinarily high DNA concentrations, with little degradation, in spite of presumably being out in the elements since the day of the crime. To me, *that* was what "didn't fit." Add to this the demonstrated errors of the "cesspool" police lab and a woefully inept coroner, and any jury finds itself faced with more questions than answers.

A lot of criticism has been directed toward the jury on reaching a verdict so quickly. I was just as stunned by the speed of the verdict as anyone else on the case. How did they reach that verdict? How does *any* jury reach a verdict? It differs each time. A juror may come to a vote truly and honestly heeding the judge's instructions to leave bias and assumption outside the jury room. But jurors bring their lives into the room with them—their experience, their values, their ability to make careful judgments. Jurors (like lawyers and judges) are human beings, not computers, hence the term "jury of your peers." And as humans, they cannot help but respond to what they see and hear. They heard Fuhrman impeach himself, and they heard Vannatter deny O.J. had been an early suspect. They listened as Dr. Lee said, "Something wrong." And they saw O.J. try on the murderer's glove, which did not fit.

If, in the same amount of time, the jury had come back with a verdict of guilty, would there have been the same accusation that this jury failed to deliberate properly? After all, everyone watching the case had already formed their opinions. Why should we have expected that the jury had not at least come to some tentative conclusions of their own? The trial, and their feelings about it, was the only thing these people had in common, the *only* reason for them to be out of their normal lives and living with strangers. But for nine months, it was the one thing they could not discuss. When that prohibition was lifted, what's the first thing they did? They asked each other, "What do you think?" Is that incorrect jurisprudence, or is that logical human behavior?

Contrary to the prosecution's plea, the jury wasn't there to do justice on behalf of Nicole Brown or Ron Goldman. Contrary to the defense's plea, they weren't there to do justice for past wrongs to black Americans. They were there to decide one thing only. Had the People proved O.J. Simpson guilty of first-degree or second-degree murder beyond a reasonable doubt?

I contend that the same result would have been reached if they'd spent two months in deliberation, poring through each witness's direct and cross-examined testimony, every item of evidence, and seeing, over and over again, the areas of real and reasonable doubt. I stand by that contention not just on behalf of this jury, but on behalf of any other jury of twelve impartial citizens you want to place in the jury room and present with this case.

∞

I never believed that O.J. Simpson was being victimized by a racist police organization because he was black. I didn't believe that his life and career had ever been viewed as a symbol of black America or that he was seen as a black hero. He was a brilliantly talented sports legend, a charmingly successful commercial spokesman, a sometime movie actor, and to many, an American hero; hence, my hope and intention that race would not be a deciding factor in the case.

Not until the media began separating out their poll queries—what black Americans think, what white Americans think—did the case begin to split down racial lines. Racism also rode in on the back of Mark Fuhrman's credibility. Who or what Fuhrman hated wasn't pertinent except to the degree that it pointed to his credibility as a witness—and, not incidentally, to the credibility of the entire L.A.P.D. As one sheriff's deputy said in a letter to me after the trial, "When he stated he never used the *n* word, we knew he was in deep fecal matter."

Mark Fuhrman should never have been investigating a crime in June 1994. He should have long since been shown the door by his police colleagues and supervisors, who knew what he was and turned a blind eye to that. Is he credible? Not very. At the very least, he lied; at the worst, he planted evidence. However, Fuhrman is an anomaly. He's neither a typical cop nor a typical American. And where else except in Hollywood will you find a rogue cop undone by an aspiring screenwriter?

Our country has experienced a great deal of growth in race relations since the civil rights movement. Granted, not enough. We are not color-blind. In fact, the question increasingly raised is whether Americans *should* be color blind, which would imply a denial of color rather than respect and acknowledgment of the diversity of individuals. But whatever gains we've made have been more than set back by the polarization that grew out of this case. As Jimmy Breslin wrote, "The devil played the race card on the day the world began, and now, all these centuries later, it's still on the table."

When the Fuhrman tapes were released, black America's response was "I told you so." White America's response was "I don't believe it." We still, it seems, have a lot to learn about each other.

∞

As for fortune and fame: Contrary to headlines, there were no fortunes made here. Indeed, all the defense attorneys and experts are still owed large sums of money. Throughout my time on this case, I had a law practice to maintain, with law associates and employees to pay, and all the expenses of running an office. I sustained that practice with loans, not from any money I received from O.J. Simpson. I'm not complaining about economics, however. I've been blessed in the practice of law and my success in it.

As for fame: I've had clients who, because of their celebrity, must live their whole lives in their homes, and those homes are behind walls. They don't go out for dinner or to malls or amusement parks, they don't go to watch their kids play sports. Their entertainment is inside their own walls; if you want to see them, you go there.

I never understood that way of life. I thought it had more to do with Hollywood than reality, and that these people were either eccentric or arrogant. And then I saw the flip side. When even panhandlers call you by your first name, it's hard to ever have privacy again. Fortunately, most people who come up and greet me on the street are wonderfully kind and respectful.

However, the autonomy that comes with privacy is gone, and with constant scrutiny comes constant judgment. I am occasionally taken aback when an angry voice shouts "Guilty!" from across a street, especially when my wife and children are with me.

Add to that the constant attacking nature of the thousands of words written about all the lawyers, and it becomes easier to understand the downside of a case with this kind of notoriety. Said Andrea Ford of the *Los Angeles Times:* "What I found most disturbing has been the attitude in the press corps and in newsrooms that is anti-defense. A disdainful, dismissive attitude taken toward the defense . . . automatically seen as sleazy and dishonest. . . . The prosecution is automatically seen as virtuous."

Was this the Trial of the Century? I don't know. Consider the Lindbergh kidnapping, the trial of the Rosenbergs, the Chicago Seven, the Watergate hearings, Oliver North, Iran-Contra, and any number of gruesome murder trials such as Manson and Dahmer. Certainly the Nuremberg trial fifty years ago was a legal arena where mankind and morality were put under a bigger—and ultimately more important—spotlight than was ever shone on the O.J. Simpson case. If anything, the Simpson trial was the Media Trial of the Century.

There are fourteen hundred murders in Los Angeles County each year. This trial was about one of them, made larger (in scale, not in import) by its celebrity, by the issues it raised, and by being televised. Millions of people learned about sidebars, the nature of objections to testimony, sanctions on lawyers, the First Amendment versus the Fourth—in short, the process, however unwieldy, of a criminal trial. It was a remarkable civics lesson.

In the trial's wake, we'll continue to debate the social, cultural, and legal issues it raised long after the spotlight has moved on to something else. However, there is nothing in or about this trial to occasion either an overhaul or eulogy for the American system of justice.

∞

When this case began, I made a commitment to O.J. and Skip Taft that I would devote all my energies and resources to the defense, and I did that. I'm proud of the stance and positions I took. I knew that the case would provide the pinnacle of my career as a criminal defense lawyer; at any rate, I suspected that it would be the last major criminal case I would try. The experience was grueling, not unlike going through surgery. You know you'll feel better once it's all over, but you can't imagine how you'll get through it while it's going on.

Like any other life experience with peaks and valleys, time will help me continue to put it in perspective. As a name partner in a major law firm, I'm now looking forward to new and different challenges, ones that don't include the day-to-day roller coaster rides of a criminal defense attorney.

As for my family, we're gradually returning to what used to pass for normal. Thanks to the patience and forebearance of my law partners, we've had time to spend together. Working on this book has given me many reasons to think of my family with a heightened awareness of their great importance to my life. Fortunately, my parents are in great health, and I have the luxury of spending more time with them as well. My focus now is on growing into the future with my boys as they become men, and in renewing the relationship with my wife.

The difficulties that Linell endured during those months were enormous, and starkly different from my own. As a woman raising two sons, she often found herself empathizing or identifying with each of the three families—the Browns, the Goldmans, the Simpsons—in ways that were particularly painful to her. She made no secret of wanting me to leave the case, yet she knew I would not, and struggled to support me in that decision. She had private doubts, public courage, and even at her angriest never stopped being my champion. She is a strong, independent woman, and her overall attitude toward life has always been a positive one. I love her dearly and hope that one day soon she will say that at the very least, the experience taught us something about ourselves as a couple, as parents, and as a family.

∞

As for that dinner that Judge Ito had hoped for, I suspect it won't ever take place.

I haven't seen or talked to Johnnie Cochran since immediately after the verdict, and I was not included on the list of those invited to attend a Christmas celebration with the jurors. I brought Cochran into this case knowing full well that he was a leader. We differed in many areas of strategy and I wasn't surprised that he tried to take over; in fact, he had every right to do so. Unlike the friendship between Lee Bailey and me, Johnnie and I had no longtime personal bond, no preexisting relationship. Just because I brought him in didn't mean he had to be loyal to me at the expense of what he thought was best for this client and for this case. Nor did it mean he had to be in any way subservient to me or my judgment. He moved ahead and made decisions as he thought fit, and he gained O.J.'s confidence in the bargain. That's what happens when a team defense, which was essential to the success of this case, is employed. That's not to say I don't regret the tensions, the words spoken in anger or disappointment, or some of the ultimate choices that Cochran made. I acknowledge the strength of his ability, and the risks he chooses to take as a man and as an attorney; however, I won't work with him again.

I did see Judge Ito at a fundraiser for a local judge sponsored by the Chinese American Bar Association, and we had our picture taken together. We shared a few private moments there and we agreed that someday the two of us would sit down and have the long talk that's been so long in coming.

I've spoken with Chris Darden at two or three charity

events and congratulated him on his courage and hard work. He was looking forward to a year-long sabbatical, working on his own book, and going back to teaching. His students will be fortunate to have him as a teacher and mentor.

Barry Scheck and Peter Neufeld returned to New York, where their Innocence Project will push science and advocacy as far as the system will allow.

One day I ran into Marcia Clark at a restaurant. She was having lunch with her agent, Norman Brokaw, the genial and gracious chairman of the William Morris Agency. During the trial, Brokaw had often raised the possibility of my being represented by William Morris. Flattered by his attention, I nevertheless felt at the time that it was too soon for me to make a decision that required careful thought and some perspective. Now, when I passed the table where they were sitting, I greeted them both. Brokaw extended his hand. Marcia, however, turned her head away and concentrated on the menu in front of her.

I saw Bill Hodgman at a reception for his assistant, and my dear friend, Norman Shapiro, who had been appointed as a judge of the superior court. I talked with Bill at great length, and I hope to do it many more times. I suspect that he, Judge Ito, and I would have a lot to talk about.

And finally, I spoke with O.J. not long ago. He asked my advice about life after the trial, and I willingly gave it. However, we were not friends before the case; as is common in a criminal representation, it was a one-time thing. I suspect our relationship will be what it was before: professional acquaintances in a large city. Our professional business relationship ended the day the verdict came back. We never had a personal relationship before, and we won't have one in the future.

Acknowledgments

The transcript for the O.J. Simpson trial totals more than fifty thousand pages; the pages of this book seemed just as daunting when I first confronted the possibility of writing them. This book was in no way intended to be the definitive book on the Simpson case. If such a book exists, it will be written by any of the numerous and talented writers who watched the drama unfold both in- and outside the courtroom, and whose perspective and purpose differ significantly from my own.

The attorney-client privilege is one of the most sacred, if not the most sacred, tenets of the law. It allows an individual to freely consult with a lawyer on a confidential basis, knowing that the communication between them cannot be divulged. In that respect, it resembles the communication between doctor and patient, priest and penitent.

The privilege is held by the client, not by the lawyer, and only the client can waive it. It attaches at the moment the client first seeks legal assistance, and it doesn't cease unless and until the client says it does. Even when communication between lawyer and client is positive—that is, reflecting positively on that client, or supporting a theory of his innocence—it remains privileged.

The privilege, and my respect for it, governed the writing

of this book. I cannot share confidences. I can take the reader into a room; I cannot, in all instances, repeat what was said there. Readers should not draw negative conclusions from what they think may or may not be missing from this narrative. This is not the story of O.J. Simpson's innocence or guilt; rather, it is about my experience of the months between June 1994 and October 1995, and the resulting effects on me, my wife and family, our friends and colleagues.

With hindsight, the Simpson case might not have been the best one for me to take. In retrospect, I am proud of my work on it. It's an experience I wouldn't want to duplicate; it's also one I wouldn't have wanted to miss. In the wake of the verdict, there were a lot of stories being told, a great deal of second-guessing, and not a few bittersweet feelings. I received many letters and phone calls, some laudatory, some critical, some kind, some not. One call in particular meant a great deal. It came from my friend and colleague Alan Dershowitz, who phoned my wife, Linell, after he saw me on Larry King's show. "I was there from the beginning of this case, I know what went on behind the scenes," he told her. "And Bob was the architect."

My great thanks go to the following people:

My wife, Linell, and my two boys, Brent and Grant, for their public grace, their private patience, and their love.

My parents, Marty and Mary, who worked so hard and sacrificed greatly for my education. They instilled in me the values that were important to them and that I maintain today, and they gave me the confidence that I could accomplish anything I set my mind to do.

The dear friends who have always been there for me, many of them from grammar-school days, who are never reluctant to remind me of what is real and good in this life.

Bonnie Barron, my longtime assistant, who during the Simpson case put in as many hours as any of the lawyers, virtually seven days a week for seventeen months, without ever losing her common sense or humor; and my talented associates, Sara

Caplan, always available, day or night, and Karen Filipi, who virtually ran our criminal practice while I was in trial.

This book was made possible through the encouragement of my dear friends film critic Joel Siegel, who has been cheering me on since the sixth grade; Michael Nasatir and Larry Feldman, my twin consciences and advisors; and Christine Forsyth-Peters, who not only insisted I write it but personally interviewed literary agents and then introduced me to Sterling Lord, to whom I am deeply indebted. Sterling agreed that the book would not be auctioned to the highest bidder but placed instead with a leading publishing house and a superb editor. That goal was more than achieved with Larry Kirshbaum and Warner Books. Larkin Warren, my collaborator, knew what questions to ask, when and how hard to push, and how to wrestle a voluminous amount of material into something readable.

Finally, I want to acknowledge the lawyers and partners of Christensen, White, Miller, Fink, Jacobs, Glaser and Shapiro, who treated me like a partner long before I was one, who allowed me virtually total access to their vast resources, their brainpower, their insight, and the physical facilities that allowed me to defend this case.